SOUTH-EAST ASIA—
RACE, CULTURE, AND NATION

By the same author

STUDIES IN MANAGEMENT (University of London Press, 1961)

THE NEW SOCIETIES OF TROPICAL AFRICA
(Oxford University Press—Institute of Race Relations, 1962)

EDUCATION FOR A DEVELOPING REGION (Allen & Unwin, 1963)

INDUSTRIALISATION AND RACE RELATIONS
(Oxford University Press—Institute of Race Relations, 1965)

The Institute of Race Relations is an unofficial and non-political body, founded in England in 1958 to encourage and facilitate the study of the relations between races everywhere. The Institute is precluded by the Memorandum and Articles of its incorporation from expressing a corporate view. The opinions expressed in this work are those of the author.

South-East Asia—
Race, Culture, and Nation

GUY HUNTER

Published for the
Institute of Race Relations, London

OXFORD UNIVERSITY PRESS

NEW YORK 1966 LONDON

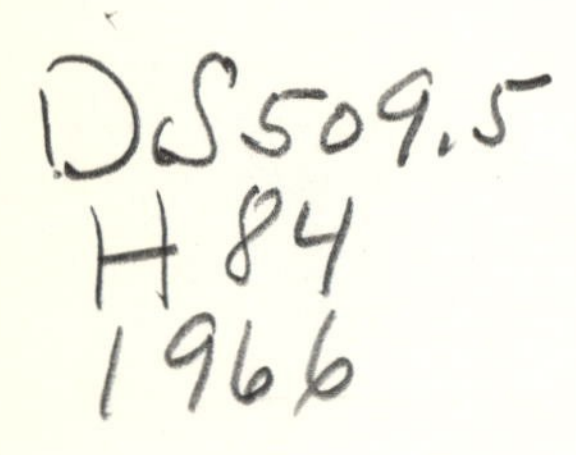

PRINTED IN THE UNITED STATES OF AMERICA

CONTENTS

Author's Preface vii
Foreword by Philip Mason ix

PART ONE

I Introduction—The General Theme 2
II The Countries of the Region 13
(1) Some General Figures 13
(2) The Buddhist Mainland 16
(3) The Malay World 27
III The Immigrant Races 36
(1) The Chinese 36
(2) The Indians 53

PART TWO

IV Colonial Authority—Effects and Responses 60
V Variants in the Nationalist Idea 73
VI Economy and Administration 86
VII Education and Society 104
VIII Education—Language and Minorities 119
(1) The Language Situation in Independent States 120
(2) Some General Considerations 131

PART THREE

IX The Impact of Modernity 136
(1) The Transfer of Institutions 136
(2) The Effects of Industrialization on Race Relations 141
(3) Education and Science 144
(4) Science and International Aid 147
(5) Religion and Secularism 148
(6) The Texture of Social Life 151
(7) Some Common Themes 155
X Conclusion 157
(1) Economic Growth 159
(2) The Continuity of Culture 161
(3) Religion 163
(4) Politics and Policies 165
(5) The Outer World 168
Index of Authors Quoted 174
General Index 177

LIST OF TABLES

1 Population and Economy (1962) 14
2 Population—Ethnic/Racial Balance (Rough Estimate—1962) 15
3 Education (1962) 15
4 Numbers of Indians in Burma 18
5 Indian Population of Malaya 31
6 Chinese Population of Malaya and Singapore 31
7 Population of Federation of Malaya, by Race 31
8 Malaysia—Population Percentage, by Race (1961) 32
9 Ethnic Chinese in South-East Asia 38
10 Percentage of Chinese to Total Population in Certain States (1957) 70
11 Selected Occupations, by Race (1957) 71
12 Populations of Sabah and Sarawak, by Race (1960) 80
13 Populations of Sabah and Sarawak, over Ten Years Old: Educational Attainment, by Race (1960) 80
14 Increases in Total Enrolments in Primary and Secondary Education (1950–61) 109
15 Primary and Secondary Enrolments (1961–2) 111
16 Percentages of Survival through School Grades (1950–62) 111

MAPS

I Mainland of South-East Asia
II Malaya, Singapore, Indonesia and the Philippines
between pages 13 *and* 14

AUTHOR'S PREFACE

DURING 1963 and 1964 my wife and I had the opportunity to spend a total of six months in South-East Asia, visiting all countries except Laos and North Viet-Nam, in the course of preparing a report on manpower for the Research Programme on Higher Education in South-East Asia undertaken jointly by U.N.E.S.C.O. and the International Association of Universities.[1]

The study of manpower involves detailed work not only on the educational system but also on the occupational structure of the economy and the economic development plans. An extremely interesting part of all the economies of South-East Asia is the special contribution of the immigrants, not only Europeans but Indians and, more particularly, the overseas Chinese. When Mr Mason, as Director of the Institute of Race Relations of London, asked me if I could contribute a short book to a major series of studies of race relationships in various regions of the world, I was therefore extremely interested, and had a certain background of detailed modern material to start from. I was, however, very conscious of not having specialist knowledge of the area. Partly for this reason, and partly because the area is so large and varied, it was clear that I could only attempt to put forward certain rather wide and general thoughts. These are concentrated on the special problems which arise in newly independent countries as they set about building modernized nations from traditional societies in which there is a marked racial, ethnic, and cultural diversity.

This book is therefore written, not for specialists, but for the intelligent reader who is interested in the social, cultural, and political problems of developing countries. I have included in Part One a good deal of straightforward description, so that the main argument in Parts Two and Three can be intelligible without assuming that the reader is already fully familiar with the area.

I am therefore much indebted to the Institute of Race Relations for the opportunity and finance which enabled me to collect extra material and complete this book, and to U.N.E.S.C.O.–I.A.U. for permission to use some material collected in the course of work for them.

As to the book itself, I owe an immense debt of gratitude to five

[1] The full Report on the Programme, and the Consultants' Reports, are published by U.N.E.S.C.O.–I.A.U. under the title: *Higher Education and Development in South-East Asia*, Paris, U.N.E.S.C.O., 1965.

people in particular. First and foremost to my wife, who worked with me in South-East Asia and collected a huge volume of notes, and who has at all stages made a critical contribution to the thinking and form of the book, as well as a mass of detailed improvements. Secondly, to Professor Edward Shils, who read the first draft and contributed a very large number of perceptive and valuable comments on it. Thirdly to Professor Hugh Tinker and Professor Maurice Freedman, who each contributed some wide general comments on form and structure. Fourthly, to Philip Mason, who has taken immense trouble, in comment and discussion, to question generalizations and point out contradictions in the text. Although I am responsible for the opinions expressed, I can only say that any value the book may have has been greatly increased by the help and criticism which has been so generously given. Finally, I would like to express my thanks to Mr Simon Abbott and Miss Claire Pace of the Institute of Race Relations for their work in preparing the final manuscript for the publisher.

G.H.
October 1965

FOREWORD

by Philip Mason

Director of the Institute of Race Relations

THIS book is the first of a series, linked by a common purpose, but dealing with widely separated geographical areas and approaching what I believe is one problem from extremely different angles. It is the problem of what is felt to be diversity between groups of people included in one political system—and in particular of what is believed to be racial or ethnic diversity. The purpose is to analyse the different ways in which that felt diversity is expressed, to see how it has arisen, to consider how far it is an obstacle to progress, and whether as an obstacle it can be overcome.

The series sprang from the thought—simple, perhaps obvious, no doubt grossly oversimplified—that while in some parts of the world race seemed to be the main criterion for deciding social status, in others it was only one factor in many. In South Africa, the extreme case, the Government was trying to define precisely the racial category into which every one of its subjects fell and to make more rigid the barriers between categories. Meanwhile, in Brazil and Jamaica, with a similar range of difference—though the proportions in which the categories are mixed are different—there seemed to be no rigid definitions, much easier interplay between groups, a society based on class with some possibility for the individual of rising in the social scale whatever his race. Perhaps in these easier, more open, societies race counted for more than was officially admitted, but there could be no serious doubt that the structure of social life and the way racial difference was regarded was quite different from South Africa's. Would it not be possible to examine and compare various societies and try to reach some conclusions—or at least make some suggestions—as to the reasons for such very different views and behaviour? And could any practical conclusions be drawn from such an analysis?

A start was made in Africa. The Institute of Race Relations in London, with the help of a generous grant from the Rockefeller Foundation, published a trilogy of books on Rhodesia and Nyasaland and two on the former Belgian Congo. These endeavoured to trace the historical development of the social structure, which in these areas is synonymous with the relationship between the races. They were followed by Guy Hunter's *New Societies of Tropical Africa* (financed by British industry), a study of a different kind, concerned less with historical analysis than with the present as a guide to the future, aimed less directly at social structure and more at the probable development of the whole economic, cultural, social, and political complex, a complex in which racial attitudes were likely to operate among the other factors.

At this stage it seemed necessary to carry the inquiry a stage farther by studies of other parts of the world. The Ford Foundation generously provided funds to make these further studies possible. They deal with large regions and every one of the authors concerned has felt a scholarly reluctance to cover a field wider than that in which he has a specialized competence. But I think all have in the end found that the areas with which they are dealing have much in common as well as many differences and have found their thought enriched by both. Julian Pitt-Rivers, whose published work has dealt with Spain, Mexico, and the Mediterranean, is dealing with those parts of Spanish-speaking America in which there were pre-Columbian high cultures—Aztec, Maya, or Inca; this means, broadly, Mexico, parts of Central America, and the Northern Andean republics. David Lowenthal's area is the Caribbean; his most detailed field-work has been in Dominica. David Maybury-Lewis, whose previous work has been in the Central Province of Brazil, has agreed to compare the situation there with that described by other writers in other areas; the whole will constitute a review of the literature on race and social structure in Brazil. There is also a more detailed study of Trinidad by Donald Wood. Guy Wint is writing on India; there is a symposium on divisive and unifying influences in India; and there is the present volume on South-East Asia. With the single exception of Thailand, all the states in these areas were once ruled by Europeans. But in Asia the problem has a very different look and is formulated in terms in which 'race' hardly plays a part. The term 'plural societies' is familiar, but what are the dividing lines between these societies and how do they make up a nation? What are the distinguishing marks by which an individual is recognized and put into these categories? In what way do categories that are defined by language, culture, or caste differ from those defined by race? How far do these divisions affect national development?

To answer these questions in respect of South-East Asia we were fortunate to obtain Guy Hunter, whose knowledge of Africa is so varied and whose *New Societies of Tropical Africa* combined so wide a range of insights. He had been working in South-East Asia for U.N.E.S.C.O. and it seemed that there would be a real advantage in bringing to the study of this region a fresh mind with experience of another. It was with perhaps even more diffidence than the others that he accepted the invitation, but his study does, in fact, provide just the stimulating contrasts for which we had hoped.

There is, as I have already suggested, a contrast in the first place between the New World and Asia, with Africa sharing some features with both. 'Race' is certainly not a central concept in Asia; it is perhaps hardly meaningful and is usually subsidiary to questions of culture and language. But in the New World, the physical differences between the broadest divisions of mankind—and here it would be an irrelevance to try to define those divisions—are an essential part of that often barely conscious social diagnosis that is in operation wherever men meet each other outside the family. Ants from different nests pause when they meet, apparently to explore, investigate, and judge, and something like this happens whenever two human beings meet for the first time; later meetings are conducted on the basis of an initial judgement that is continually modified by fresh experience. The part played by the concept of 'race' in this process of continuing diagnosis varies between Peru and Mexico, between Kentucky and New York, São Paulo and Bahia, Barbados and Guadeloupe, but it is never absent. What concept, if any, takes its place in Asia?

Let us dwell a little longer on the American scene. The United States lie outside the scope of this series; there are already so many intelligent people thinking about the American dilemma that it seems more sensible for non-Americans to look elsewhere. But the most powerful nation in the world cannot be insulated from any social phenomenon, wherever it occurs, nor can its problems be left out in consideration of any other. In another book in this series, which is still in preparation and which deals with parts of Spanish-speaking America, Julian Pitt-Rivers has distinguished between the position of the Negro and that of the American Indian. The Negro was brought to the United States as an individual and thus has to be part of American society because he has no other, but the American Indian in the States is an Indian for only so long as he belongs to an Indian community. He can be a part-time Indian; he can leave the Reserve and become an American not very definably different from any other and then he can go back and resume his Indian status. But being a Negro is whole-time; the status is genetically defined.

In the Spanish-speaking areas, particularly the Andean, this distinction between the Negro as an individual and the Indian as part of a community holds good in a different way and with very different results. The Indian is still indubitably Indian for so long—and only for so long—as he belongs to an Indian community and speaks an Indian language, but once he leaves the Indian community his identity is much more difficult to determine. The Spaniards in the days of Empire tried to define status in terms of ancestry, but the attempt broke down, partly because of the complexity of racial mixture and partly no doubt because of the general social and economic drift from defined status towards more flexible stratification by class. The result is definition by 'social race', in which diagnosis is partly by appearance and what is known and guessed of ancestry, modified by habits, occupation, education, and wealth. What we have now in parts of Spanish-speaking America is 'a class system wearing the trappings of ethnic distinction'—with the added complication of some communities which can really be distinguished ethnically, because, among other differences, they speak an Indian language.

Can concepts of this kind find any application in the territory of South-East Asia with which Guy Hunter is concerned? There is no doubt about their relevance in the Caribbean, another area with which the series will deal. Nor is it difficult to see a fruitful comparison with the society of India, whose traditional stratifications were based on heredity and fortified by religious belief, and which also has outlying tribal communities which are ethnically distinct. But Burma, to take one only of Guy Hunter's territories, is, in one sense and with obvious additional complications, more like Peru before the Incas had consolidated their rule than Peru today. The Kings of Ava and Mandalay had never extended their rule over the whole of what is now Burma; the suzerainty they claimed over some areas was only acknowledged when they were strong enough to enforce it, and over some it was not even claimed. English rule was a brief intermission; the successor state resumes where the Kings of Mandalay left off and has no central language with the prestige of English or Spanish, nor would, let us say, the Shans recognize Burmese culture as superior to their own. The problem is to reconcile a number of societies which are not stratified in horizontal layers but are arranged in vertical segments. The additional complications—unknown to the Incas—include not only international trade, world ideologies, and the neighbourhood of China, but the presence of two communities, Chinese and Indians, who have an outside allegiance.

Let me list these factors again—indigenous but distinguishable minorities, linguistic diversity, alien communities with allegiance to an external power, and a variety of international pressures. They are present in varying degrees in each of Guy Hunter's territories. These have long been thought of as plural societies rather than superordinate and subordinate societies and this, of course, is a basic difference from the American scene. Both in North and South America, Europeans not only conquered but stayed as settlers and their culture completely dominated that of the people they found and of those they introduced. In South-East Asia the various European nations found strong and ancient cultures which let them thunder by; they came and went; the flotsam of empire in one sense—that of direct legacy—was little more than froth on the beach. There is, of course, another sense in which the presence of Europeans changed everything; it destroyed ancient unquestioned ways and set everyone asking questions. But it did not establish a permanent superordinate society. There was nothing remotely comparable with the conquest of Mexico. And this surely is one basic reason why the concept of 'social race' is not applicable; a Negro in the United States will try to 'pass for white' because he accepts the superordinate status of white society, and this is not usually the case between the parallel societies of South-East Asia. And again, he is recognized not as a member of a Negro community but as an individual. But it is essentially as members of communities, not as individuals, that Indians or Chinese or Malays are identified in South-East Asia and in this they resemble the Amerindians in Southern Mexico.

A high emphasis in Hunter's book goes to the priority which the new rulers assign to the search for national identity in political terms. It is seen as an end in itself as well as a means of achieving progress; the first need is a loyalty that will transcend loyalties to the smaller community. But in America and the Caribbean it is of a search for *personal* identity that men write and speak with passion. In Africa both are sought; a nation has to be found to replace the cement of the colonial power and the need for some more personal and emotional link with a shared past produces such concepts as *négritude* and African socialism. Perhaps this difference between Asia and the New World reflects in part the length of time since independence from an imperial power; perhaps it has something to do with the age and strength of the local cultures. Be that as it may, it is with political unity and national identity that the new leaders in Asia and Africa are concerned; administrative detail, all that Anglo-Saxons think of as efficiency, comes as a poor second. And, since the unifying leader must appease his followers, any community felt to be alien, however useful economically, is a convenient scapegoat.

This is one of the dangers on which Hunter insists. It is a danger that is direct for the alien community. Those with an outside allegiance, European, Chinese, Indian, are more obvious targets than the tribesmen, but the aliens can at least withdraw, while Dyaks or Karens feel they are threatened with loss of their existence as a separate people. But it is a danger for the majority as well; often an economic danger, because the threatened community would not be where it is if it did not perform a service—but also a moral danger, because one act of injustice and aggression leads to another, as with the Nazis and the South African Nationalists.

Serious as this is, and central to his subject, Hunter feels almost as deep a disquiet at the dangers of cultural discontinuity, the gap between traditional village life and the international rootlessness of the great cities, between peasant and bureaucrat, between parents brought up with known duties in an ancient system of faith and reverence and children who have been introduced to a system of education. Those who complete it are divorced from their parents but have at least some anchors. But for those who drop out the system seems almost as wasteful of human beings as nature of male sperm. It is designed to produce university students in physics and history, but provides neither jobs nor philosophy for those rejected on the way. Looking at the intrusion into their ancient societies of forms of enterprise which have developed in another setting, Hunter feels in a far more acute form the misgivings of a botanist at an ill-judged interference with the natural ecology of a pond. We foresee profound ill health which provides, of course, just the kind of anger and frustration which is deflected on to minorities.

This problem is not, of course, confined to South-East Asia; it is of world importance. Outside the wire fence of the international airport there are men living in huts of dried mud and thatch; what do they think of the giant airliners that roar overhead, of the passengers sipping gin and tonic under the striped umbrellas? What do they now believe in? Not, surely, with the same faith as before, in the godlings of tree and rock and waterfall, who are powerless before these flying monsters? Can they be helped to any system of belief and hope linked with their own past and compatible with what Hunter calls modernity and Pitt-Rivers's Indians, if they speak Spanish, call *progreso*?

In Latin America the dividing line between modern and traditional is often defined by what is spoken of as ethnic difference; this, as I have said, is less often the case in South-East Asia. But however the difference is signposted it is there, and in both regions it can be brought into the terms of an historical process which is described by Pitt-Rivers in

Latin America and which he suggests is of wide application and might be called a dialectic of imperialism. Imperialists or colonizers must, he suggests, once they have established themselves as rulers, impart some of their skills to the conquered, if for no better reason than to save themselves trouble. And so, inevitably, they prepare the ground for rebellion; once the natives can do it themselves they see no reason to submit to people whose interests are different. There is tension and opposition between colony and mother country; this appears for a brief moment to be solved by independence, but in fact all that happens is that the point of tension moves; it lies now within the colony, between the *élite* who have learned from the imperialists how to do it themselves and the mass of the natives who have not. In America—North or South—the *élite* were 'settlers', racially of the same origin as the people in the mother country; in Asia they are usually of the same stock as the people they rule. But in either case, however it is defined in words, the gap is really one of thought and habit.

The sharply contrasted interests and barriers to comprehension between the modernist few and the traditional many are familiar. Hunter points out that it is the essential nature of this misunderstanding to introduce into new nations techniques which are unsuited to the soil, and he is sceptical about the commonly held view that urban life and the introduction of industry will break up traditional forms of hostility between communities. He is particularly well qualified to form an opinion, having recently edited for U.N.E.S.C.O. a symposium on *Industrialisation and Race Relations*. But this is surely a matter in which there will be immense differences between different areas and institutions; it may well be that in the long run some hostilities will be reduced and others take their place. Industrial life is almost bound to introduce into the life of a recent arrival from the village an ambivalence and a variety of roles in different contexts which he did not know before; he may find himself working on quite friendly terms with a man he would not ask to his house. The rigidity of caste is likely to be modified, but tribal links may even be strengthened for a time. Hunter is deeply aware of the stresses of this new life and refreshingly sure that its needs will not be met by bread alone. A faith, and a faith with symbols, will be needed. This is an individual need as well as a national need.

The new societies of South-East Asia, segmented vertically by ethnic and religious differences, horizontally by the distinction between traditional and modern, searching for national unity, have to find symbolic expression for their nationhood; so have those of Africa. But while African nationalism has in most cases to discover symbols which have really very little relevance to the present—Ghana and Zimbabwe are examples—the Asian societies, with a much richer recorded past, have the embarrassment of too many symbols, each of which has associations for particular communities. What flag, what song, what hero can fire the blood of Malays and Chinese alike? Yet some such symbols are essential if nationalism is the best alternative to Communism. In Spanish America, again, the quest for identity and symbol assumes different proportions and finds a different answer, but here, too, there is something artificial. The symbol of the pre-Columbian Indian is often associated with a mythology about the Indian's place in society which sometimes carries, as Pitt-Rivers puts it, a rather low factual content.

How different is the part played by religion in America and Asia! The Conquistadors were—ideally or mythologically—Roman Catholic missionaries before anything else; the other motive, symbolized as Don Dinero, Sir Money, was alluded to less openly. They suppressed the indigenous religion, but the clergy carried to the Indies a long-standing conflict with the nobility and attempted to build up, in the Indians, the powerful constituency which the commons had provided for them in Spain. (I do not suggest that this was the only motive for their attitude.) A struggle to prevent the enslavement and exploitation of the Indians followed, with the Church as a liberal champion; a transposition of forces followed and by the time independence from Spain was achieved, the Church was usually the supporter of the *status quo*, that is to say, of landed aristocracy and oppression. But in South-East Asia the colonial powers (excepting the Portuguese, who do not fall within the scope of this book) came as merchants and did not obtain political power until a more sceptical age had begun. As Hunter points out, they found 'higher religions' in being and on the whole left them alone; they had themselves already settled the relation of Church and State and that unhappy quarrel was not among the luggage they brought with them. Religion, though deeply rooted in the life of the people, played little part in the development of the nation, except in two negative respects. It has been a divisive factor between communities, while the trappings of religion—social adhesions such as caste and purdah—have become an obstacle to 'progress' or modernization. Only in former French territory was there a significant identification of any religious body with the colonial power and a ruling class. But this is not the place to open the vast question of the different effects of the Spanish attitude to religion compared with English, Dutch, and French.

With so many points of difference between New World and Old, there are certain depressing constants. Poverty, ill health, ignorance, apathy, hunger; how can these be cured? How can modern knowledge be applied to them without the destruction of traditional values that Hunter has painted so vividly? There must be, as he says, a continual movement from the shelter of closed societies and known ways to dangerous uncharted open country—and everywhere there is at once a frightened impulse to get back into cover again. Despotism, the one-party state, Communism—these are all ways of avoiding the isolation and loneliness of the open. And here there is the difficulty that closed political and social systems present an immediate appeal, while it is much more difficult to persuade people whose horizons are near at hand of the advantages of tolerance and a free individual society. The forms of democracy mean that any idea that is to hold people's emotions has to be expressed simply, perhaps ultimately in the form of a slogan, and it is not easy to preach the virtues of capitalism to a society which is short of capital. Why should people who have so little fight to keep out Communism, which promises so much? On the other hand, the emotions to which appeal *can* be made are just those which hinder progress. Hunter emphasizes the advantage to society in general of a Chinese trader who works until midnight compared with the bureaucrat who goes home when office hours are over—and yet generally throughout this region it will seem a patriotic act to install an indigenous bureaucrat instead of an alien individualist.

Mr Hunter is not without hope. He quotes Professor Frankel's saying that 'different countries have a different language of social action and . . . peculiar aptitudes for solving problems at their own time and place'. He hopes that institutions more deeply and basically linked with the past of these countries can emerge and a new kind of education linked with and aimed at rural administration; he hopes that religion may rid itself of superstitious accretions and resume 'its essential dialogue with the human spirit on the meaning of life'. He believes that the fundamental issue is the struggle for human freedom against bureaucracy and he says, 'Every policy which delays advancement of the mass of rural people while enriching the metropolitan few; every policy which hampers education—as linguistic nationalism does; every policy which destroys economic initiative—as racial policy does; every concession to prejudice and prestige weakens the chance of the survival of freedom.'

This, of course, raises the question of how many people in South-East Asia want freedom, and how they conceive it. To hungry people freedom has a much greater appeal if it seems likely to bring food;

further, because of racial dominance in the past, the peoples of South-East Asia, like other ex-colonial peoples, are highly suspicious of Western talk of freedom and other Jeffersonian ideals. It is easy for them to put the United States in the same bracket with Britain, Holland, and France, as rich and white, and once that is done it is easy to regard talk of freedom as a cover for capitalist exploitation. It is one of Hunter's virtues that he sees this struggle for the mind as central and yet as never dissociable from problems of population and agriculture, schools and health. He sees them as one wide and immensely complex problem and yet he is continually bringing himself down to questions of how many schoolchildren are in a given class in Secondary education. This ability to combine breadth with detail is one of the rarer gifts.

To summarize, what Guy Hunter does in this book is to explore these themes as part of a single process in the development of the nations of South-East Asia:

(*a*) the transition from tradition to modernity;

(*b*) the establishment of national identity, legitimacy, and unity out of a diversity which reappeared when the colonial blanket was whipped off;

(*c*) the complications introduced into (*a*) and (*b*) by racial and ethnic diversity.

In this foreword, I have done no more than touch lightly on a few of the comparisons, mainly with one other region, which Guy Hunter's book provokes. But there is one possible criticism of the basic idea of this whole series which is likely to occur at this stage. No one person can be familiar in detail with the structure of society in such widely different regions. Students of even a single region find it embarrassingly diverse; they cannot produce scientifically measurable results with anything like the exactitude of the physical sciences. Can any comparison, then, have validity? Further, it might be argued, the writers approach their problems from widely different angles; one is an anthropologist, one a geographical historian, one is interested in development and education, and so on. This, it might be said, reduces even further the areas of valid comparison. These points have some force. The answer is that each human situation is unique. Mix the same chemicals in the same proportions and you get the same results—so long as they really *are* the same proportions and the same chemicals without any impurities. But with mixtures of people, neither the proportions nor the constituent elements are ever the same. Comparisons therefore can be illuminating, but they will never provide a formula of universal application, nor even an exact parallel between any two situations. 'Validity' is really the wrong word; comparisons of this kind will have value, but not perhaps 'validity'. They can provide insights and understanding and they suggest further lines of inquiry.

This kind of understanding of the structure of society and the forces at play within it have never before been so desperately needed; the Western world, with riches and physical power beyond the dreams of any past age, stands faced with world problems of a delicacy and complexity such that they can never be solved by force, such that pressure rashly and excessively used will put them beyond solution. It is in the hope of contributing some understanding of these problems that this series has been conceived.

December 1965

PART ONE

I

INTRODUCTION—THE GENERAL THEME

MUCH the same forces, much the same human aspirations and weaknesses have attended the growth of new nations from the old colonial empires, whether in Asia or in Africa or in the New World. But in each country and in whole regions these forces play upon a different historical and cultural heredity and give a different character and sequence to the processes of growth. It is not without reason that South-East Asia, for all the variety of its countries, has been looked upon as a single region among the developing nations. Both the mainland countries and the islands hang upon the fringes of two great civilizations—Indian and Chinese—from which they have been greatly influenced. Yet for centuries they maintained an independence from their great neighbours, and developed cultures of their own, richer than those of Tropical Africa, more capable of persisting through the period of European colonial rule. All in varying degree are plural societies, containing much-differentiated ethnic groups and, in particular, a share of the long-continuing emigration from Southern China. All live in a context of Asian politics which has a character increasingly its own.

The broadest range of thinking within which this book is set is the study of how the common forces and common problems which attend the creation of modern nationhood have affected this South-East Asian world. But within this range there is a sharper focus. It is directed to the relations of cultural, ethnic, and racial groups—these words will need more definition—within the parallel processes of modernization and of nation-building through which all these societies are now passing.

Although there is a world of South-East Asia, felt as a reality by its members within its outer limits of India, Japan, and Australia, it is a world which may usefully be divided, for many purposes, into two. One half is the mainland world down to the Kra Peninsula—Burma, Thailand, Cambodia, Laos, Viet-Nam. The other is the Malay world—the Malay Peninsula, the huge arc of Indonesia, and the Philippines, with the city of Singapore, now independent, and the Malaysian strips of Borneo as political outliers.

By its geography and the movement of peoples within it, the mainland world might be roughly called Sino-Himalayan. High in the eastern buttress of the Himalayas, in the Tang Lha ranges, three great rivers spring from the Tibetan plateau—the Salween, the Mekong, and the Yangtze Kiang. All three first strike southwards through parallel gorges. The Yangtze is the first to strike off to the east, through the whole width of China to Shanghai. The Mekong bends less sharply, running past the Burma border, through Laos, circling Thailand, on through the rice lands of Cambodia to its delta in Viet-Nam. The Salween plunges straight to the south, through the Shan hills, with the shorter Irrawaddy now parallel in the plain to the west, until both find the Indian Ocean within the boundaries of Burma.

The rivers, with the great rice plains in their lower courses, and the mountains, with their forested ridges stretching a thousand miles to the south and east, tell us something of the distribution of peoples on the mainland who form one half of the South-East Asian world. Many of their peoples moved down from Tibet and China, and the strongest of them established powerful kingdoms in the river plains—to the east, the Chinese on the Yangtze; farther south, the Thais, the Khmers of Cambodia, the Annamites of Viet-Nam, peoples of the foothills, the rice plains and the Mekong delta; to the south, the Burmese, first centred on the Irrawaddy at Mandalay. In the mountains which surround these plains, and right down the backbone of Malaya which stretches on to Singapore, there remain many smaller peoples and tribes, never fully absorbed by the great kingdoms. Such are the Chins and Kachins of Burma, the mountain tribes of Northern Thailand, Cambodia, and Viet-Nam, the original forest-dwellers of the Malay Peninsula. Separate in many elements of culture and language, these and many others form the indigenous minorities of the modern nation-states. The history of this patchwork of South-East Asian states, a history of constant wars and movement, is mentioned very briefly in the next chapter.

The Malay half-world is in many senses different. It is formed by the Malay Peninsula and the great crescent of islands curving round from Sumatra through Java and the Celebes up to the Philippines, enclosing Borneo, dotted out in islands across to New Guinea and the Pacific. In early history its power at times seems to have stretched to the mainland, reaching Viet-Nam, Cambodia, and Thailand. Although repulsed from there, it colonized and held the Malay Peninsula, gripping every river mouth and driving the mountain peoples deeper into the forest. The Malays of Malaya are from Sumatra, Java, Celebes, Borneo; Malaya, geographically just attached to the mainland world, is culturally of the islands.

The Malay world is in some senses a world of the sea. As once in the Mediterranean Ionians and Achaians, Phoenicians and Cretans and Egyptians moved, conquered, and settled on coasts and islands, so for thousands of years peoples from the Indian Ocean, the China Sea, and the Pacific have moved within the Malay archipelago, trading, exploring, fighting, intermarrying; the ports of these islands have long been crowded with many different types and tongues, with the coastal Malay language gradually gaining ground. But inland, in the mountains of Borneo and in many other islands, less mobile forest people live on, often in a culture of shifting cultivation closely comparable to that of Central Africa. The Malay world thus has its own minorities. It has also its full share of immigrants from China.

In culture and religion deep differences have also grown up in the two half-worlds. At the eastern fringe China's influence spread down into modern coastal Viet-Nam. Farther west and south both the mainland and the islands seem to have received their first high cultural influence from India, at least as early as the beginning of the Christian era. Hindu art spread as far as the Annamite mountains on the mainland and far eastwards down the chain of islands, giving them their name of Indonesia. But in later centuries there came a cultural division. Theravada Buddhism, spreading from Ceylon, captured the mainland until it merged into Chinese cultures at its eastern fringe. In the Malay world the Muslim faith, largely carried via India and with many Hindu influences, gradually became supreme, though it lost most of the Philippines to the Catholic Christianity of the seventeenth-century Spanish conquerors. The Malay Peninsula and large parts of Indonesia became a world of mosques and sultans; the mainland a world of Buddhist priests and kings. This division was well established before the European trading and colonizing invasions of the seventeenth century; it is still significant today.

Of the 200 million people of South-East Asia, probably four-fifths live in mainly rural surroundings, still deeply held in a traditional culture. Every problem in South-East Asia finds its scale and nature in relation to this fact. Of the last fifth perhaps 15 million live in or around the great capital cities, within sight of the most Westernized techniques and ways of living; the rest in smaller towns[1] with less sophistication yet still unlike the peasant village. In religion more than half live within the dominantly Islamic areas of Malaya and Indonesia, a third in the Buddhist mainland countries, less than a sixth in the Christian

[1] Indonesia has twelve towns with over 100,000 population, and both the Philippines and Malaya are, for South-East Asia, relatively highly urbanized.

Philippines. Yet, in fact, below these blanket titles lies a strong foundation of village and tribal cultures, far older than Islam or Buddhism, often Hindu-influenced, manifested partly in animist and magical beliefs and in the systems of family and clan upon which village society is built.

Leading the nations into which these great masses of peasant peoples are divided are two to three million men and women who have had a full modern education[2]—the teachers and doctors, lawyers and Civil Servants, politicians, businessmen, and engineers upon whom the burden and the opportunities of leadership have fallen. They have set out to lead their peoples on a long pilgrimage. It is a road which will lead towards the modern nation-state and the modern society, made rich from the store of scientific knowledge which now lies open to all who can find a way to take and use it.

In the tangle of complexities in South-East Asia it is perhaps useful to restate these broad divisions. First, the Buddhist mainland of ancient warring kingdoms, each based on a dominant people, with hill-tribe minorities and the separate problem of immigrant Chinese (and, in Burma, Indians). For all of them China is a vast and in varying degrees threatening neighbour. Second, the Malay world, again with both indigenous and immigrant minorities, now divided into four states—Malaysia, Singapore, Indonesia, Philippines; Muslim in Malaya and much of Indonesia (there are strong Christian groups in the Celebes and Moluccas), Chinese in Singapore, Christian in the Philippines save for a minority of Muslims in the south.

Finally, there is China, apparently an outside power, yet far more deeply interwoven with every local issue than any outsider, not only from its size and power, not only from its history of contact (India had as much), not only from its vigorous minorities in every state, but from the challenge of its politics. For Burma, Thailand, Laos, Cambodia, Viet-Nam, Malaysia, Singapore, and Indonesia, Chinese Communism and Chinese power are burning issues; only in the Philippines are they not.

This basic geographical, ethnic, and religious structure of South-East Asia provides only a background upon which the forces of modern history play. By far the most significant of these forces has been the influence of the Western colonizing powers. This period of colonization has been much studied and described; it is not necessary to repeat

[2] Those who hold jobs requiring either university degree or some post-Secondary training amount to between 0.5 per cent of population (Burma) and 2 per cent (Malaya)—perhaps 1¼ per cent for the whole area. The numbers with *some* higher education, especially in the Philippines, are higher.

the historical story here. On the economic and administrative side, and in education, certain peculiar distortions caused by it, which are relevant to this book, are mentioned in later chapters. At the most general level it is the influence of Europeans, seen as the channel through which ideas originating in Western developed countries reached South-East Asia, which is of significance.

It was not only that Europe brought in applied science and technology, with their corollaries of economic development and progress. Certainly, these in themselves were new and dynamic concepts in Asia. It was the overflow of scientific thinking into the humanities which was really revolutionary; the coming of certain elements of secular, pragmatic, sceptical thinking (touching even subjects considered sacrosanct), and certain elements of social egalitarianism which were so profoundly disturbing (and exciting) to religious and traditional societies. 'All that is solid melts into air; all that is sacred is profaned; and man is at last brought face to face with his real conditions of life and his relations with his kind.' These words from the Communist Manifesto of 1848 prophesy the ultimate effect of applying the narrow logic of science and materialism to human societies; they scarcely overemphasize the practical effect of Western values applied to Asia. The bearers of these values, whether in Africa or Asia, would not have acknowledged them as stated. But colonized peoples have always had an oversimplifying directness in cutting through the ideals of the colonizers and fixing upon what they feel to be the true sources of their power. These sources they identified as technology and economic advance, the replacement of a feudal type of authority by a more progressive one, the relegation of religion to the sphere of private life, and, perhaps above all, the creation of the unitary nation-state.

Such ideas may be slow-acting—be they poisons or fertilizers—and much that is traditional, feudal, religious, provincial, and particularist survives in South-East Asia; only in China did revolution break through in one enormous bound. In certain ways the new ideas may tend to blur the old distinctions, even those which divide the mainland and the Malay world; to devalue, in subtle ways, the old distinctive and divisive elements of ethnic, historical, and religious culture. In their place the tiny group of progressives begin to share common values oriented to the future, to 'modernity', science, economic progress, democratic criticism of authority—including, first and foremost, the authority of the European colonizers themselves.

But the effect is not so simple. The creation of a nation-state, and the 'nationalism' which is used to power that process, may tempt the new leaders to use highly irrational and regressive emotions—racialism, religious fanaticism, intolerance of political minorities—which are wildly at variance with scientific modernity, not to say democracy. Even where the worser aspects of such policies are absent, the search for unifying factors may seize upon 'Buddhist tradition' or 'Malay culture' to give an historical and emotive background to the nationalist surge. Thus there will emerge a constant tension between the attempt to build on tradition, which will use all the ethnic, religious, and cultural distinctions which have been outlined, and the attempt to build on modernity, where the emphasis will be on rationalism, economics, and technology, functional rather than cultural divisions. As a wide generalization, the political leadership is apt to play upon the traditional themes, which have greater emotive force; the emerging middle classes, in commerce and the professions, will tend to find common ground, across ethnic and religious frontiers, in a 'modern' culture which is, in fact, international. The progress and the tensions of modernization form a vital part of the central theme of this book.

Next, it is necessary to give a working description—it is not a strict definition—of the meaning which will be given here to the terms 'racial', 'ethnic', and 'cultural', applied to the differences between peoples in the societies of South-East Asia.

Biologists, social anthropologists, and psychologists all have their special approach to the definition of race among human beings. Even if there were full agreement about the origin and classification of certain physical differences between large human groups—which there is not—such a purely biological definition would not, in fact, cover the range of meaning which the reasonable man intends to convey in using the word 'race'. I am therefore using it pragmatically as a useful indication of a type and degree of difference which is felt as more fundamental in certain respects than the difference between 'tribes' or 'ethnic groups'. In the first place it implies a physical difference, usually a number of hereditary characteristics commonly found together which serve to distinguish broad categories such as 'European' from 'Negro'. There can be huge physical differences between 'Europeans'—short or tall, dark or fair, long-headed or round-headed—but in certain respects this normal range is distinguishable from the normal range of Chinese. Further, 'race' is usually applied to major groups in the world, and groups which normally have developed far from each other; there are great physical differences between 'Chinese' from different areas of China, or between 'Africans' in Central Africa, but in common parlance these could not be described as 'racial'. And indeed it is natural that there should be an undertone of cultural as well as physical difference in the rough distinction between races, since groups which have developed far apart are likely to have developed different cultures.

In contrast, 'ethnic' differences will be used to describe differences between groups who have developed their own social pattern and way of life, often including their own language, *within* one of the major areas of civilization and (in the broadest sense) 'race'. Such are the differences between tribal groups within Negro Africa, or the differences between many of the groups in Indonesia or Borneo. Here there may be more or less of physical difference, but not of the same order as those commonly recognized as characteristic of the major races.

Thirdly, in speaking of cultural differences, the emphasis is clearly upon ways of life rather than physical stock. Culture is almost infinitely subdivisible, from European culture to British, to Scottish, to Scottish Highlands. But in all cases it refers to the pattern of social relationships, rather than physical differences. As one aspect of culture, differences in religion, so often a cause of group tension, almost demand a section to themselves. Finally, 'communal' tensions will refer, as the word implies, to tensions between communities who recognize each other as different, whether on racial, ethnic, cultural or religious grounds.

These descriptions do not, of course, include the emotional additions which may become attached to basic meanings, particularly in the case of race. The white invasion of Tropical Africa and the resulting slave trade to the New World have produced the largest crop of racialist attitudes, now so widespread that light or dark skin colour is temporarily a factor of social ranking almost throughout the world. This tendency for racial difference to attract emotional responses, *especially where there is a potential threat from one group to another*, cannot be neglected, and it is one reason for the particular distinctions which will be made in dealing with South-East Asia.

In accordance with these rough distinctions, throughout this book I have treated not only the Europeans but both the Indians and the Chinese as *immigrant racial* minorities in South-East Asian countries. In the case of Indians this is fairly clear. They come from a separate major civilization, and the southern Indians in particular (the majority in South-East Asia) have clear physical distinctions. But the case for including the Chinese as a separate race is less clear. Not only has there long been intermarriage and close cultural relationship between many South-East Asian peoples and the Chinese, but the shading of physical characteristics between Chinese and many local peoples is gradual and sometimes almost imperceptible. Nevertheless, the Chinese in Burma or Malaya or Indonesia come from a major, unitary, outside power, and they are seen in certain circumstances as a threat to the interests of an indigenous society. They are just as much intruders as the Indians, and the fact that physical differences are sometimes slight does not alter attitudes towards them. It is as intruders, as offshoots of a large, powerful, politically dangerous foreign state, as culturally cohesive and different, and as economically competitive and threatening that the Chinese are distinguished from internal ethnic minorities in South-East Asia; and they are identified at least as much by their culture as by their physical appearance.

In general, therefore, the Indians and Chinese will be described as immigrant racial minorities, whereas the differences between indigenous groups within a country (between the Burmese and Karens or Kachins, between the Javanese and the Ambonese or Dyaks) will be described as *ethnic*. In some cases there are local intruders (for example, Vietnamese in Cambodia) and these will also be included as ethnic minorities. It may be, in the outcome, that cultural differences will seem the most important of all.

Clearly these descriptions are not watertight, nor are they defensible in detail. There may well be a small, by now 'indigenous' minority in some South-East Asian country—one of the hill tribes, for example—which sprang originally from stock which biologists would emphatically classify as racially distinct from their neighbours. Such a group, if not powerful or threatening, if long established, if not maintaining relations with some major outside parent-nation, would be clearly distinguished by Burmese or Thais from a Chinese or Indian group; and hence may be treated as an ethnic minority.

Thus it is the question of attitude, a subjective approach, which is of main importance here. It may therefore be useful to attempt a few more generalized remarks on the attitudes in South-East Asia which are directed towards the indigenous ethnic minorities and towards the immigrant racial groups.

The whole world of South-East Asia is strongly characterized by ethnic minorities—Indonesia is the largest example. These differences are felt in two main ways. First, as cultural differences, which may involve mutual contempt—the advanced but unmilitary plainsman versus the backward but fighting hillsman—or a range of more varied and detailed cultural judgements. Second, as political differences, which are more important for our purpose. In the search for national unity the new ruling groups will be determined to include their minorities within the nationalist programme; the minority groups may be equally determined not to lose their cultural identity, their historical self-respect, or their sense of self-determination.

A more complex and generally more hostile attitude applies to the immigrant Indians and Chinese. They are felt first to be intruders who *could* be legitimately expelled—an attitude certainly not applicable to indigenous ethnic minorities, who are felt to share the country, however tiresome they may be. Secondly, they are felt almost always as culturally more widely different and less assimilable, especially the Indians. They bring with them the aura of a different, major, developed civilization, of which they are evidently proud, to which they may hope to return, whose ways they are unwilling to give up. Thirdly, the Chinese and non-Muslim Indians will have a different religion, with all that that implies. Fourthly, they will almost always be felt as economically threatening to the indigenous majority—as taking the bread from mouths which have more right to it. Finally, the Chinese may be seen both as a political minority which can be safely crushed without the loss of votes or outrage to the spirit of national unity and (simultaneously) as a cell from an outside and dangerous political power. Thus, as both weak and dangerous, they may be in particular danger of attack.

This study is based upon the proposition that racial or ethnic relationships cannot be effectively studied in isolation from the totality of social, political, and economic life. They arise in concrete, local, historical situations, and they can be greatly altered by changing economic or political events. For example, in the political field, the relations between races cannot be separated from the majority-minority situation; $2\frac{1}{2}$ million Chinese among 100 million Indonesians present a different problem from a Chinese 'minority' of 40 per cent in Malaysia. A racial minority in power creates another and entirely different situation—there is no need to quote the effects of minority racial rule in Rhodesia or South Africa. Again, if a racial minority is linked to a major outside power, or thought to be attached to an outside political ideology (for example, part of the Chinese minority in Sarawak), this will radically affect race relationships. Again, in so far as 'nationalism' is powered by an appeal to cultural or racial unity (as it often is—but in Malaysia is not), the effect on race relations may be overwhelming.

The same is true of economic relationships. If economic power, even in a single sector of a whole economy, is concentrated in a racial minority, it will give rise to far sharper antagonisms than it would in a homogeneous society. Racial factors may also become bound up with economic ideologies, as they are where a socialist government, attacking private enterprise, can bring to bear the added weapon of racial jealousy against the mainly immigrant private sector of merchants and traders.

Religious and cultural differences may also confuse the racial issue. In the emphasis on national unity it is often hard to tell if a minority is being attacked on religious or racial grounds; and the sense of social offence which arises between neighbourhoods of different cultural habits is more sharply focused where the cultural gap is also racial or ethnic—a situation which has been especially marked in the case of West Indian and Pakistani immigrants in Britain.

It is for these reasons that this book does not attempt a detailed survey of race and ethnic relationships, country by country, and including all possible groups, which would indeed be a task for several specialists. It is, rather, an attempt to consider the various issues of race relationships as they enter into the whole pattern of nation-building in the plural societies of South-East Asia, and as they affect the transition from a customary to a modern society.

If we consider these problems of nation-building, it is clear that they include at least the following five large tasks. First, to consolidate a geographical nation; and this involves, both on the mainland and in the islands, capturing the loyalty of ethnic minorities in the hills or special regions of ethnic patriotism. Second, to create a modern economy; and this will mean adopting some attitude to foreign entrepreneurs and internal racial minorities who may be important in the economic process. Third, to choose a cultural personality; and this will involve attitudes to religion, education, language, to name only three major cultural areas. Fourth, to decide a policy towards immigrants somewhere in the range from total assimilation to total rejection. Finally, to establish a foreign policy, with all that this implies in attitudes towards East and West, towards ancient ethnic affiliates or enemies (Indonesian-Malay; Thai-Cambodian; Cambodian-Vietnamese), and towards China as the bearer of an ideology and the overseas Chinese as daughter-cells. It is thus primarily in reference to these tasks that race relations are here considered; that is, as an integral part of the total national process, taking different shapes and colours in the differing national contexts within the region.

Nowhere will the evolution of attitudes towards racial or ethnic minorities run smoothly in one direction. There are strong opposing currents. In particular, the desire to achieve modernity, in its broadest sense, may well run counter to the nationalist quest for unity, with its ever-present temptation to see this in racial or ethnic terms. Upon the resolution of this conflict much of the future of South-East Asia will depend.

In two respects this account is not evenly balanced. There is a heavier concentration on Malaysia than on other countries, and on the Chinese rather than other immigrant races. In both cases there is, I think, justification for this proportion. Malaysia concentrates every ethnic and racial problem in acute form and with urgent political relevance. The Chinese, far more than the Indian, Eurasian, or even the ethnic minorities, raise political issues of world importance. On any reckoning, they deserve special treatment.

II

THE COUNTRIES OF THE REGION

1. SOME GENERAL FIGURES

SOME very general indicators of the population, economic wealth, numbers in various levels of education, and ethnic balance are given, for ease of reference, in the three tables on pages 14 and 15. The figures for employment in manufacturing industry are in some cases very rough estimates, since accurate figures are not available.

There are one or two points of special interest in these figures. The wealth of Malaysia, in terms of income per head, stands out as about double that of the next richest country (Philippines), more than double that of Thailand, and three or four times that of all the rest. It is, of course, unrealistic to give any very precise figure for Cambodia, South Viet-Nam or Indonesia. Almost half of the South Viet-Nam budget derives from American aid; and the translation of Cambodian *riels* or Indonesian *piastres* into terms of hard currency is not meaningful if the purely artificial official exchange rates are used. In fact, the figures for these two represent no more than a reasonable comparison with the general economic level of the other countries in the region, based on population and real outputs.

The figures for education are more reliable as to numbers, but they say nothing as to quality. Here the number of Philippine college students stands out as a different order of magnitude altogether. This figure includes a great mass of students in fee-paying private colleges all over the islands, in which standards vary from full international university quality to that of a rather poor and badly equipped high school. In contrast, the very low figure for Malaya covers a single university of high standard, based on thirteen years of pre-entry education (as against ten years in Burma or the Philippines).

On the production side, the universally high proportion of population in agricultural employment is evident. The lower figure for Malaya reflects not only the widespread tin-mining industry but also the higher proportion of urbanization and commercial activity corresponding to the higher income per head. The division between plantation and cash-crop agriculture is impossible to make with any accuracy

MAP I

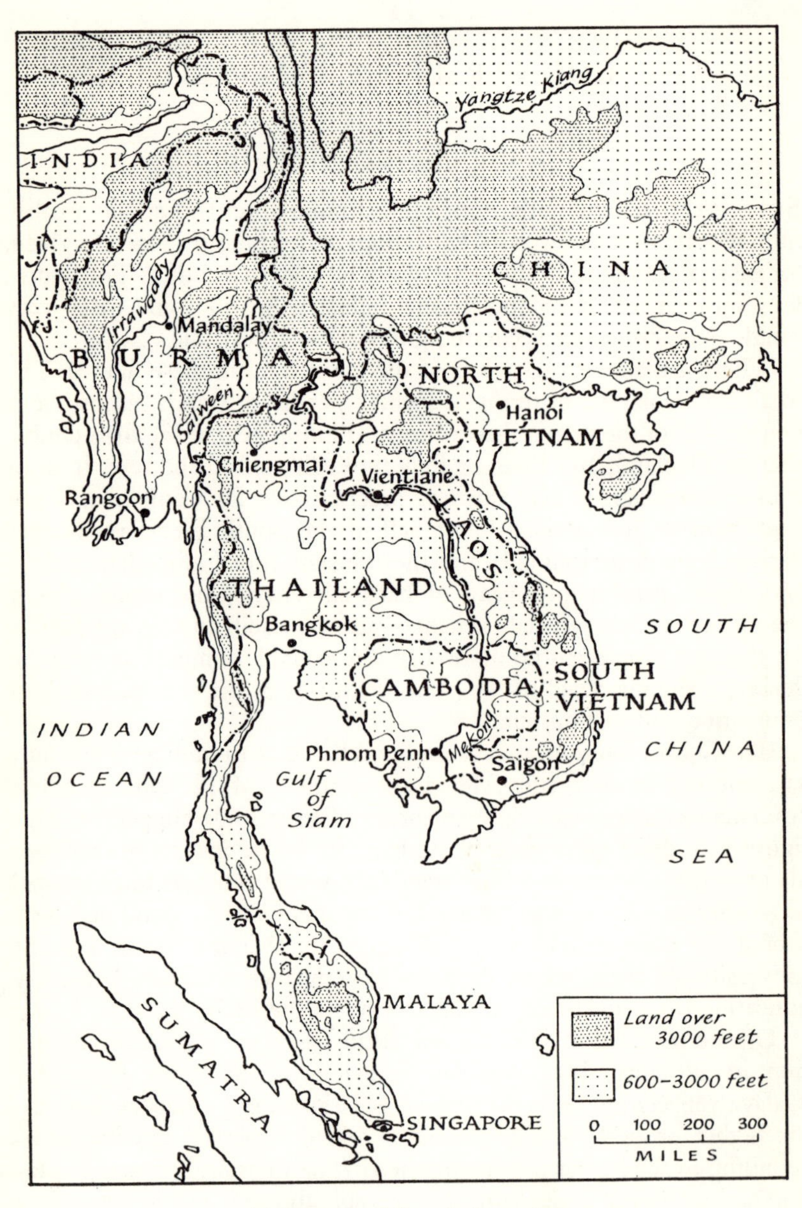

Mainland of South-East Asia

MAP II

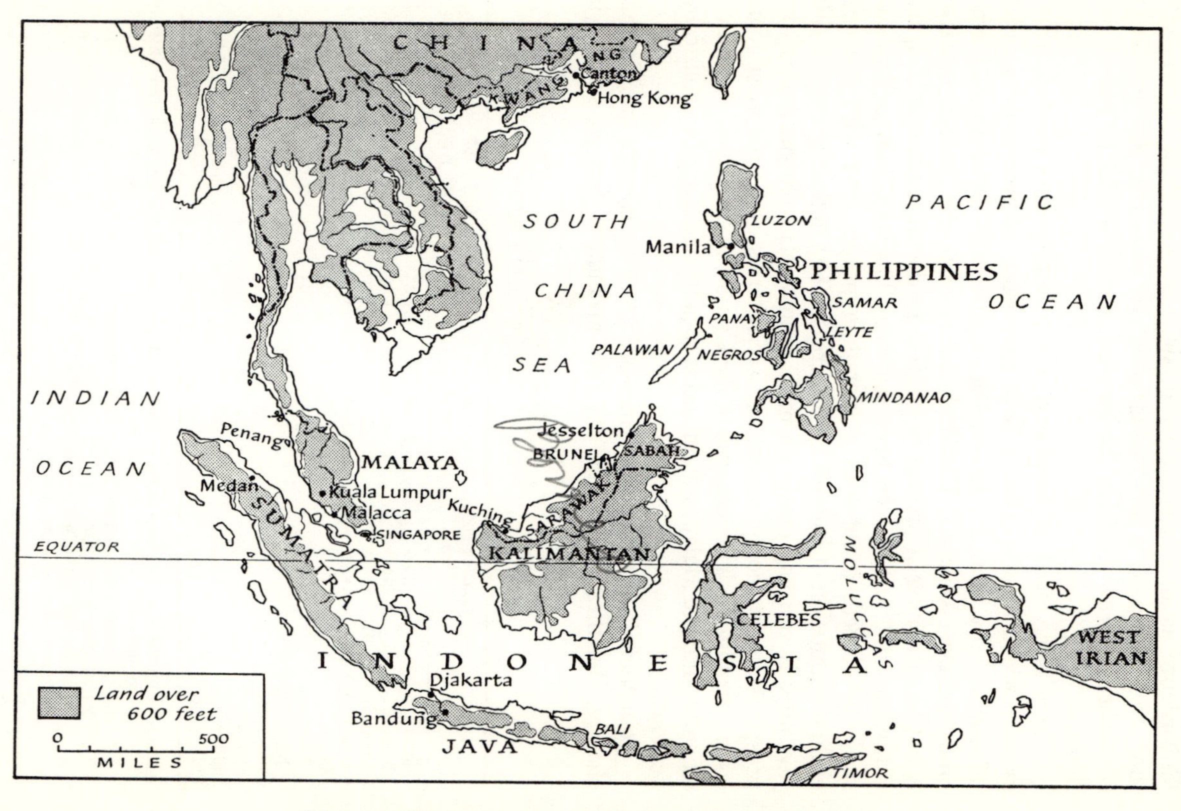

Malaya, Singapore, Indonesia and the Philippines

—Dobby[1] estimated in 1950 that about one-third of the whole population of South-East Asia was engaged in 'subsistence' farming. 'Subsistence' is an inaccurate word, since most of these farmers sell some crops for cash; 'traditional farming', on small holdings, primarily concerned to grow food for the farmer's family, would be nearer the mark.

There is no need to emphasize the daunting rates of population growth, which mop up such a large proportion of growth in national income year by year. In the smaller populations—for example Cambodia and even Malaysia, Thailand, and Burma—the absolute increase is not too alarming at present in relation to the large amount of spare cultivable land; it has even been said that Thailand, fully and intensively developed, could feed 100 million people. But with the 100 million population of Indonesia an increase of 2½ million per year, with Java already carrying nearly 60 million on a relatively small area, the prospects are far more alarming. In racial terms by far the most acute issue lies in the high growth rate of the Chinese in Singapore, for whom an outlet into the Malayan mainland is socially necessary but politically perilous.

Some details of ethnic minorities are given by country later in this chapter. But these, again, are not very meaningful figures, since it is

TABLE I

POPULATION AND ECONOMY (1962)

	Population 1962 (millions)	*Est. Annual Pop. Growth (%)*	*G.P.N. per Head*	*Industry* (Employees)*	*Agriculture (% occupied)*
Burma	23.0	(2.4)†	£23	140,000	62.9
Thailand	28.8	3.3	£37	(150,000)	82.0
Cambodia	5.4	2.7	(£30)	N.A.	(80–85.0)
South Viet-Nam	14.8	(2.5)	(£30)	(30,000)	78.0
Malaysia‡	10.5	(3.0)	£100	240,000	55.0
Malaya	7.5	3.1	£93	145,000	62.0
Singapore	1.7	3.3	£175		8.5
Sarawak	.78	2.5	£69	10,000§	81.3
Sabah	.48	3.0	£75	6,940§	80.5
Indonesia	99.4	2.3	(£15)	(400,000)	71.9
Philippines	29.0	3.2	£46	(200,000)	61.7

Notes: * Figures are for 'organized manufacturing'—normally firms with ten or more employees.
† Figures in brackets represent rough estimates.
‡ Including Singapore.
§ Figures for 'manufacturing industry'.
All figures are estimates for 1962.

Source: U.N.E.S.C.O.–I.A.U. Research Programme: Consultant's Report on High-Level Manpower.

[1] E. H. G. Dobby, *South-East Asia*, London, 1950.

TABLE 2
POPULATION—ETHNIC/RACIAL BALANCE
(Rough Estimate*—1962)

Country	*Dominant (millions)*	*Indians*	*Chinese*	*Ethnic Minorities*		*Total (millions)*
				Karens	2,500,000	
	Burmese			Shans	1,000,000	
Burma	16.0	600,000	350,000	Mon Wa	1,000,000	23.0
				Kachins	500,000	
				Chins	500,000	
	Thais			Malays	750,000	
Thailand	25.0	—	2,500,000	Hill Tribes	230,000	28.8
				Lao	?	
	Khmers			Vietnamese	350,000	
Cambodia	4.5	—	450,000	Cham-Malays	70,000	5.4
				Hill Tribes	60,000	
	Vietnamese					
South Viet-Nam	13.8	—	750,000	Hill Tribes	250,000	14.8
	Malays†			Indigenous‡		
Malaysia	4.1	983,000	4,373,000	and other	810,000	10.5
Malaya	3,709,000	843,000	2,771,000	Hill Tribes	40,000	7,500,000
Singapore	232,000	140,000	1,253,000	'Other'	39,000	1,664,000
Sarawak	136,000	—	244,400	Indigenous	387,700	777,000
Sabah	—	—	104,500	Indigenous	306,500	480,000
				'Other'	43,400	
				Java and Madura	63.1 million	
				Sumatra	15.7 million	
				Celebes	7.1 million	
Indonesia §	*Indonesians*			Kalimantan	4.1 million	
	97.0	—	2,400,000	Bali / Nusa Tenggara	5.5 million	99.4
				Malaku	.79 million	
	Filipinos			W. Irian	.7 million	
Philippines	28.3	—	700,000	(Muslims 750,000)		29.0

Notes: * Owing to rounding and different statistical sources, the figures do not add exactly.
† Malays. Strictly 'Malaysians', which includes citizens of Indonesian origin domiciled in Malaya.
‡ Note that the indigenous peoples of Sabah and Sarawak have *not* been included as Malays.
§ Source for provincial figures, *Statistical Pocket Book of Indonesia, 1961* (Provisional Census Returns). These are not ethnic minorities.

TABLE 3
EDUCATION (1962)

	Primary Pupils per 100,000	*Secondary Pupils per 100,000*	*University Students per 100,000*	*Doctors to Population*
Burma	8,340	477	70	1:14,000
Thailand	14,200	997	59	1:11,000
Cambodia	10,400	824	27	(x)
South Viet-Nam	9,800	1,772	112	1:20,000
Malaysia	15,200	2,765	53	1: 5,500
Malaya	15,000	2,700	18	1: 7,000
Singapore	18,000	3,965	250	1: 2,500
Sarawak	9,500	1,900	—	1:13,500
Sabah	12,000	1,115	—	1:10,200
Indonesia	10,000	617	91	(1:50,000)
Philippines	13,000	2,288	807	1: 2,500

Note: Cambodia has very few doctors, mainly expatriate. Health Services are largely maintained in rural areas by *officiers de santé*, with less than full medical training. If these were included, the figure would be approximately 1:36,000.

Source: U.N.E.S.C.O.–I.A.U. Manpower Report.

impossible to draw hard and fast lines among some populations where there is a general cultural affinity or a long history of intermarriage. In particular, Indonesia is a chequered pattern of cultures from end to end, with the Javanese as the biggest fairly homogeneous block.

2. THE BUDDHIST MAINLAND

Burma

The central plain of Burma, watered by the Irrawaddy, is shaped roughly like a segment of orange, with the outer (western) curve bounded by the Naga, Chin, and Arakan Mountains, and the inner side lined by the Shan Hills, through the centre of which the Salween runs. The ancient kingdom of the Burmese was based at its northern tip, at Mandalay, 500 miles north of Rangoon on the Irrawaddy. From there the Burmese controlled a kingdom of varying extent, according to victories or defeats against the hill-peoples around them and the neighbouring kingdom of Thailand. Up to 1784 the Kings of Arakan were not under Burmese control and had some sway over parts of East Bengal; by that time a considerable Indian settlement, Muslim in faith, began to grow up in Arakan. The delta, inhabited by Mons and Karens, was not originally a Burmese world.

The British advance into Burma proceeded by fits and starts. In 1824 the East India Company became involved in wars which resulted in the control of Tenasserim and Arakan; in 1852 the Irrawaddy delta was annexed, and large-scale Indian immigration followed; in 1886 King Thibaw was deposed in Mandalay and the conquest was completed. Burma became part of the Indian Empire; it was not formally separated until the Act of 1935, implemented in 1937. After the War (1939–45) and Japanese occupation, the British resumed control for two years. Full independence was gained in 1948.

During the British occupation the outlying peoples (Kachins, Chins, Shans, and the Karens of the Salween district) were treated as 'excluded Districts', outside the ministerial system which was eventually built up, on the usual colonial pattern, in Rangoon. After independence the central Government in Rangoon was faced with two political tasks. First, to deal with various army and Communist revolts; second, to bring the ethnic minorities, by force or by compromise, into a Union of Burma which would be strong enough to operate as a nation-state. By 1955 the main structure of the Union was fairly well established, in the form of a Union of five states (Kachin, Shan, Karen, Kayah (Karenni), and Burma Proper) and the Chin Special District. Since then sporadic fighting has continued, mainly against two conflicting Communist groups ('White Flag' and 'Red Flag' Communists) and strong minority resistance. This fighting, varying in intensity from serious raids and engagements to mere dacoity, continues to the present day in several areas, despite repeated attempts by the central Government to negotiate a final settlement.

Parliamentary government was maintained until 1958, when the army took control for over a year. After a further civilian ministry under U Nu, the Revolutionary Government of the Union of Burma, under General Ne Win, again took control in 1962, this time with the intention of retaining power. The Government is committed to a socialist programme; it has nationalized all major foreign enterprises and the wholesale and retail trade of Rangoon; the emphasis of its political and economic programme is on the mobilization of the common people of Burma, with a maximum of direct contact between the ruling military group and the farmers.

The problem of finding national unity in Burma, since the cataclysm of the war and the Japanese occupation, has far outshadowed all else. Political and ethnic differences have intertwined, but it is broadly true that the ethnic problem has been central. The hills and some parts of the delta provide an almost inaccessible refuge for insurgents, and the ethnic minorities have persistently resisted any but the most tenuous control from Rangoon. On several occasions in the early 1950s Rangoon itself was threatened by insurgent forces, and the central road and railway to Mandalay have constantly been cut or sabotaged.[2] The economy necessarily suffered from this constant interference (national income did not reach its prewar level until 1956–7), but the strain also gradually wore down all attempts at civilian government; it was almost inevitable that, in the end, the army should take over.

It would be unfair to attribute too much blame to the central Burmese Government. On the military side they have shown amazing persistence and a considerable degree of success in sustaining a long, wearing battle to establish internal security. On the political side, it can be argued that the main governing party (the Anti-Fascist People's League) attempted to control and 'Burmanize' the administration of the minorities unwisely. But the offers of federal relationships made from Rangoon have gone as far as it is possible to go without dismembering the country into separate autonomous states; yet they have frequently been rejected. Faced by intransigence (as the Burmese

[2] This period has been described authoritatively and in detail by Dr Hugh Tinker, in *The Union of Burma*, London, 1957.

saw it) among the minority leaders, and by a largely immigrant domination of commercial and industrial life, the Government of Rangoon has moved constantly farther towards a central military dictatorship and a left-wing anti-foreign socialism, hoping to create a solid bond of alliance between the peasant masses and the central modernizing power. Almost inevitably, the outcome of this policy, in the hands of the army, has been to antagonize almost the whole middle class—the trading and commercial community, largely Indian or British; the Civil Service, damned for being traditionalist, bureaucratic, stiff-necked; and even the universities, partly because of Communist infiltration into the student body, partly for being academic and claiming a freedom to obstruct and criticize in a time of national crisis. At the time of writing a further and predictable antagonism between the army and the Buddhist hierarchy has been manifested in demonstrations and arrests.

There are parallels to this situation elsewhere in the developing world. The African attack on 'tribalism' shows the anxiety of the central, newly established state to eradicate or crush this danger of ethnic separatism which has plagued Burma. But whereas in Ghana, for example, the ruling political party was strong enough to infiltrate and undermine Ashanti; whereas in Uganda the modernizing political leadership from the outer provinces is slowly squeezing the central kingdom of Buganda into the national mould, in Burma party leadership and influence never managed to upset the traditionalism of the Shan states or make a deep enough mark among the Karens or Kachins. The transition from civil war to politics was never fully achieved; the central power of the army was left to impose a unity which politics had failed to create.

Apart from the indigenous minorities, Burma has had both Chinese and Indian immigrants in considerable numbers, the Indians being, until 1964, by far the larger group.

Indian immigration grew rapidly throughout the nineteenth century and particularly after 1852. Apart from the old Muslim settlements in Arakan and in many other towns of Burma, Indian labour and Indian merchants were largely responsible, under British guidance, for the development of the great rice production of the Irrawaddy delta.

TABLE 4

NUMBERS OF INDIANS IN BURMA

	Total	*% of Population*
1872	136,504	4.9
1901	560,263	5.4
1931	1,017,825	6.9

Of the Indians in 1931, about 566,000 were Hindu, 397,000 Muslim, with about 30,000 Christians, 12,500 Buddhists, 11,000 Sikhs. The main groups included Bengalis, Chittagonians, Tamils, Telegus, Oriyas, Hindustanis, and Gujeratis, and Chettiar moneylenders from South India.[3]

Rangoon became more than half an Indian town (1931: 212,929 Indians out of 400,415 total population) with Hindustani as its lingua franca. The Chettiars became large landowners in the delta. By 1931 there were over 1,600 Chettiar firms, and by 1938 they owned 2,468,000 acres, or 25 per cent of all land in Lower Burma.[4]

War and the Japanese invasion resulted both in massacre and a huge exodus of Indians from Burma—it is thought that about 500,000 left, of whom many thousands perished on the way. About 150,000 to 200,000 probably returned after the War, and by the incomplete Census of 1953 there were shown to be 286,903 Indian or Pakistani people out of an *urban* population of 2,940,704; the rural Indian population might have been 300,000, making a total of about 600,000. Since the army took over in Burma, and particularly since 1964, when retail trade was nationalized in Rangoon, there has been another very large exodus amounting to 40,000 in the first six months of 1964, which may have reached 100,000 during 1964 alone.

The Chinese immigrant minority in Burma was, in the past, not only much smaller than the Indian but politically much less significant. The Indians came when Burma was part of the Indian Empire, under British protection; their continued presence was a reminder of colonialism and of the battle to secure independence from India in the 1930s. Moreover, they were far more dominant in commercial life and far more obtrusive in Rangoon. The Chinese became established in the urban retail trade and a few specialized occupations, notably as artisans and in the motor and petrol trade, but they have never been a serious focus for political feeling. Perhaps in consequence of this their numbers have grown, and they probably now amount to over 350,000, challenging the much-diminished Indian numbers. They have been torn by the faction of rival supporters of Peking and Taiwan, and it appears that Peking has won—all the Chinese schools in Burma use Peking textbooks. The close relationships between Peking and the Burmese military Government, as long as they last, will help to protect the Chinese minority. But their growing numbers and dependence on

[3] Usha Mahajani, *The Role of Indian Minorities in Burma and Malaya*, Bombay and New York, 1960. I have relied heavily on this most useful book.

[4] ibid.

private enterprise points to the possibility of more troublesome times for them later on.

Wherever the blame for Burma's suffering lies—and Britain must bear a heavy share for failure to protect in war or to re-establish a viable nation afterwards—the grim history of the postwar years in Burma shows how real are the dangers which other South-East Asian states have faced. An economy dominated by expatriates; a political structure wired together by the administration of a now-vanished colonial power, rather than by any common sense of nationhood; the infiltration of Communist ideas—these were a heritage not only for Burma but for Indonesia, Viet-Nam, and Malaysia.

Thailand

Thailand has an ancient monarchy, stretching back to the thirteenth century, extended or contracted by wars with Burma and by the occasional occupation of provinces of modern Cambodia and of Laos. The Thais themselves are known to have entered their present country from Yunnan in China, probably in the twelfth and thirteenth centuries. Their earliest settlements were in the Chiengmai area, and they fought their way south, mainly against the Khmers, to successive capitals at Sukhotai (1238–1350), Ayuthia (sacked by the Burmese in 1568 and 1767), and finally Bangkok. They now occupy the immense rice plain which leads down to Bangkok, sharing the surrounding foothills with some indigenous mountain tribes. The monarchy and Theravada Buddhism have combined to give Thailand a strong religious-monarchical system, with an aristocracy which has transformed itself largely into an educated *élite* with the prestige of high birth still retained. It is typical of this social transition that Thailand's oldest university, Chulalongkorn, grew first from a school for royal pages, was transformed next into a college for Civil Servants, and finally grew to be a university.

The revolution of 1932 transformed the autocracy of the kings into a constitutional monarchy, and political history since that time has been marked by a succession of *coups d'état*, attempted or successful (about thirteen have taken place since the revolution), marking changes in the possession of power between individual leaders who usually relied on one or more of the branches of the armed forces or the police. At present parliamentary government is in suspense. The *coups* have not, however, resulted in great bloodshed or bitterness and have left the main life of the country remarkably undisturbed.

In some ways it is difficult to avoid giving too idyllic a picture of

Thai society. There is plenty of land at present (Thailand is about as big as France, with half the population), and parts of it are much favoured, with good rice land and an unusually good supply of animal protein from the abundant fish in the rivers and irrigation systems. However, the large north-east plateau, with low rainfall, much poorer soils, and inadequate rivers, presents a less satisfactory picture. Population, now (1965) estimated to have reached over 30 million, is growing at an exceptionally high rate (3.5 per cent to 3.6 per cent per annum) and the problem of agricultural development will soon become far more urgent.

National income has been rising at between 6 per cent and 7 per cent per annum, giving an income per head of about £36 per annum in 1962. The wealth of Thailand lies in her agriculture, and particularly in the exports of rice and rubber which account for over 50 per cent by value of all exports. Although rice yields are higher than in Burma, and Thai rice is of good quality, they could still be very greatly increased. On the industrial side Thailand has given a warm welcome to foreign enterprise, and Bangkok in particular has had a long period of boom conditions in construction and industrial growth. There are small beginnings even of heavy industry and a remarkable growth of lighter enterprises, in which Thai citizens are playing an increasing part. Little of this new industry has, however, spread out into the provinces; the second town of Thailand, after Bangkok-Chonburi with its 2½ million population, is Chiengmai, with approximately 56,000. Out of a total of 9 million people economically active in 1960, 82 per cent were in agricultural pursuits, and only 5.6 per cent in commerce, 3.4 per cent in manufacturing industry, including cottage industries. Employment by manufacturing firms employing ten or more people probably did not exceed 150,000 in 1962 and may have been as low as 100,000.

Over and above the hopeful economic outlook, the national structure of Thailand is strong. Thai language and Buddhist religion are almost universal and there is a deeply felt sense of national unity. The Thais are surrounded by the evidences of a splendid Buddhist culture,[5] and sustained by a customary life deeply rooted in their history. The ruling classes have, for many generations, sent their sons overseas for education, so that in many ways the aristocracy has kept pace with the times. There is, indeed, a slightly alarming gap between the luxury and sophistication of Bangkok and the simplicity of the rural areas; and

[5] The magnificent Thai temples, often in a landscape of very simple peasant agriculture, remind one (socially, not architecturally) of the mixture of simple life and impressive Gothic cathedrals of England in the twelfth and thirteenth centuries.

the younger middle-class generation is becoming more impatient with dictatorship and the inevitable intrigue and corruption which go with it.[6]

There are minority problems, although they do not have the urgency of similar issues elsewhere in South-East Asia. In the hills there are some thirty tribes, mainly small, numbering about 230,000 in all; these form only a small fringe of ethnic difference which gives little anxiety. A larger and more problematic minority consists of the Malay Muslims on the Kra peninsula bordering Malaya. The Thai Government is always concerned lest an irredentist movement should gain ground there; but the Government of Malaya has not given any encouragement to this, and there is no immediate threat of trouble. The area is, indeed, largely alien, even in language, and Thai administrators have to speak Malay and accommodate to Muslim culture when they are sent there. The area which gives most concern to the Thai Government is the North-East, where a Lao element on the border may be infected with Pathet Lao and Communist ideas, and where the Khmers of neighbouring Cambodia are unfriendly. A good deal of economic effort has been devoted, in current development plans, to developing the North-East, and a university is being established at Khonkaen. Moreover, if the vast plans for the control of the Mekong River system come to fruition, the agricultural development of the North-East could make a major advance. No doubt the Thai Government is wise to see that this area does not remain a backwater in which opposition could breed.

Finally, Thailand has a large Chinese immigrant minority, probably now numbering over 3 million. The history of Thai-Chinese relationships is more fully dealt with in the next chapter. It is enough here to mention that, although there is a good deal of friction and jealousy, and although at some periods there has been downright persecution of the Chinese, it is a heated rather than a major or dangerous political issue. The Thais outnumber the Chinese by ten to one, and they are completely self-confident. Indeed, they have even a somewhat ambivalent attitude, one side of which is dominated by economic jealousy of Chinese commercial success, the other by a belief that a little Chinese blood in the family is not a disadvantage. Indeed, some of the most rich and powerful Thais may be thought to have profited from it.

Cambodia

The Khmer people of Cambodia present one of the mysteries of ethnic history. They are believed to have entered their present country on

[6] Even the tolerant Thai society was shocked by the revelations of the late Prime Minister Sarit's immense fortune.

the Mekong River from the north-west earlier than 2000 B.C., and they speak a language which is not obviously related to those of their neighbours, the Lao, Vietnamese, and Thais, but is grouped with the Mon language of southern Burma. By the first century A.D. three kingdoms occupied the lower Mekong—the people of Fu-nan, the Chams, and the Khmers—with Fu-nan dominant, and with extremely strong cultural influence pouring in from India. At some time in the sixth century the Khmer Kingdom of Chen-la, north of the Mekong, appears to have conquered Fu-nan, only to fall under periodic vassalage to the great Malay kingdom of Indonesia.[7] In the centuries 900–1200 the vast temples of Angkor were built, still within Hindu cultural tradition. The end of this great period of Khmer glory came in 1353 when the Thais conquered Angkor. After about 1430 (and a second Thai conquest) Brahminism gave way to Theravada Buddhism. After centuries of Khmer warfare against both the Vietnamese and the Thais, the French Protectorate was established in April 1864, and in June of that year King Norodom was crowned in Phnom-Penh by representatives of France and Thailand. It could be said that French protection saved Cambodia from greedy neighbours on both flanks. The monarchy continued under French protection, Prince Sihanouk succeeding as king in 1941. After an attack by Thailand in August 1940, aided by the Japanese, peace was concluded in 1941, Thailand regaining the border provinces. Independence was gained in 1954, and in 1955 Prince Sihanouk abdicated as King and took over as Prime Minister.

The foreign policy of Prince Sihanouk has been neutralist, with considerable hostility to both Thailand and Viet-Nam, always suspected of ill designs on Cambodia. A quarrel over the ownership of the Prek Viharn temple, resolved by the International Court of Justice in Cambodia's favour in June 1962 has soured Thai-Cambodian relations lately, and there is a running sore over the Viet-Nam border demarcation, by which at present half a million Khmer people are said to be included in South Viet-Nam. In 1963 Prince Sihanouk, wishing to avoid all entanglement with the Cold War, rejected further American aid, and Cambodian-U.S. relations have been further strained by American and South Vietnamese bombing of allegedly Cambodian villages on the Viet-Nam border. Aid from France, however, is still accepted, particularly willingly since France decided to recognize the Peking Government. Prince Sihanouk, who has established a remarkable paternal ascendancy over his people, personally guides policy. His apparently needless hostility to America (and, to a less degree, Britain)

[7] Sri Vijaya Kingdom, based on Sumatra, *c.* A.D. 630–1300.

is most easily understood as a recognition that, in the long term, Cambodia must establish a relationship with China akin to that of a tributary monarchy. He dare not risk association with China's enemies, however good and even generous their intentions may be. For one who lives next door to Laos and Viet-Nam this is scarcely an unreasonable point of view.

The population of modern Cambodia is not known with any accuracy. A reasonable estimate for 1962 would be 5¾ million. Income per head is probably not above £30 though it is hard to estimate realistically, because the international value of the *riel* is artificial. The economy is overwhelmingly agricultural, and 70 per cent to 75 per cent of exports consist of rice and rubber. The latter, under French plantation management, is some of the highest yielding in Asia. Rice yields and quality are, however, poor, and there is room for great expansion. Industry is in the infant stage, with a few foreign enterprises. The main development has been in road-building and the construction of the port of Sihanoukville. Cambodia is, however, making strenuous efforts to develop native resources (*Le Cambodge s'aide lui-même* is a favourite official slogan), and has achieved much, in small ways, over the last five years.

Cambodia has indigenous minorities[8] in the form of hill-tribes (about 60,000), often called *phnong* (barbarians) as a collective term, and a group of Cham-Malays, a rigidly Muslim remnant of the Champa Kingdom who had intermarried with their Malay conquerors. They live their own life in villages north and east of Phnom-Penh and were estimated to number 70,000 in 1950.

The main immigrant minorities are Vietnamese and Chinese. It has been almost impossible to establish the number of these minorities. Estimates of Chinese numbers vary from 100,000 to 425,000,[9] with the latter figure probably much nearer the truth. The Vietnamese numbers are probably within the range 300,000 to 350,000. Thus the Khmer people represent 80 per cent of the population. In Phnom-Penh, however the immigrant population is heavily concentrated, and 30 per cent of the city's population was estimated in 1950 to be Chinese, 27½ per cent Vietnamese. While the Khmers are in some degree jealous of Chinese merchants (and in late years they have been driven out of the

[8] Much of the following material comes from D. J. Steinberg *et. al.*, *Cambodia*, Human Relations Area Files, New Haven, 1956 (revised ed., 1959).

[9] D. E. Willmott, *The Chinese of Semarang*, Ithaca, N.Y., 1960. Much depends on the criterion used to identify 'Chinese'. Willmott's higher estimate is based on the numbers who describe themselves as Chinese (including a large number who have Cambodian citizenship).

import-export trade), they respect Chinese energy, and there is some intermarriage—about 68,000 Sino-Cambodians were recorded in 1950. On the other hand, the Khmers dislike and despise the Vietnamese, who are mainly engaged in service occupations in Phnom-Penh, and as artisans, fishermen, and plantation-workers on the French rubber estates. The French favoured the Vietnamese, and used them in the Civil Service; they were, in contrast, hostile to the Chinese, partly from commercial rivalry. It may be that the good Khmer-Chinese and bad Khmer-Vietnamese relations reflect an anti-colonial reversal of the French attitude as well as historical hostility towards Viet-Nam.

South Viet-Nam

The Annamites, who form the main population of both North and South Viet-Nam, are reputed to have come from Tibet (as are so many of the nations of South-East Asia today) well before the Christian era. From the second century B.C. to the second century A.D. they were pressed upon by Imperial China and finally subdued and Sinicized during many centuries of Chinese rule. In the seventh century they were attacked by the Chams from the south, but repulsed them; in the tenth century they finally broke free from the Chinese and also began their drive to the south which ended in the conquest of the kingdom of Champa and the final occupation of the Mekong delta in Cochin China. There followed a long period of Annamite empire, following the Mandarin system of administration and a strong Confucian philosophy. Bitter rivalry between Tonkin in the north and Cochin China in the south, led by the Trinhs of Tonkin and Nguyens of the south, was in existence long before the French invasions. This rivalry gave the first opening for European intrusion, the Trinhs enlisting Dutch support and the Nguyens Portuguese. The French, who gradually ousted their European rivals, finally established Gia-long (Nguyen Anh) as 'Emperor of All the Annamites' in 1802. French conquest of Cochin China followed in 1863, and, after an abortive expedition in 1873, a French Protectorate over Cochin China, Annam, and Tonkin was finally established in 1884. Over the whole of this period occasional wars were waged against the ever-present threat from China, and at many periods there was forceful expansion into Cambodia. This history of passionate resistance to Chinese control and of rivalry between North and South is worth remembering.

After the Second World War the French were never easily in the saddle again, and the confused internal fighting, partly a war of independence and partly a struggle against Vietminh Communism, was finally closed by French defeat and the partition into North and South Viet-Nam made by the Geneva Accord in 1954.

In its early years the régime of President Diem had considerable success in re-establishing order and administration and some important measures of land reform. But gradually the rising tide of guerrilla warfare, led by Communist sympathizers, and the growing dissatisfaction with the autocratic methods of the Diem régime led both to the downfall of Diem and to a military emergency. Only massive American aid has (at the time of writing) prevented a total collapse of the quickly changing Saigon governments.

Despite parliamentary forms, democracy, in any widespread sense, has never penetrated South Viet-Nam. Provincial government has remained highly autocratic, in the Mandarin tradition, and the central Government has been a dictatorship supported by an *élite*, French-trained bureaucracy, or resting solely on the army. In the provinces, riddled with underground or overt guerrilla warfare, it is a desperate struggle to maintain administrative control and to give any effect to the modernizing social and agricultural policies of a Government which is attempting reform in the midst of a bitter struggle for survival.[10]

South Viet-Nam retains the French educational system, with something of its high quality. Three universities have been established: at Saigon, as the southern successor to the University of Hanoi, teaching in English, French, and Vietnamese; at Dalat, which is a French Catholic institution; and at Hué in the North, which is purely Vietnamese. During the endless civil war many of the French-educated Vietnamese preferred to stay in France, despite a shortage of educated manpower in their native country, and 3,000 to 4,000 of them are there to this day.

South Viet-Nam is as confused culturally as it is politically. Theravada Buddhism has formally replaced Confucianism to a large extent, although Confucian political and social ethics still in many ways remain the stronger force. French Catholicism, favoured by the Diem régime, has been a strong rival; it was in part responsible for provoking the Buddhist priesthood to revolt and to the symbolic martyrdoms by fire which preceded the fall of the Diem régime. There have also been powerful religious sects, notably the Hoa Hao, Binh-Xuyen, and Cao-Dai movements, which became involved in politics and were finally crushed in a considerable civil war in 1955. American influence,

[10] Viet-Cong have followed a policy of murdering or intimidating Government officials in rural areas (teachers, medical personnel, agricultural extension staff) which has crippled even the most well-intentioned efforts at social and economic reform.

intensely resented by the French and by some Vietnamese, has further complicated the scene. Caught in the Cold War, and between conflicting French and American policies, South Viet-Nam is not master in its own house.

One last complication is found in the presence of the Chinese, thought to number about three-quarters of a million, heavily concentrated in the towns and above all in Cholon, the 'Chinatown' of Saigon. A vigorous attempt to force them to assimilate was made in 1956, when they were, in effect, given the choice of accepting citizenship (offered to all locally born Chinese) or of deportation; and at the same time sweeping occupational restrictions for all non-citizens were announced and Chinese schools temporarily closed. These measures met with vigorous opposition and have been only partially effective; the Chinese remain, awaiting the outcome of the civil war.

3. THE MALAY WORLD

Indonesia

It is impossible to give a satisfactory thumbnail sketch of the vast area and 100 million people of Indonesia. Its unity is not, indeed, wholly and solely the result of common administration by the Dutch. Racially, it is in a broad sense 'Malay', with the many sub-mixtures which can be included in this word, with more marked homogeneity in the groups running North-East to Borneo from Java and a greater admixture of Pacific or 'Melanesian' types in the eastern islands, from Sulawezi (Celebes) as far as the quite different Papuans of West Irian (New Guinea). Again, four-fifths of the present population profess the Muslim faith, though a somewhat lax and much Hindu-influenced variety. Throughout history this great archipelago has been an area of constant sea-movement of peoples, slowly built into what might broadly be called a civilization[11] in terms of the distribution of local trade, local movement, a level of skills, broad similarities in the range of climate and agriculture, and wide extension of common language and religious belief.

Indian influence deeply affected these lands at least from the first century A.D., though many settlements appear to date from much earlier times. Two vast Indonesian-Malay empires are believed to have

[11] The nearest word would be the Greek οἰκουμένγ (ecumenical), meaning a circle of inhabited lands within which men move about and have relations with each other; but this is too broad.

flourished—Sri Vijaya from Sumatra (about A.D. 650–1300) and Majapahit from eastern Java, overlapping Sri Vijaya but continuing to the fifteenth century. These kingdoms are reputed to have made vassals on the mainland (Viet-Nam, Cambodia, Thailand, and Malaya) and at times reached out to Taiwan (Formosa) and New Guinea.

The Muslim influence was also very old, coming partly through Arab traders but also reaching the archipelago through India, carried by Gujerati merchants. The main period of Muslim occupation (as against mere trading contact) seems to have run from the thirteenth to the sixteenth centuries. By the end of this period Majapahit had fallen, Sumatra and Java were converted to Islam, and Hindu faith had taken refuge in Bali.[12]

The Dutch were already on the doorstep. In the first thirty years of the seventeenth century they established their key controls in the Moluccas, Java and Sumatra, and continued to expand and tighten their grip until in the late nineteenth century it was administratively and politically complete.

Whether, but for the Europeans, there would ever have been a political separation between the mainland Malay peninsula, colonized from Indonesia, and the Indonesian islands, or where the centre of power might have been found, it is hard to say. Certainly, when the British seized the Dutch island territories in the Napoleonic Wars, Raffles (as British Governor of Java) had dreamed of a Malay federation. But in 1824 an exchange of settlements and rights between the British and Dutch Governments settled a division between the Malay Peninsula and the islands which has lasted until now. It is not unnatural that Indonesia should look back to a precolonial era in an attempt to reunite a Malay empire which foreigners had sundered.

Dutch power was broken by the Japanese invasion, and the Allies after the reconquest were not prepared to go on helping Holland re-establish it by force. A considerable Dutch 'presence', in commerce and administration, remained until 1958, when President Sukarno, having painfully secured ascendancy over all Indonesia save New Guinea, made the final break. One major immigrant community remained—the overseas Chinese, numbering perhaps 2½ to 3 million, mainly in Java, with many centuries of history and much intermarriage behind them, playing their accustomed role as city merchants and traders, as the purchasers of peasant crops and the small distributors and retailers in the village stores.

[12] C. Robequain (trans. E. D. Laborde), *Malaya, Indonesia, Borneo and the Philippines*, London, 1958.

The characteristics of Indonesia in these troubled postwar years have been the intense concentration of the Government on politics and an equal neglect of economics; the sagging of agricultural production mainly through lack of management skill to maintain and replant the Dutch estates; the rise of a powerful Communism, balanced by the power of the army; mutterings and occasional outbreaks of revolt, in Sumatra, Celebes, Kalimantan (Dutch Borneo), and the South Moluccas; a remarkable extension of education at all levels, with the foundation of twenty-five skeleton universities (Djakarta, Bandung Institute of Technology, Jogjakarta and one or two more are establishing high quality); a passionate nationalism, with nationalization of foreign enterprises as a sop thrown to the Communists from time to time; a desperate inflation and shortage of foreign exchange, which has led the President to cling to American aid despite the Cold War and the Communists; an ambitious programme of industrialization, largely but not quite wholly frustrated by the prevailing economic chaos; and, finally, 'confrontation' with Malaysia.

It is tempting for any Westerner to criticize Sukarno. Indeed, Indonesia, with its rich resources and highly intelligent people, has come to a sad state of poverty and economic chaos. But it is more to the present purpose to notice the amazing power which one independence leader can exercise. For millions of Indonesians, despite all their troubles, Sukarno is still the man who led them to freedom and re-established their pride. That he could hold together these vast territories for almost twenty years, despite rebellions and hardships, is a measure not only of the man but of the immense force of nationalism in the hardest times. The Dutch, despite their great virtues and economic achievement, seem of all the colonial powers to have generated the most hostility. The man who symbolized their defeat could impose untold strains and sacrifices without losing popular support.

Perhaps, too, the continued existence of Indonesia as a unit points to the relative weakness of ethnic divisions, many as they are. Only Sumatra was big enough to challenge the power of Java, and Sumatra is not one community but a patchwork of cultures with little recent history of unitary patriotism. The islands to the east of Java were neither united nor individually strong enough to hold out against Java's power.

Sukarno, by highly skilful handling of Communist and religious movements, and by dealing with local revolts one by one, managed to avoid the simultaneous wars on many fronts which almost brought the Government of Burma to its knees.

Malaysia

The Malay Peninsula and Singapore stand in sharp contrast to every other state of South-East Asia. Both, as they stand today, are newly made. The remainder of the original inhabitants of Malaya are found now only in the mountains—Negritos in the north, called *Semang* in Kedah and Perak, *Pangan* in Kelantan; Senoi scattered in the central mountain chain, Jakuns in the south (Negri Sembilan, Malacca, and Johore). They were gradually driven back by the Malays invading from Indonesia, who seem to have moved in from the twelfth century onwards, first to the river mouths, then up the rivers, and later strung out along the tracks and roads and eventually the railways. The original golden age of Malay settlement was the period of the Malacca sultanate, founded in about A.D. 1400, which set the pattern for the sultans' rule in the later states. Slowly the Malays became organized into the nine states which formed the Federation of Malaya in 1948.[13] The Malays spoke a common language, and held a common Muslim faith. By themselves, they might slowly have formed a fairly small agricultural nation with a common culture and small hill-tribe minorities.

But they were not left alone. The earliest European invasions of Malaya go back 450 years. The Portuguese, under Alfonso d'Albuquerque, captured Malacca in 1511 and ruled for more than a hundred years, until the Dutch defeated them in 1641. The Dutch continued in power until the Napoleonic Wars, finally yielding to the British (who had meanwhile occupied Penang, Province Wellesley, and Singapore) in 1825. Until this point the Europeans had been primarily interested in control of the rich trade route through the Straits of Malacca. They had done little more than burden the growing Malay sultanates with onerous trade restrictions and harry the sultans if agreements were broken. It was the development of the tin and rubber industries in Malaya and the growth of Singapore which brought in Chinese and Indians, both as labourers and as merchants, and turned Malaya and Singapore into the perilously balanced plural societies which they are today.

The Indians, almost wholly Tamil-, Telegu-, and Malayalam-speakers from South India, began to come in large numbers, as indentured labour for the rubber industry, in the second half of the nineteenth century.

[13] Before the 1939–45 War there were: (*a*) the Straits Settlements—Singapore, Malacca, Penang, and Province Wellesley, a British colony united in 1826; (*b*) the Federated Malay States—Perak, Selangor, Negri Sembilan, Pahang; (*c*) the Unfederated Malay States of Johore, Kedah, Perlis, Kelantan, and Trengganu.

TABLE 5
INDIAN POPULATION OF MALAYA

		% *of total population*
1871	33,390	11.0
1911	267,170	10.1
1921	471,514	14.2
1931	621,847	14.3
1947	599,616	10.25
1957	735,038	10.0

Of the 1957 total, 635,000 were Tamil, Telegu, or Malayali (556,453 Tamil), and 61,400 Sikhs, Punjabis, or Pathans. The remainder were composed of Ceylon Tamils (24,600), Ceylonese (3,300), and Pakistanis (10,900). They were heavily concentrated in the states of Perak and Selangor (385,000), either in the rubber estates or in service occupations or retail trade in the towns.[14]

The Chinese, unlike the Indians, did not come in as indentured labour under government-to-government arrangements. They were recruited by contractors direct from China, or they came simply as immigrant settlers to make a life in Malaya. They quickly dominated the tin industry on the mainland; they increased fantastically in the port of Singapore and in Penang; and they settled to market-gardening and small rubber production wherever they could. The immigrants who came for a short time and returned vastly outnumbered those who settled permanently—the records show that 5 million Chinese entered in the nineteenth century and 12 million between 1900 and 1940. The numbers of residents recorded in Malaya and Singapore at various dates are:

TABLE 6
CHINESE POPULATION OF MALAYA AND SINGAPORE

1871	(Straits Settlements)	104,600
1901	(Malaya and Singapore)	301,463
1941	(Malaya and Singapore)	2,418,615 (44% of total population)

The estimated population for all races of the Federation of Malaya only (Census Department projection) is:

TABLE 7
POPULATION OF FEDERATION OF MALAYA, BY RACE

	Malaysian	*Chinese*	*Indian*	*Other*	*Total*
1962	3,709,000	2,771,000	843,000	140,000	7,463,000
1967	4,381,000	3,282,000	1,014,000	154,000	8,831,000
1972	5,158,000	3,888,000	1,230,000	—	10,450,000

[14] 59.5 per cent in primary, 33.2 per cent in tertiary, only 7.3 per cent in secondary occupations. 85 per cent of those in primary occupations were on rubber estates. See Ooi Jin-Bee, *Land, People and Economy in Malaya*, London, 1963.

In Singapore, the 1960 figures are:

Malaysian	*Chinese*	*Indian*	*Other*	*Total*
232,000	1,253,00	140,000	39,000	1,665,000

Thus, in Malaya and Singapore, Malays could barely muster 50 per cent of the population. The addition of Sabah and Sarawak, with a mainly indigenous population which, though part of 'the Malay world', is not narrowly Malay in speech or culture, and with a large Chinese[15] population, tipped the balance of numbers against the Malays, while Singapore was still part of the Federation.

TABLE 8

MALAYSIA (INCLUDING SINGAPORE)—
POPULATION %, BY RACE (1961)

	Malaya	*Singapore*	*Sarawak*	*Sabah*	*Total Malaysia*
Malays	50.1	14.0	17.5	—	39.2
Other indigenous	—	—	50.3	67.2	7.0
Chinese	36.9	75.2	31.1	23.3	41.2
Indian/Pakistani	11.2	8.3	—	—	9.4
Others	1.8	2.5	1.1	9.5	2.2
	100.0	100.0	100.0	100.0	100.0

The Borneo territories which joined Malaysia in September 1963—Brunei refused and remains under British protection—are a twentieth-century relic of an earlier style of colonization. The British stumbled into this coastal strip in the days of naval and trade rivalry with other European powers, partly for strategic reasons, partly as merchant-adventurers, partly by mistake. Brunei was and still is a Muslim sultanate with a mainly Malay population. Sabah (British North Borneo), with a population (1960 Census) of 454,421, is the mountainous, forested north-eastern corner of the island, with 67.5 per cent indigenous population, and 23 per cent Chinese. Sarawak (1960 population 744,529) has barely 50 per cent indigenous population, 31.5 per cent Chinese and 17.5 per cent Malay. Both countries have made great strides in education and the beginning of a road system since the Second World War. But they remain, in effect, undeveloped, with a high proportion of subsistence agriculture, 25 per cent literacy, and, in the forests and mountains, a tribal way of life.

Politically, this finely balanced plural society of Malaysia was at first managed in three separate blocs. The Alliance Party in Malaya, grouping Malays, Chinese, and Indians, gives in effect a Malay political domination and holds at bay extremist racial and religious groups,

[15] 105,000 in Sabah; 244,000 in Sarawak (1960 Census).

notably the Pan-Malayan Independence Party (P.M.I.P.), which represents the extreme Malay-Muslim nationalists. Singapore runs its own Chinese politics, with the moderate left in control. The Borneo territories have mainly elected indigenous ministers, served by expatriate or Chinese senior Civil Servants.

Thus the picture of Malaysia divides into three parts. First, mainland Malaya, with its nine Muslim states with 87 per cent of Malays in rural occupations and 62 per cent of urban population Chinese[16] ruled by Malays, with a Civil Service in which four-fifths of senior posts are reserved for Malays. Second, Singapore, the greatest Chinese city in South-East Asia. Third, Sabah and Sarawak, democratically ruled by its indigenous majority, but, for at least another five years, staffed mainly by English and Chinese, and coloured by a strong local patriotism. After Federation, the possibility that Singapore political parties would campaign on the mainland was a clearly foreseen danger. When it materialized the strain on Malay nationalism proved too great: Singapore had to go.

Economically, Malaysia is by far the richest country of South-East Asia, with an annual income per head (about £100) double that of any other.[17] Its economic prospects (if at least economic links with Singapore are sensibly managed) are excellent, if it can survive the heavy balance of payments and budgetary deficits of its large development plan over the next four years. Politically, and in its racial relationships, it faces by far the most difficult problem in South-East Asia. Internationally, it faces the hostility of Indonesia, and is able to do so only by incurring the accusation of sheltering behind 'the imperialist powers'.

The Philippines

Both geologically and by their flora and fauna the Philippine islands belong to 'the Malay world', particularly to the curve from Java through Borneo. Quite possibly most of the population moved in along this curve; they are described as Malay and Proto-Malay (Indonesian), with some admixture of Negritos, Vedda, and Papuans. The Negritos are now a very small primitive group, probably numbering 30,000 to 40,000, mainly in the interior of Mindanao and in the western Visayas.

At least from the earliest centuries of the Christian era Indian influence was reaching the Philippines, and through the great period of Indonesian empires (A.D. 700–1500) it had reached at least to Manila. Islam followed closely, and was first felt in Mindanao in the fifteenth

[16] Ooi Jin-Bee, op. cit. [17] See Table 1, p. 14.

century; it has retained the allegiance of about three-quarters of a million inhabitants of the southern Philippines.

The Chinese from Kwantung were also early settlers, and by the sixteenth century may have formed as much as 10 per cent of the island population.[18] Although modern Philippine statistics, which record only Chinese citizens as Chinese, give a figure of about 100,000,[19] it has been variously estimated that there are at least 700,000[20] or 1,000,000[21] Sino-Filipinos, mostly from intermarriage with Tagalog women from Central Luzon.

Three hundred years of Spanish rule naturally left a deep mark on the Philippines, and today there are thought to be at least 200,000 Filipinos with mixed Spanish blood, who form much of the Philippine *élite*. Spanish capitalists play a large part in the Philippine economy, ranking only after the Americans and Chinese, and are especially prominent in the sugar and tobacco industries.

The total population of the islands is estimated to reach 32,422,000 by 1965 (27,455,800 in 1960; 29,000,000 *plus* in 1962) with a growth rate of over 3 per cent per annum. Income per head was £45 to £50 in 1962. Economic growth was extremely rapid in the early 1950s (over 6 per cent per annum), but fell off at the end of the decade. It has probably recovered to a high figure now, thanks in part to increased quotas for sugar in the U.S.A. owing to the exclusion of Cuba.

The economy of the Philippines is primarily agricultural (61.7 per cent of all those economically active). Agriculture is divided into major plantations (sugar, tobacco, abaca, coconut), much of it of high productivity; large landed estates with small tenant cultivation (much of it highly unproductive); and peasant holdings. Rice yields are low and rice is now imported (over 200,000 tons in 1964).[22] As elsewhere in South-East Asia, despite the fundamental importance of peasant agriculture, attention had been mainly concentrated on industrialization. Manufacturing industry accounts for less than 12 per cent (1961) of total employment, and the World Bank Report (1960) reckoned that organized manufacturing (employing five or more workers) employed about 250,000, less than 3 per cent of the labour force. While industrialization has been much concentrated in or near Manila, there are now major schemes for heavy industry based on proposed iron and steel plants in Rizal Province (Luzon) and in Mindanao. Textiles, oil

[18] Beyer, quoted by Robequain, op. cit. [19] 100,971 in the 1947 Census.

[20] Robequain, op. cit. [21] Kolb, quoted by Robequain, op. cit.

[22] It is ironical that the International Rice Research Institute, magnificently equipped and well staffed, is situated in the Philippines, yet the results of its research work have not been used in Philippine agriculture; indeed, they have been better used in Thailand.

refining, food milling and processing, sugar refining, logging, cement, and car assembly represent other growing industries.

The most striking characteristics of the Philippines are the deep and near-universal influence of the Catholic Church; the markedly American emphasis on free capitalism and American-type democratic political life; and the immense development of a system of private, profit-making colleges and universities (with nearly 300,000 students, or 1 per cent of total population enrolled). In all these ways the country differs totally from all its South-East Asian neighbours. In three respects, however, it is alike—in the preponderance of one capital city, Manila-Quezon City, with nearly 3 million inhabitants in the conurbation; in the backwardness of peasant agriculture and the maldistribution of wealth and educated manpower as between Manila (and some provincial towns) and the whole peasant economy; and finally in the nationalist jealousy and dislike of Chinese small traders and merchants, especially in the rural economy. The social/political problems of the Philippines, with a high number of unemployed (about 2,000,000) among whom are 30,000 to 40,000 college graduates, and a glaring gap between ostentatious wealth and acute poverty, could be serious, particularly if the present commercial and plantation boom should collapse.

Catholic, capitalist, much Americanized—the Cambodians say Filipinos are more like Americans than Asians—yet by race and ancient contacts part of the Malay world, the Philippines represent a nation in search of a personality. Their dealings with Indonesia reveal one side of this. There is a strong pull towards 'Maphilindo' and pan-Malayanism; there is perhaps an even stronger terror of Communism in Sukarno's camp. Again, there is a wish to be Asian, not American—and yet a pride in American democracy, modernity, economic vigour. There is a proud Spanish tradition and Catholic obedience—and a secular, egalitarian, nationalist youth. Even if the quarrel between Sukarno and Malaysia were settled, it seems doubtful whether the Philippines would live happily in a Muslim-Malay-Chinese world. More probably a somewhat anonymous modernity will keep Philippine policy opportunist, seeking friends and profits where they can be found. Manila and the big landlords and capitalists would feel more at home in the 'big league' of international commerce, with close contacts with America, Japan, Hongkong, Singapore, and Bangkok, than with the peasant-socialist-revolutionary countries. It is neither minority problems nor the search for nationhood which dominate Filipino thinking: it is the internal problem of managing a corrupt capitalist democracy superimposed on a backward peasantry.

III

THE IMMIGRANT RACES

1. THE CHINESE[1]

Origin

Throughout history the Chinese have been in close contact with the countries to the south. Within the Christian era we hear of quite large movements of pilgrims to India who broke their journey in Nanyang,[2] between the fifth and eighth centuries. By the eleventh century, under the Sung Dynasty (920–1279), merchants were developing a fast-growing trade, particularly with the coast of Viet-Nam. In 1293 a huge fleet carrying 20,000 Chinese made a reconnaissance of Java as a possible point of settlement, though no large colony seems to have been established. The next great period of overseas adventuring comes with the famous voyages of Admiral Cheng-Ho between 1405 and 1433; a system of state trading was built up with Nanyang at this time. By 1500, overseas Chinese were widely established in Brunei (which then included much more of Borneo), the Philippines, Java, Sumatra, and the mainland of Viet-Nam, Cambodia, and Thailand. Significantly, there are tales of local massacres, notably in Luzon in 1603[3] and again in 1639.

A critical date is reached in 1644, when the Manchus overcame the Ming Dynasty in China. For forty years the Manchus were fighting Ming rebels in South China, and the rebels drew extensively on the communities of Nanyang for help. The constant warfare in South China and the special political affinity of the rebels with the Nanyang Chinese reinforced both the tendency to emigrate and the narrow concentration

[1] The 'overseas Chinese' have been much studied by many scholars, and I could not hope to add new, specialist knowledge in this book. Much of what follows is drawn from Wang Gungwu, *A Short History of the Nanyang Chinese*, Singapore, 1959, and V. Purcell, *The Chinese in Southeast Asia*, London, 1965. Other authorities extensively used are: Willmott, *The Chinese of Semarang*; Ooi Jin-Bee, *Land, People and Economy in Malaya*; Robequain, *Malaya, Indonesia, Borneo and the Philippines*; R. J. Coughlin, *Double Identity: The Chinese in Modern Thailand*, Hong Kong, 1960; G. W. Skinner, (1) 'Overseas Chinese in South-East Asia', *The Annals*, Jan. 1959; (2) 'Chinese Assimilation and Thai Politics', *Journal of Asian Studies*, Vol. 16, No. 2, Feb. 1956; and (3) *Leadership and Power in the Chinese Community of Thailand*, Ithaca, N.Y., 1958.

[2] 'Nanyang' is used by the Chinese to describe all Chinese settlements in South-East Asia.

[3] See Purcell, op. cit. The accounts from Spanish sources suggest a rising by the Chinese. Some say over 20,000 Chinese were killed.

of emigration in the South China provinces of Kwantung and Fukien. From the mid-seventeenth century to the nationalist rebellion of Sun Yat Sen in 1911 the Chinese of Nanyang came from an area generally hostile to the Manchus, eager to find a better home overseas, and therefore more prepared to assimilate. Especial force was given to this emigration by the T'ai-p'ing-T'ien-kuo Rebellion of South China against the Manchus in 1850–64.

In the eighteenth century the Chinese flourished greatly in Thailand. Europeans had been expelled in 1688, and King Taksin (1767–82), who was himself said to be the son of a Chinese immigrant, greatly aided the immigrants, particularly the Teochius, who were to become the dominant group in Thailand and whose language became the lingua franca for the whole Chinese community there. They flourished also in Java, despite the Dutch-organized massacre in Batavia in 1740, caused by Dutch fears of the growth and aggressiveness of the Chinese power in Java. The arrival of the British in Penang in 1785–6 and later in Province Wellesley (1800), Singapore (1819) and Malacca (1825) gave a tremendous opening to Chinese immigration; they were welcome both as middlemen and settlers for their economic contribution to new colonies. They were to follow the British flag, not only into Malaya but into Sarawak (Rajah Brooke, 1841) and North Borneo (British North Borneo Company, 1881). By 1871 there were over 100,000 overseas Chinese in the Straits Settlements alone. From the last half of the nineteenth century until the start of the Second World War the rate of immigration was high, and it was only finally brought down to a trickle when the new independent states began to think seriously of limiting their minority problem. Skinner[4] gives the following table for ethnic[5] Chinese in South-East Asia in 1959 (p. 38 below).

It is important to note two major changes in this period. First, from the Sun Yat Sen Revolution of 1911 onwards there was more sympathy between the Nanyang Chinese and the mainland Government. Second, since the turn of the century, and particularly after 1920, Chinese wives began to come in large numbers to Nanyang. The sex ratio of Chinese, which had been totally out of balance, became almost normal, and in consequence intermarriage with nationals of the host country fell away sharply. To give examples from different areas, the alien Chinese in Thailand[6] numbered 205,470 men and only 54,724 women as late as

[4] *Annals*, loc. cit.

[5] Ethnic (includes local citizens) as against 'alien'. The Cambodian figure is probably too low, perhaps by 100,000 or more (see Chapter II, p. 24).

[6] Coughlin, *Double Identity*.

TABLE 9

ETHNIC CHINESE IN SOUTH-EAST ASIA

	Ethnic Chinese	*Chinese % of Population*
North Viet-Nam	50,000	0.4
South Viet-Nam	780,000	6.2
Cambodia	230,000	5.5
Laos	10,000	0.6
Thailand	2,360,000	11.3
Burma	320,000	1.6
Malaya	2,365,000	37.8
Singapore	965,000	76.0
British Borneo*	270,000	27.0
Indonesia	2,250,000	2.7
Philippines	270,000	1.2
Total, South-East Asia	9,870,000	5.3

Note: *Includes Sabah, Brunei, and Sarawak.

1919, whereas by 1947 figures on the same basis were 319,196 men to 157,386 women; the ethnic Chinese in 1947 were divided 495,188 men to 340,743 women. In Semarang (Java) there were 90 Chinese women to every 100 men by 1954.[7] Both these factors weighed against assimilation.

The Kuo-Min-Tang Government of China, established firmly after the long period of battle with 'war-lords' up to 1928, was finally defeated by the Communists in 1949. Thus a large number of the present older generation of overseas Chinese came to Nanyang in the Kuo-Min-Tang period and many (an unknown proportion) retain their sympathies with the exiles of Taiwan rather than the Communists of Peking. From 1949 a great fragmentation of loyalties in Nanyang began, and still continues.

Immigration has been greatly slowed down over the last twenty years. Some restrictions date from before the last war, notably in Thailand in 1927–31, Malaya in 1928–37, the Philippines technically since 1902. In consequence, by now a far higher proportion of Chinese are locally born than used to be the case. The figure is over 80 per cent in Java, 75 per cent in Malaya (1957),[8] probably as high in Thailand, although there was a major influx between 1918 and 1931 (about 370,000)[9] and between 1945 and 1947 (about 170,000), when all restrictions were relaxed. However, this open door in Thailand was closed by a restriction of quota to a mere 200 per annum since 1949. Short of forcible expulsion, the Chinese are, in the main, no longer temporary

[7] Willmott, *The Chinese of Semarang.*

[8] Ooi Jin-Bee, *Land, People and Economy in Malaya.*

[9] Skinner, *Leadership and Power in the Chinese Community of Thailand.*

immigrants but a permanent part of the local population in the areas where they live.

The Nanyang Chinese belong to a number of different dialect groups, according to their region of origin in South China. The largest groups are Hakka from Kwantung, Hokkien from Fukien, Teochiu from Swatow, and Kaouchow, Cantonese, Hainanese, and Hoktjia from Foochow. These dialects are mutually unintelligible, so that Chinese schools teach a demotic Mandarin. But in most areas, and particularly in rural districts, the dialect groups keep together, and to some extent immigrants from a single village in China will join up with earlier settlers from the same village.[10]

Occupations

The Chinese have been mainly referred to in this book as merchants, retailers, traders, except for the rubber-growers and market-gardeners of Malaysia. But by origin the great bulk of them were peasants from poor and often overcrowded agricultural districts of Kwantung. Certainly very few indeed came as merchants with any capital, and most as penniless immigrants with a very high percentage of illiteracy. By the 1937 Census in Thailand, out of 576,000 Chinese aliens only 20,000 had completed Primary education. How did they so quickly outstrip the local peoples in the skills of commerce?

Professor Maurice Freedman has pointed out[11] that the rural Chinese were constantly involved in a network of debt and moneylending, though the sums of money involved might be a matter of only two or three Chinese dollars. He quotes extensive evidence for this from the Rev. J. Macgowan, a missionary working in Fukien province and elsewhere early in this century, who concludes by saying: 'The whole Chinese Empire may be said to be in a perpetual state of borrowing and lending.' Moreover, the Chinese had invented 'Money Loan Associations', a system (familiar to students of West Africa) by which a group pays in a monthly subscription and the whole amount is taken out month by month by each member in turn.

On arrival in some new country of Nanyang, the immigrant will be temporarily looked after by members of his own dialect group and especially by his own village clan. He may join up with the typical occupation of his dialect group—Hakka usually go into agricultural

[10] See W. H. Newell, *Treacherous River* (a detailed study of a single Chinese village in Province Wellesley, Malaya), Kuala Lumpur, 1962.

[11] M. Freedman, 'The Handling of Money', *Man*, Vol. LIX, Apr. 1959, quoting the Rev. J. Macgowan, *Lights and Shadows of Chinese Life*, Shanghai, 1909.

work, Hainanese into coffee shops, Teochius into the grocery trade,[12] and so on; or he may find any labouring or casual work which is available, often work which local nationals are unwilling to do. He works hard—far harder than the easygoing Buddhist or Malay populations. He saves, though from the poorest wage. Quite soon he goes into business on his own, as a small shopkeeper or a pedlar in the villages. He sets up at crossroads, gets the agency for a petrol station, or finds a job supervising slaughterhouses, or in the opium trade.[13] Alternatively he may set himself to learn a trade and soon becomes a competent craftsman. The background of dire poverty left behind in China; the sheer insecurity of his position as a newly arrived alien in a strange country; perhaps the extra energy and greater working persistence of those from colder climates; a long habit of frugality; and finally a shrewd knowledge of how to turn one dollar into two—these are the essentials which have ensured Chinese success. In agriculture the Chinese have generally avoided rice-growing, which is the least profitable crop in South-East Asia, and gone for the cash crops—vegetables, rubber, pepper and spices, fruit, abaca.

Naturally, for every success story there are scores of failures, or, more often, stories of men who meant to stay for a year or two and have stayed fifteen or twenty years, still without saving enough to complete the dreams of returning as a rich man to China. Ju-k'ang T'ien quotes an old saying of Fukien province: 'Of every ten who go abroad, three die and six stay and one returns.'

The Chinese success in retail trade is most often noticed because the visitor to South-East Asia sees, in every town, the long rows of Chinese stores. It is indeed remarkable. Chinese were thought to control 36 per cent of all retail assets in the Philippines in 1951,[14] even 23 per cent of total commercial investment (1955), and 30.6 per cent of foreign trade (1948; but this has been halved in recent years). In Semarang (Java), Willmott[15] found that the 60,000 Chinese in a population of 360,000 owned at least 70 per cent of all retail stores, and possibly more than 80 per cent if those with 'dummy' Indonesian owners were included. Much the same could be said of other parts of South-East Asia.

[12] See particularly the list of dominant occupations of the Chinese in Sarawak given by Ju-K'ang T'ien, *The Chinese of Sarawak*, L.S.E. Monographs in Social Anthropology, No. 12, 1950.

[13] See particularly Robequain, op. cit., for an admirable description of Chinese industry and enterprise.

[14] S. Appleton, 'Overseas Chinese and Economic Nationalizations in the Philippines', *Journal of Asian Studies*, Vol. XIX, No. 2, Feb. 1959.

[15] *The Chinese of Semarang.*

But the modern Chinese are not to be thought of solely as small traders or even merchant-millionaires (of whom there are many). They have shown the same energy in education as they have in trade, and in Malaysia in particular they are found as a professional class of engineers and graduate scientists, and as the technicians of the new industries, as teachers and doctors, as professional employees in the largest international companies. The Malaysian and Singapore universities, the universities of Taiwan and Hongkong, and many of those in Australia and New Zealand and farther afield have a large quota of Nanyang Chinese, studying every possible advanced subject; the Malaysian universities themselves are heavily dependent upon Chinese teaching staff. It is thus not only into the cash sector of an agricultural and trading economy, old style, that the Chinese have learned to fit themselves; in the modern sector of major new development plans in post-war Asia they are equally prominent.

Culture and Religion

The discussion of the culture of the Nanyang Chinese requires a heavy emphasis on the distinction between culture as meaning the whole way of life of a people, which is roughly the anthropologist's sense of the word, and culture as meaning, in T. S. Eliot's phrase, 'the culture of the cultured classes'. In this latter sense the Chinese brought extremely little, if anything, of Chinese 'culture' as it is admired by the 'cultured classes' of other nations throughout the world. The emigrants were poor peasants or labourers and knew little of the fine art and literature of classical China.

Even of culture as a way of life they brought with them only a local fraction—by no means all the ways of cookery or the rituals of religion practised in their region came with them in the packed transports or sailing junks on the long journey to Nanyang. They brought peasant habits and a peasant outlook, as did many an Italian or Greek or Levantine who emigrated, for the same reasons, to the United States of America.

Yet, if they were not 'cultured', in the narrow sense, they were deeply attached to the only way of life they knew. Above all, the family system remained strong, their own language remained precious, their outlook on life—strongly materialist, as their particular answer to the pressure of poverty—remained steadily unchanged. Both to the mainland Buddhist peoples (except perhaps the Vietnamese, who are more closely allied) and to the Malays this materialism, this endless pursuit of money and success at the cost of grinding labour and self-denial, seems the most outstanding Chinese quality. It shows not only in working life but in Chinese religion and magic. If there is one petition more than any other which is made to the Chinese gods of the household or the greater gods outside, it is the prayer for success, for prosperity, good fortune, luck in enterprise.[16] As in Tropical Africa (and indeed in tribal animist societies all over the world), religion, care and reverence for ancestors,[17] and magic are almost inextricably interfused in Chinese life, so that success may come through a wise consultation with ancestors, a timely petition to the right god, and the choice of an auspicious day.

There is one quality of Chinese religious outlook which is of some importance in considering their relationships with the peoples of their adopted countries. It is tolerant and eclectic. In Buddhist countries particularly there is felt to be some affinity. Below the highest spiritual level of Buddhism in mainland South-East Asia lies a large layer of animism and magic—the belief in *nats* (spirits) which in Burma and Thailand is, in effect, perhaps more real and earnest in the business of daily living than the pure doctrines of Buddhism. These animist beliefs —and magical beliefs, too—are easily shared by the Chinese, who have a parallel system, though the names and qualities of spirits differ and the magic works to different rules. Even at the more spiritual level, Theravada Buddhism of the mainland (related to the Hinayana branch) and Chinese religion (a Mahayana cognate with Taoism and Confucianism added in) are not too far apart. There are Mahayana monks in the Chinese temples, with a saffron robe (though different from the Theravada robe) and an easily recognizable similarity of attitude. Chinese will use Thai Buddhist monks for intercession in adversity or for healing and will enter to say a prayer to the Buddha figure in many Thai temples. Willmott notes that in Semarang the Chinese have adopted some Javanese customs and visit Java's holy places; a Chinese party for the 'birthday' of a Chinese god at Welahan (near Semarang) made a four-hour side-trip to a mountain tomb of Sultan Muria of Demak, supposedly a very powerful spirit to whom, as the Chinese typically remarked, 'You can pray to become wealthy.'[18]

Chinese eclecticism is exemplified by the fairly large numbers of converts to Protestant or Catholic Christianity, by the varieties of Confucian, Taoist, and Buddhist beliefs, including the 'Three Religions Society', which is devoted to an amalgam of the three, and by the

[16] Coughlin quotes some names for the God of the House, such as 'Silver tree has bloomed', or 'Gather together Treasure Hall'.

[17] I avoid 'ancestor worship', which has been given a quite false 'idolatrous' connotation in Christian societies, mainly through the attitude of missionaries.

[18] Willmott, *The Chinese of Semarang*, p. 186.

occasional (though rare) conversion to Islam. There is little which is rigid in belief—Chinese Buddhists will send their children to a Catholic school, because it happens to be the best; many families will maintain the family altar although one or more members have become Christian.

It is clear that such societies are not likely to become involved in passionate religious quarrels with the host country where it is Buddhist; but the relation with Islam—where fanaticism and memories of religiously inspired '*jehads*' against the unbeliever are never far below the surface—might be more difficult or even violent. That this difficulty has not arisen markedly in Indonesia may be due to the more relaxed and Hindu-influenced character of Islam in the archipelago—it is stricter in mainland Malaya.

Organization

The Chinese of Nanyang are immensely and intricately organized—by family, by class, by dialect, by commercial grouping; in literary, religious, economic, regional, political, occupational, and secret societies. This facility, if not passion, for organization is noted by every writer for every country. In terms of good relations with a national majority, it is both a useful and a dangerous quality. It is useful for self-defence, for political pressure, and for commercial power. The Chinese in Malaya made a far better job of political representation, through the Malayan Chinese Association, than ever the Indians could manage through the Malayan Indian Congress.[19] The depth of Indian particularism—by language, region, caste, religion and general culture—is so deeply felt, the points of difference (rather than of common interest) so sharply defined by the Indian mind, that common action with the compromises which it demands eluded the Indians in Burma as it did in Malaya and as it has within the Indian subcontinent itself. For this reason the Chinese are always a more formidable minority than the Indians.

Yet the Chinese habit of organization is a major danger to race relationships. Few things enrage a majority more than to believe that a minority 'stick together'. In the majority's eyes, they become, by this very act, non-national (even if they are citizens), and potentially enemy. For their grouping is not one of the scores of groupings which nationals make, by special interests. They are together not as trade unionists or liberals or music-lovers or grocers, but as Chinese; as aliens, therefore, whatever the slip of citizenship paper may say. Economic jealousy in particular is fanned by the belief—and it is well founded—

[19] See particularly Usha Mahajani, *The Role of Indian Minorities in Burma and Malaya.*

that Chinese traders form a tight ring, with private channels of communication and intelligence, into which the outsider cannot break; they are not out on their own as individuals in the common open field of competition in which the nationals must make their way.

Naturally, the Chinese are not always and everywhere a monolithic block. There are savage divisions between them, particularly where secret societies flourish. The bitter warfare of Chinese *kongsis* in the early tin-mining industry of Malaya led to such rioting and bloodshed that the strongest government intervention was needed to suppress it. In Singapore, inter-Chinese politics are vigorous, and the split between Taiwan and Peking gives a special edge to partisan feeling in many parts of South-East Asia. But *vis-à-vis* the non-Chinese the ranks are largely closed whenever any threat to racial interests arises.

Education

It is natural enough that the Chinese immigrants should have insisted on their own Primary schools. The different dialect groups were unable to understand each other, although the written ideographic language is understood in common. The teaching of Mandarin (*kuo-yu*) in school gave a common language to all groups and preserved essential Chineseness. In almost all countries the Chinese also set up High Schools, if they were allowed to; and the various edicts banning them were deeply resented, not solely because much money had been invested in them. The wealthier Chinese who were determined to give their children higher education in Chinese might engage a private tutor or send them to Hongkong or even back to China.

Obviously, there is some disadvantage in the change-over to a new language at the Secondary level—now compulsory, in effect, all over South-East Asia, save in Singapore. 'Bridge' classes have to be introduced, and the Chinese boy or girl will need an extra year in the school stream to match up with national students. But this is a handicap which the Chinese can well carry. Both they and the Indians come from societies where education is esteemed and where the pressure of competition has been inordinately strong. They see clearly enough the link between formal education and personal economic success in the new world of bureaucracy and development which lies ahead, and the habits of frugality, hard work and unquestioned parental control drive the Chinese pupil to the limits of his ability.

In some areas at least, the nationals with whom Chinese compete take a far more easygoing view. As nationals, they expect political favour in the struggle for jobs. Government employment, which counts so heavily in the total of all wage-paid labour, may well be partially or totally reserved for them.[20] Besides, they are living in their own society (not as immigrants, with the threat of insecurity always with them), and one which provides a continuing, homely social structure within which their ancestors lived, and they can live, at many different levels. The view of life as a constant upward struggle for success—so much a Western and an immigrant Chinese view—has not entered so deeply into the native societies of the region, save in the largest towns, where the struggle for survival is more bitter.

At the top level the Nanyang Chinese are producing men of the highest attainment—scholars able to hold their own in any academic company, first-rate engineers, men of wide culture who have travelled to foreign universities and become part of the international educated world. At present these intellectuals may not be as highly esteemed within the Chinese community as the successful businessman—Richard Coughlin certainly asserts this of the highly educated Chinese in Thailand. But in the political and managerial society of the future they will come into their own.

Assimilation

In most countries of South-East Asia the Chinese were, in a sense, much more assimilated in 1900 than they are today. They had been in the region not for scores but for hundreds of years; and in all the early period they had intermarried—or at least begotten children—very widely. Chinese ancestry two or more generations back must be a characteristic of South-East Asian families in numbers which will never be known but must be very high. Perhaps this is least true in the tin and rubber areas of peninsular Malaya, where the Chinese came to areas scarcely inhabited by Malays—newly cleared forest and newly opened mines quite a long way from the Malay kampongs by the rivers and the coast. By the time that the Chinese represented more than a third of the nation in Malaya, 'assimilation' became scarcely a relevant word to use. But in other countries, too, the stronger racial nationalism since independence, and the fact that Chinese have brought their wives and intermarried with local people less often, have made their communities more separate.

There have been significant differences in the extent and nature of assimilation in different countries in South-East Asia. One vital

[20] A university tutor, urging an exceptionally able Malay student in Kuala Lumpur University to aim at a first class in his final degree, was told: 'Even if I get a third and the Chinese gets a first, I shall be director and he will be my deputy.'

difference is emphasized by Skinner[21] in the Thailand context. There was no European ruler in Thailand; it was therefore possible for Chinese to achieve an upward social climb into the ruling group itself—which was not possible where that group was English or French or Dutch. In Thailand a policy of ennobling prominent Chinese had been followed from the earliest dynasties, certainly back to the fifteenth century.[22] In the seventeenth century scores of Chinese had been appointed to official posts, some as Governors and Chief Justices; it was royal policy to include them as part of the Thai nation and to win their loyalty by the gift of responsibility and honour. In the centuries up to 1900 few Chinese women came in, and the Chinese founder of a family in Thailand married a Thai girl. The children became Thais, and the daughters, known as 'Lukhsin', were much sought after in marriage, even by royalty. The grandchildren were probably fully Thai-ized.

It is significant that, in this earlier period in Thailand, when Chinese were not forced into assimilation but tempted by the possibilities it offered, assimilation was rapid and effective. But the tide turned after King Wachirawut came to the Thai throne in 1910. He was personally hostile (he wrote a pamphlet on the Chinese entitled *The Jews of the East*), and pursued a policy of forcing assimilation, at just the time when Chinese women were beginning to enter Thailand and when the Sun Yat Sen Rebellion had engaged Chinese loyalty. The result was bitter hostility. Again, in 1938, under Prime Minister Phibun, there was violent anti-Chinese legislation—schools closed or controlled, immigration fees raised, occupations barred, prohibition of land purchase. After a brief relaxation (1944–7) repression started again; in 1948 all Chinese Middle schools were closed; in 1949 the immigration quota was reduced from 10,000 to 200 per annum, and in 1952–3 the screw was turned even harder. Only since 1956 have these repressive measures been somewhat relaxed.

The reaction of the Chinese leadership to these later phases has been analysed by Skinner[23] in a detailed study of great importance. The Chinese community in Bangkok (numbering over 500,000) chose as leaders those men of wealth and ability who had close connexions with the Thai rulers. Increasingly these leaders built up a close association with a very senior official or service chief, while in business prominent Thais were invited into partnership with Chinese firms. The Thais gained dividends, the Chinese political protection. Skinner

[21] Skinner, 'Chinese Assimilation and Thai Politics'. [22] ibid.
[23] Skinner, *Leadership and Power in the Chinese Community of Thailand.*

found that 36 per cent of the most 'prestigeful' Chinese leaders had genuine Thai names and 83 per cent of them spoke Thai fluently; about 5 per cent of them had been decorated by the King. It is interesting, however, that only 23 per cent were Thai citizens, 70 per cent held Chinese nationality only, 72 per cent had been born in China (of whom nearly half were genuinely first generation in Thailand).[24] Thus even where considerable assimilation was desired there was evidently a good deal of resistance to acquiring citizenship.

There is an obvious corollary to this situation where protection from discriminatory laws is needed—protection may have to be bought, and the Thai police have not been slow to seize opportunities, at all levels, for a little personal taxation of their Chinese fellow townsmen. Some say the Chinese pay about 20 per cent more 'tax' than Thais, by this simple method, not only to police but to every Government official, large or small, who has power to grant a licence or wink at a regulation.[25] But despite the element of monetary blackmail in this situation, at the top level a considerable community of interest has grown up between Thai notables and Chinese business; and as the industrialization and commercialization of the Thai economy proceeds (and it is proceeding fast in Bangkok) these bonds will proliferate and deepen. To a very considerable extent Chinese blood and Chinese money are now so deeply embedded in the metabolism of leadership, bureaucracy, and industry in Bangkok that the city could scarcely survive without it.

This situation in Thailand is at present unique in South-East Asia. Before looking at some possible implications—and they may be important—it is worth mentioning some contrasting attitudes in other countries.

Perhaps the nearest parallel might be expected in Indonesia, where the Chinese have been in considerable numbers for many centuries and have intermarried freely. Yet the situation is different, quite probably for the reason that Skinner mentions—that Dutch, not Indonesians, were the ruling group and assimilation to them was impossible. True, in various ways and at certain stages, the Dutch treated the Chinese as fellow immigrants, applied Dutch law to them, allocated some estates to their management and admitted some to Dutch schools. But there was never any question of real assimilation. Chinese-Dutch intermarriage was virtually unknown. The Chinese, in the main, married Indonesian wives in the early days and spoke Indonesian.

[24] The remainder would have been sons of older Chinese residents in Thailand, born when their fathers visited China to marry.

[25] The same source of gain is valued by Filipinos in administering the Retail Trade Nationalization regulations.

It is necessary to mention here that the Chinese community is fairly sharply divided into 'Peranakans'—Chinese who have an Indonesian ancestor, normally on the mother's side, who speak Indonesian, have adopted Indonesian citizenship, probably (though not invariably) send their children to Indonesian schools, and have no intention of returning to China—and 'Totoks', who, in brief, remain essentially mainland Chinese, temporarily overseas, but with continuing bonds with mainland China. The Peranakans represent the majority—probably 80 per cent of Chinese in Java are locally born and a quite high proportion would have some Indonesian blood in their veins. The Totoks, however, some of whom may be locally born, are perhaps slightly the richer and more influential. Interestingly, they attribute their superiority to the fact of having Chinese blood—an example of racial superstition which is unpleasantly familiar all over the world.[26]

The Chinese were given the opportunity to choose local or Chinese citizenship (between December 1949 and December 1951), retaining Chinese citizenship only if they positively rejected Indonesian, becoming Indonesians if they took no action. More than three-quarters of the Chinese in Semarang[27] became Indonesians. However, in 1955, after the Bandung Conference, the situation was reversed, and the Chinese who had gained Indonesian citizenship by this passive procedure, except for a certain group to be named by the Indonesian Government, were required to opt for Chinese or Indonesian citizenship; failure to opt would leave them as Chinese, and children born to them would be Chinese.[28]

But the purely local assimilation of the Chinese Peranakans was an 'assimilation trap'.[29] They moved half-way to integration in Indonesian society and there they stuck. For the Indonesian wives came into Chinese homes, in a Chinese quarter of the town, into the Chinese family system—it was they who were assimilated to a community which remained, in all essentials except language, Chinese. As to language, Willmott shows that in Semarang the vast majority of families where neither parent was China-born used Indonesian as the language of family conversation, with the remainder using Javanese, Dutch, and Chinese in roughly equal proportions. Language might well have been assumed to be a vital factor; it is generally felt to be of the very essence of a culture. It certainly greatly reduced the importance of dialect-

[26] See particularly Willmott, *The Chinese in Semarang*. [27] Willmott, op. cit.

[28] Skinner, 'Overseas Chinese', and see Willmott, *The National Status of the Chinese in Indonesia*, Ithaca, N.Y., 1956.

[29] ibid.

group associations (most Peranakans cannot speak a dialect but only Mandarin). Nevertheless, the Peranakans, and, of course, still more the Totoks,[30] remain a Chinese society, their associations for sport or culture are Chinese, they are 100 per cent identifiable as non-Indonesian, although they may have lost much of Chinese culture and any close continuing connexion at least with a local region of China. It is in this sense that they are poised between two worlds. Peranakans suffered equally with Totoks in the various Indonesian anti-Chinese campaigns of 1956, 1960, and 1963.

Thus intermarriage and even the adoption of a local language have not led to complete assimilation in Java, and the same is true in the rest of South-East Asia, outside Thailand; for example, the Chinese in Burma and in the Philippines and in Cambodia have all intermarried very considerably, and can speak the local lingua franca; but they remain an easily identifiable separate group, always in danger of attracting nationalist persecution. Malaysia is a special case, considered below.

Attitudes to China

Even in Thailand assimilation is a dangerous word to use, for it is far from complete, as the attitudes of Chinese to China shows; and this is even more true in many other parts of South-East Asia. The Thai Chinese still visit China, and many send a son, at the age of about twenty, to find a wife in his original home district there. They are divided about Chinese metropolitan politics in the strongest way. Their 'leadership' is itself a sign that the community is regarded and regards itself as separate, requiring protection and diplomatic intercession with the Thai Government. Throughout all South-East Asia Chinese Primary schools are maintained, Chinese festivals are observed, Chinese newspapers are printed, the rituals of Chinese marriage and funerals are observed. Despite the loss of some elements of home culture, in some areas at least the immigrants (as so often in any part of the world) are 'more Chinese than the Chinese'. Ju-K'ang T'ien[31] remarks that in Sarawak Chinese weddings are celebrated with the full Ming customary rituals which are very rarely encountered in China today. He records the extremely close ties with the home village, both in sending remittances (there were, in 1949, forty-four 'remittance-

[30] Peranakans: Chinese with (almost invariably) some Indonesian ancestry, speaking Indonesian, and with few links with China; Totoks: Chinese usually without Indonesian blood, looking mainly to China as their cultural base.

[31] op. cit.

shops' in Kuching alone for arranging dispatch of money and messages and even for financing remittances at low rates); in the reading of 'home news' of local dialect regions in newspapers published from Singapore; and above all in clan relationships across the sea. He found a group of Henghua fishermen, all with the surname Ch'eng, who had clubbed together to have an 'ancestral hall' built by their clan in their home area in China and each had a photograph of the hall pinned to the house wall in Kuching.

Communism in China has somewhat weakened these ties in some cases, just as opposition to the Manchus in earlier times inclined the Nanyang Chinese to be thankful for their escape overseas. But even where Communism is feared or disliked, links may remain, particularly within the family group. Some of the richer Thai Chinese have been sending money and relief to relations in China whose land was 'divided' by the Communists. Moreover, in the nineteenth century, China was war-torn and internationally powerless. Today she is potentially one of the greatest world powers and already of great international significance among the developing countries. Although few Chinese traders and merchants would wish to return to a Communist society, all no doubt have some pride in China's resurgence, and some may be glad to think that, if they were to suffer local persecution, they might have a powerful patron to defend them.

South-East Asian Attitudes to the Chinese

Just as the mass of fairly humble Chinese immigrants feel themselves separate, so no South-East Asian country—Malaysia partially excepted—is under any illusion that the Chinese immigrants are just local citizens. They are seen to be different for the reasons just given. In Thailand they are politically second-class citizens, in that regulations for voting in both local and national elections require of Chinese voters educational and Thai-language qualifications not demanded of Thais. In both the Philippines and Indonesia there is commercial discrimination by the Governments—in Indonesia 70 per cent of all capital is supposed to be in purely Indonesian hands. There has been discrimination against them, as immigrants, in Burma, Cambodia, Viet-Nam; in Malaya there is the famous bargain on the proportion of government posts which they may hold,[32] preference to Malays in government scholarships, reservation of vast areas of land as 'Malay reservation'. Nowhere has even the grant of full citizenship resulted in the kind of

[32] This was made as part of the general settlement between racial groups upon which independence was based (1957).

indiscriminate equality which applies in theory to every American citizen and in practice to at least the citizens with white skins, whatever their country of origin and however recently arrived. Except possibly in Burma, where pure Burmese blood is so heavily emphasized at present, the Eurasians are more accepted as local nationals than either Indians or Chinese.

Thus, from both sides of the fence, assimilation is barely a term which can be used, at least of whole communities. It is most real in Thailand in the upper classes, where several generations of intermarriage have indeed produced Thais with Chinese blood, rather than Chinese with Thai blood. This class element in assimilation is, to a lesser degree, true elsewhere—some Burmese leaders have Chinese blood, many Filipinos, many Cambodians, many Dusuns in Sabah, a few of the leading Indonesians. This is not an assimilation of communities but of individuals and families and it may well continue. For while the Chinese are regarded by the Thais, or the Khmers, not only as grasping and materialist but also as vulgar, noisy, crude in certain manners and habits, there is none the less some admiration for Chinese energy and intelligence. A little Chinese blood is no disgrace for an Asian who is not thereby absorbed into the Chinese community; and this is most likely to be the case among men of standing. Further, as Westernization and a certain cosmopolitanism spreads, there will be mixed marriages more often among the educated classes, creating slowly an *élite* less narrowly based on purely national origin.[33] The assimilation of individuals does exist in Thailand to a considerable extent; there is no sign of whole Chinese communities being lost in the general mass of nationals.

The Malaysian Case, and the Future

The Europeans, as a ruling group, have left South-East Asia. Could this mean that the opportunity to assimilate, at least at the top level, is now open to the Chinese in other countries, as it was in non-colonial Thailand? It is true that the second factor tending to assimilation—the lack of Chinese women—is no longer there, but this might not prove decisive.

The creation of Malaysia was an immense gamble on this possibility. Indeed, the near-equality in numbers, with its corrollary of mutual fear, ultimately implies assimilation or division and failure. There are at least some factors which are on the positive side. In Kuala

[33] There are many Anglo-Thai and some Franco-Thai links and marriages in the top level of society (and a fashion for golf!).

Lumpur the new generation of Malay Civil Servants has come through the university with Chinese fellow students and they mix constantly in social gatherings with Chinese. There is already some intermarriage, and considerable adoption of Malay names, and occasionally the Muslim faith, by a few Chinese and rather more Indians. There has also been a fashion for a few wealthy Malays to adopt a Chinese child, as in Tunku Abdul Rahman's own family. At the top level, it would seem that fusion may well increase. In the Borneo states again the Chinese are the best qualified and the richest, extremely eligible as husbands; many of them are anxious not to overplay Chinese dominance for fear of creating persecution; they could well emulate the Thai Chinese in making marriages within the indigenous group and taking business partners and political patrons from among the elected national ministers and leaders.

Unquestionably the main difficulties in Malaysia have been the fear on the Malay headland of Chinese Singapore; the fact that the proposed fusion was between Muslims—not Buddhists—and Chinese; and the geographical division of mainland Malaya into huge areas, in the mountains and on the east coast, which are overwhelmingly Malay and overwhelmingly poorer than the west coast strip where the Chinese are concentrated. The Malays feared that assimilation would mean assimilation of Malays to Chinese wealth and power, leaving the rural areas as a poor though large 'native minority' in a wealthy and effectively Chinese-run state. Even if the aristocratic Malay leaders were still to wear the formal trappings of power, the real facts could not long be concealed. Islamic Malay nationalism, the high voting power of the Malays in a carefully organized democratic system, and the bargain for continued power which they have secured would be thrown against this solution. Yet in the long run, considering Chinese energy and their long educational advantage, a fused society under joint Malay and Chinese leadership, with the Chinese in fact economically dominant, would seem the most hopeful and the least violent prospect. Pan-Malay Islamic revolt, with the evident possibility of pro-Indonesian intrigue to level up the balance against the Chinese, is a prospect of violence and economic ruin which neither the more responsible Malay rulers nor the Chinese can view with less than the gravest fears. Future events in Indonesia, when Sukarno's domination ends, may open up various possibilities of allowing for the recombination of political forces between Malays and Chinese, since there is always pressure on the Chinese to come to terms rather than face isolation or Peking Communism.

There is one further factor which may affect the future of race relations—'modernity'. The industrial revolution, secular education, science, commercialism, international contact—all these act, in many cases, as a solvent of old cultural and communal patterns. They will act with equal force on Buddhist, Muslim, or Chinese ways of life, blurring the sharp communal differences, spreading new values shared in common. They are so acting already; but they need time to make much headway against the new instinctive forces of social suspicion. The secession of Singapore has proved once again how quickly and powerfully these forces can strike back.

2. THE INDIANS

The Indians are an important minority only in Burma and Malaysia, although they may be found in very small numbers in all the other countries of South-East Asia. Some brief details of the Indians in Burma and Malaya have already been given in Chapter II; it is only necessary here to emphasize a few more general issues, and in particular the contrast between the Indian position in the two countries, some special characteristics of individual groups, and their prospects in the current situation.

The Indian penetration of Burma was far more generalized and widespread than that of Malaya. Among the one million Indians in Burma before the Second World War there were quite large numbers of Indian peasant landholders, in addition to the large Indian labour force in Rangoon and the other main towns. In commerce they played the part of the Chinese in Malaya, not only dominating the large-scale commerce of Rangoon but also largely controlling the retail trade, sharing this with the smaller group of Chinese. In industry, Indians far outnumbered Burmese employees in transport (particularly railways), much of manufacturing, and in a host of domestic and menial services. In 1934 Indians accounted for 145,715 male wage-earners out of 198,700 in Rangoon, and paid more than half the total of Rangoon municipal taxation.[34] The Indian Chettiars controlled great areas of the delta rice lands as moneylenders and landlords.

Because Burma was in effect a province of India until 1937, the Indians were in a strangely ambiguous relation with the Burmese. Burmese nationalists, seeking freedom from the British Government of India, contracted this, in word and largely in thought, to 'Freedom from India'. On the other hand, the Indian nationalist struggle against

[34] Usha Mahajani, op. cit.

the British quite naturally attracted Burmese sympathy. In broad outline, the anti-Indian feeling in Burma predominated in the period from 1918 to 1937 (when the link with India was broken). There was then a confused period, under Japanese occupation, when the Indian Independence League and the Indian National Army, led by Subhas Chandra Bose, were fighting in South-East Asia against the British and were thereby attracting some sympathy from anti-British Burmese nationalists. Finally, the third period of Burmese independence and nationalism is one of growing hostility to the Indians (as aliens, as capitalists, as competitors), leading to the wholesale expropriations and exodus of the last three years.

There is thus no need to labour the reasons for Burmese opposition before and after the last war. The Indian minority was so large, so well-placed commercially, and so closely identified with British rule that it was bound to be unpopular. The fact that a large section of the Indian community opposed the separation of Burma from India in the 1930s, or insisted that guarantees for minorities should be sanctioned by the British Government, was an obvious source of political bitterness. Moreover, Indian unskilled labour competed directly with Burmese, and attempts to unite workers against employers in a trade-union movement foundered on communal differences—'communal loyalty overshadowed class loyalty', as Usha Mahajani succinctly puts it. The 1930 dock riots were a direct outcome of this competition.

A second source of possible friction was religion. About two-fifths of the Indian community were Muslim, and, partly by intermarriage, in some areas (notably in Arakan) quite large numbers of Burmese were converted; indeed, in Arakan district a community of 'Zerbadis'—Indian Muslims with Burmese wives—grew to quite large proportions.[35] The extremely serious riots of 1938 started with a battle between Burmese Buddhists and Burmese Muslims, spread to an attack on Indian Muslims, and finally to an indiscriminate slaughter of Indians, including Hindus, by Burmese.

Religion is but one aspect of total culture; there were many other causes of friction or dislike such as are bound to arise where an alien group insists on retaining, within a closed circle, its own habits of dress, domestic manners, family cohesiveness, and language. With some exceptions, Indians in Burma remained quite obviously, and often proudly, Indians. Despite efforts of the Burmese Government to prevent them, they continued to send constant cash remittances to members of the extended family in India, to speak of India as 'home',

[35] 122,000 in 1931.

and to identify themselves as a community by political agitation for communal minority rights. Neither before nor after the War was there any real sign that they were fully identified with Burmese aspirations, or that they genuinely regarded themselves as Burmese first and Indians only by origin. It was natural for the Burmese to feel that, not by their own wish but by the invitation and with the connivance of the British, huge areas of their national life had been penetrated by foreigners, as though by the fine threads of a parasitic fungus. Indian separation was further shown in Burmese eyes by the unwillingness of the majority to accept Burmese citizenship (renouncing Indian citizenship) after the Second World War, when an opportunity to adopt it on reasonably generous and simple terms was offered by the Burma Government—and this despite the fact that almost 50 per cent of Indians in Burma (1947) were locally born.[36] The Indians felt that they must retain an avenue of escape (however uncertain or even illusory) in case the new nationalism of the adopted countries should turn against them in racial violence.

Thus in Burma the Indians reached just that position, in numbers and economic privilege, which made them most liable to attack. Unlike the Chinese in Malaya, they never became so large a proportion of population as to compel recognition as almost half the nation; the Indian percentage in Burma rose only from roughly 5 per cent in 1872 to 7 per cent by 1931; it must be nearer 3 per cent today. Nor were they a really small and compact minority which could have been treated as an isolated ethnic group. They were heavily concentrated in Rangoon, where they were most visible to politicians, and they were spread in a wide range of occupations which made them highly visible to the ordinary Burmese citizen. The Indian poor were accused of undercutting Burmese labour by their acceptance of shockingly low wages and conditions; the Indian rich were even more violently abused as extortionist landlords, moneylenders, and middlemen. The end of British rule was bound to expose them to the full force of Burmese resentment.

In contrast, the Indians in Malaya and Singapore (they are a negligible factor in the Borneo territories of Malaysia) never entered so widely into the Malayan economy or caused equivalent hostility. Although in total they represented before the Second World War a higher percentage of the Malayan population than they did in Burma (14 per cent in 1931; 10 per cent in 1957, against the Indian maximum

[36] Exactly the same reluctance was shown in East Africa when local citizenship was offered by the newly independent governments.

of about 7 per cent in Burma), they were shut off from the mainstream of life in camps or villages on the rubber estates, and thus heavily concentrated in a few states. The Chettiars did indeed come into Malaya as moneylenders and bankers—there were about 800 firms in 1959—along with some Gujeratis and Marakayars, both of whom were found in commerce. But as late as 1939, from 700,000 Indians only 4 per cent were classified as in trade and commerce, only 10 per cent in skilled or semi-skilled occupations. Today Indian merchants are to be found in the towns; Sikh night-watchmen sleep on camp beds on the streets (the Sikhs also are found in the police); Indian and Ceylonese clerks are fairly common, and a few more senior posts in the Civil Service—but more especially in railways, public corporations, public utilities, and the medical services—are held by professionally educated Indians.

In terms of racial friction the Indians are, in Malaya, as it were in the rain-shadow of the Chinese. There are not a great number of jobs for which Malays compete wholly or mainly with Indians; but for almost every job in Malaya there is a Chinese competitor. The Indians have indeed organized themselves politically into the Malayan Indian Congress and form the third element of the ruling Alliance Party. There is a long history of political manoeuvre, protest, and claims which forms part of the political detail of twentieth-century Malayan politics. For the Indian voice in politics is that of a tolerated minority—in a society where communal toleration is a necessity for survival—speaking in a debate which has other and far more vital concerns.

There are both similarities and some subtle differences between the attitude of Indians and that of Chinese as immigrants in South-East Asia. Both come from major civilizations, with a long tradition of power and culture which they feel to be stronger than the traditions of their host countries. India and China were greater than the Burmese, the Thais, the Khmers of Cambodia, the Annamites or the peoples of the Malay world. Few of them are willing to submerge this age-old cultural identity in any local civilization; only in so far as some members of their host country enter into the modern international culture of science and technology and business do the most educated immigrants join with them, as it were on culturally neutral ground. But the great mass of immigrants from both India and China came as poor men and uneducated men, deeply held in their traditional ways and beliefs, and finding an emotional shelter and security in a strange land by holding to their own roots. In this sense, they have been unassimilable to the traditional cultures of their new domicile.

Of the two, the Indians are perhaps both the more particularist, the less flexible in culture, and (partly in consequence) the less politically effective. Their strongest organizational achievement has been within the trade-union movement, both in Burma before the war and in present-day Malaya. But caste, religion, and provincialism seem to divide the Indians more deeply than the Chinese. For although there has been sharp division among the Chinese of different local origin in China, and although the split between adherents of Peking and Taiwan is deep and bitter, yet there seems less of an impassable gulf between them than between so many Indian groups. In some ways the Chinese materialism and the vague boundaries of their religious thought have enabled them to adapt more sinuously to the civilizations they have entered. More outward-looking and pragmatic, they are more willing to experiment than the deeply introspective Indians. Moreover, their common sense of ultimate Chinese nationality enables them to organize more easily across boundaries of local origin or vernacular than the Indians. Indeed, the differences in origin are, in fact, less wide. Almost all the Nanyang Chinese come from South China, most of them from the single province of Kwantung; but the Indians come from areas stretching from the southern tip of India to the Himalayas, and from classes which had not been fused into a single national identity. Tough, flexible, immensely hard-working, quick to take to modern education, the Chinese seem unlikely to be dislodged from any country of South-East Asia except by direct and brutal force. The Indians are already in retreat from Burma, and although a large community may live on quietly in the rubber forests of Malaya, they are not likely to play any major part in the political issues of the future.

PART TWO

IV

COLONIAL AUTHORITY—EFFECTS AND RESPONSES

THE complexity of the South-East Asian scene, the product of a long historical process in which major cultures have been involved, makes it extremely difficult to isolate neatly the general factors which have been shaping the character of its separate countries. This is true even in tracing the effects of colonial rule, where generalizations applicable to other areas might seem most likely to apply. For example, in Tropical Africa there was, indeed, great complexity when the colonial powers took over; but this cultural complexity was at a technical and political level so undeveloped that it was largely submerged—though by no means destroyed—by the impact of the invading culture. South-East Asia offered a tougher cultural resistance; there are, certainly, similar effects and responses, but the process as a whole has peculiarities which can only be described in South-East Asian terms.

Before looking at the effects of colonial authority on an existing racial and ethnic scene, we must recall that, in the simplest sense, the European colonization changed its composition. It was the British who brought Indians to Burma and Malaya, largely for their own purposes; and although the stream of emigrants from Southern China had found its way much earlier into South-East Asia through many cracks and fissures, the European invasion opened a breach through which it poured in far faster. It has been said that Chinese trade followed European flags[1]; and if this is true of Indonesia, Burma, French Indo-China, and the Philippines, it is even more true of Malaya and Singapore, where the stream became a massive flood. While it is not so true in Asia as in Africa that racial problems are a direct product of the colonial period—for Chinese immigration antedates the arrival of Europeans—the colonial powers must bear responsibility for making it vastly more serious and complex.

European motives for introducing this 'third force' in the Asian scene are plain enough, and similar to those which prompted the introduction of Asians into South and East Africa. Commercial development

[1] Wang Gungwu, *A Short History of the Nanyang Chinese.*

of the Irrawaddy delta, or of the tin mines and rubber estates of Malaya, required the introduction of large numbers of people more used to a higher commercial and technical culture and to a money economy than were the peasantry on the spot. It required both a labour force and a supply of traders and distributors more mobile and more used to paid employment than the owner-cultivators of a subsistence economy who were slow to leave their traditional security—their land. There was no secret about this policy. Purcell quotes W. H. Treacher, the Governor of British North Borneo in 1891: 'Experience in the Straits Settlements, the Malay Peninsula and Sarawak has shown that the people to cause rapid progress in Malayan countries are the hard-working, money-loving Chinese, and these are the people whom the Company should lay themselves out to attract to Borneo.'[2]

At the present day, when one of the most bitter criticisms levelled against the colonial record by developing countries is that the colonial rulers failed miserably to develop them economically in the days of their power, it is perhaps strange to criticize them for taking what was certainly the shortest route to getting development started. The long and expensive process of education which by now enables the indigenous people to play a full part in a modern economy was financed by this first period of railway-building, or mining, or plantation agriculture for which immigrant skills were needed, whether in East Africa, Zambia, Burma or Malaya. If there is a debit balance to the whole colonial process (and the debits are much emphasized here), there are credit items too.[3]

The long-term debits of introducing immigrants are indeed heavy. They are essentially the costs of treating a society only as an economy, of taking short cuts to economic progress without regard to social factors—the costs of Benthamism in nineteenth-century England or of the slave trade. They have been repeatedly and comprehensively analysed by J. S. Furnivall in the context of South-East Asia. His main thesis is that 'the cult of efficiency' created a plural economy without creating any social integration: 'Instead of building up a national society, the effect of British rule was to call into existence a plural society comprising numerous groups living side by side but separately, and meeting only in the market place.' Or, again: 'The cult of efficiency merely built up a monumental Western skyscraper on Eastern soil,

[2] Purcell, *The Chinese in Southeast Asia.*

[3] Where Chinese or Asians were introduced, the cost of development was, in fact, far lower than where (as in West Africa) European expatriates had to be imported in large numbers to do jobs which an Asian contractor could have done at half the price.

with the natives in the basement; all inhabited the same country, but the building was of a different world, the modern world, to which the ordinary native had no access.'[4]

The economic pattern which resulted from this policy is described more fully in Chapter VI. To ask whether development could have taken a different course is futile. Both the ideals and the shortcomings of the colonial system, its motives and the ways by which it was financed, hang together inseparably; they reflect a hundred complex factors which made Europe what it was. It may, however, be a useful warning to modern economists and statesmen—especially those responsible for aid—not to treat whole societies as economies in the attempt to find a short cut to that rapid development which dominates our ambitions today.

While the colonial powers sharpened the danger of racial conflict by the influx of immigrants whom they encouraged or allowed, they also did little in South-East Asia to bring local ethnic minorities within a common sense of nationhood. It may well be said that this was true in Africa; but there were important differences between the two. African cultures, elaborate as they were later found to be by anthropologists and historians, were dismissed by colonial rulers as too primitive to respect or preserve, not least because techniques were of the lowliest and religions unlinked to the major known religions of the world. Moreover, the multiplicity of small tribes in Africa, with their individual cultures, gave little choice to missionaries and administrators but to instil Western language, Christianity, some variety of European outlook and values throughout the continent to as many Africans as their influence could touch; and this had at least some unifying effects.

But in Asia there was a difference. For centuries the great religions had been at least heard of in Europe; 'the wisdom of the East' was proverbial. For thousands of years stories of rich courts and temples, of philosophers and holy teachers had reached the West. For those who went to South-East Asia, the Buddhist temples and the great monuments of Hindu culture at Angkor Wat or Borobodur were enough by themselves to impress. These were at least civilizations to respect, even if the Europeans were, in latter days, to bring industrial and economic techniques which had not before been turned to making wealth in Asia. In general there was much less attempt to transform the cultures of Asia into a European image.

There is an exception in the Philippines. There the Spanish Catholics, in their long reign, did indeed imprint a Western culture; it

[4] J. S. Furnivall, *Progress and Welfare in South-East Asia*, New York, 1941.

was altered in many ways but also strongly reinforced by a fresh and vigorous injection of American values from 1900. In a sense the Philippines have lived for more than three centuries on the fringe of the changing history and ideas of the West, from almost medieval Catholic authority to the other extreme of American freedom. To see, on the gate of Sta Thomas University in Manila, the date '1624' gives but a hint of this long story. But in the rest of colonized South-East Asia there was less attempt to turn Asians into Dutchmen, Frenchmen, Englishmen. A European language was imposed for government and education at the top level. Missionaries strove to alter religions; but they never had the unequivocal backing of colonial governments, who had far more respect for Buddhism or Islam than for African animist religions, which were damned as witchcraft and superstition.[5] There was less talk in Asia of a 'civilizing mission'; the monuments of high culture from the past, the quiet assurance of the Buddhist monks, were enough to silence it, if not in Europe, at least for those who made their lives in Asia.

On the Asian side, too, there was a difference. Although the Europeans' power, their purposeful, self-assured effectiveness, the steel framework of their administration, their fearlessness in nailing down their railways or their dams across the powerful forces of Nature—although all this was in some degree awe-inspiring, it was seen as *human* power, not as the overwhelming magic which at first dumbfounded Africa. For one thing Asia was 'discovered' so much earlier—not, as was the interior of Africa, in the mid-nineteenth century, when the scientific and industrial revolution in Europe had already carried the white man so infinitely far ahead of Africans in practical techniques. The early European traders in Asia were often deeply impressed by what they saw in luxury, jewellery, fine workmanship, and handicraft. European and Asian grew up more or less together into the scientific and industrial age, from schooner to steamer, from steamer to aircraft, although latterly the technical initiative came always from the European side. At all times there were both richer and more cultured men in India and China than the Europeans among them, as there are today in many parts of South-East Asia. While in some ways this longer contact deepened the European influence, creating a larger group of Asians far more thoroughly imbued with Western culture, in another sense long familiarity and their own stronger cultural assurance gave Asians a more realistic judgement of their Western rulers. Burmese, Malays,

[5] Significantly, the British accepted that no missionaries should teach in Islamic Northern Nigeria.

Chinese had a culture of their own, which they preserved—the Chinese were always convinced of their superiority. Seen at close quarters the Europeans, however powerful, were also, in some contexts and for some Asian minds, barbarians.

Because the colonialists' impact (outside the Philippines) was less, in this last sense, so their unifying influence on the regions which they temporarily ruled was less. As in Africa, the colonial power was little concerned with nation-building. It was concerned to rule, to keep law and order. If there were existing local rulers who could be used, the colonial power ruled through them. If there were many languages and cultures under one colonial régime, then languages were left intact, even taught in schools. To tamper with religious belief was, as seen by the Government, unnecessary and apt to lead to civil commotion. Further, if there was danger of communal hostility or riots, segregation was advantageous; in Malaya, the Chinese tin-miners and Indian indentured labourers were kept apart. It was casually assumed that they would one day return to their homes.

Moreover, in the most backward areas the British at least adopted an attitude typical of much British administration in India and Africa. Backward or 'primitive' groups required protection from the Indian or Chinese moneylender; from towns and their accompaniment of vice and disease; from disruption of their culture, seen to some extent as a curio, to some extent as a state of blessed innocence and virtue. Malay culture in Malaya was thus to some extent embalmed; even more markedly in Borneo the administration, right up to 1963, was cosseting the Dusuns and Bajaus, or the Dyaks in their longhouses, protecting them from the more energetic, clever, commercially minded immigrant Chinese. The British attempt to protect indigenous peoples from the effects of British commercial policy naturally resulted in emphasizing the segregation of the three tiers of society. Whatever the moral or political issue here—and a case for the British attitude can be made—the result did not make things easier for succeeding rulers. The Masai in East Africa, or the Dinka and Nuer in the Sudan, were left, when British rule came abruptly to an end, wholly unintegrated in the larger state whose citizens they unwittingly or even reluctantly became. The new Governments of Burma and Malaysia could make the same complaint; the British had encouraged the individuality of their minorities.

Again, there was little restriction on movement by the colonial powers. The seas of the Malay world continued to carry emigrants, small groups seeking fortune in a new land, labour which was often much desired. Sabah today holds Filipinos, Hongkong Chinese,

Chinese from Kwantung and Canton, Malays, Indonesians, men from the Celebes and the islands of the Sulu Sea. The archipelago remained an open highway and men were used to seeing a dozen different races and faces in the trading ports from Penang to Manila. While the colonial powers maintained an overarching unity there was little—too little—thought of how these diverse groups could one day find a unity of their own.

It might be argued that at least the problem of ethnic minorities was less acute in South-East Asia (save in Burma and Indonesia) than it was in Tropical Africa. In Asia there were larger kingdoms, founded on long tradition. The whole political experience was on a larger scale and more advanced. The great extension of Buddhism on the mainland gave greater areas of common understanding in South-East Asia than in, say, Nigeria, where the Muslim north of Hausa and Fulani were poles apart from the Yoruba or Ibo civilizations of the south and south-east. There were possibly fewer acute local tribal differences than those, say, between Kikuyu, Masai and Luo in Kenya, Baganda and the outer peoples in Uganda, Creoles and the peoples of the interior in Sierra Leone. But this is certainly not true of Indonesia, and on the other side of the balance the size and vigour of the Chinese colonies in South-East Asia represented a more serious threat to unity than, say, the 'Asian' groups in East Africa (where they count for barely 400,000 from an African population of nearly 25 million) and far more serious than the sprinkling of Syrians and Lebanese in the African West Coast states. Singapore is 75 per cent Chinese; Malaysia (including Singapore)[6] 42 per cent; the 2½ million Chinese in Thailand hold a fair grip on the commercial life of Bangkok; in Sarawak and Sabah, where they represent 31 per cent and 23 per cent of the total population respectively, over 80 per cent of all local citizens with Secondary and post-Secondary education in 1960 were Chinese. In Java many thriving townships were dominated commercially by Chinese, as was much of the distributive system until, in a series of evictions and some massacres since the War, their power was sharply reduced.

It is an irony that the dangers of this process were largely masked by the very fact of colonial rule. As in other continents, the European rulers created a social hierarchy with the white man at the top. Sometimes there was an arrogant insistence on this ranking—the Dutch in Semarang[7] at one time insisted that Indonesians must dismount

[6] Without Singapore the porportion (1962 figures) was 35.6 per cent.
[7] Willmott, *The Chinese in Semarang*.

and walk when entering the Dutch quarter, and there were times when the British were as bad.[8] But the hard facts of power were enough to create this ranking without insistence. The very existence of such an upper class, towards which so many faces were turned for favour or protection or, indeed, in admiration, overlaid in some degree the violence of feeling between different subordinate groups; they saw each other not quite full-face but in relation to a third. Certainly they were aware of a difference between their relationship with each other and that with the foreign rulers. The foreigners, few in number, totally alien in habit, who might disappear as arbitrarily as they came, were altogether outside the local plural community, in which neighbours of different culture would always be a part, even though a hated part. Save for moments when provocation burst through their self-control, local rivals would be content with a certain wariness, a suspension of active attack or defence.

It was thus the existence of a firm authority, and one largely impartial, which quietened both the anxieties and the aggressiveness of conflicting groups below it. But when this power is suddenly removed; when one group claims to rule the other by its own standards, with its own interests dominant, fear and antagonism are face to face without arbitrator or appeal. This is when violence may come, as it came in India and Ceylon, or in British Guiana; as it came between Tutsi and Hutu in Rwanda-Burundi; as it threatens in Fiji; as it smoulders and blazes in Cyprus. Even where race is not the issue, but only politics, the sudden realization that there is no ultimate appeal to an outside metropolitan power, that the power of government must be self-legitimized and self-supported within a diverse, unintegrated society weighs heavily on the post-colonial statesman. It may lead to an aggressive assertion of authority, provoking violent response. Thailand, a single ethnic community, never colonized, provides a contrast which in part explains the greater assimilation of the Thailand Chinese.

If colonial ethnic policy was to lay up trouble for the succeeding independent rulers, there are elements in administrative policy which also were to make the process of modernization more confused. The side-effects of indirect rule, in reducing the respect given to native rulers who came to be seen as the agents of colonial government rather than the protectors of their people, have often been described. Despite

[8] Philip Mason records such a period between about 1880 and 1910 in India, when the youngest subaltern demanded instant respect even from venerable Indians.

its disadvantages, indirect rule at least preserved some element of cultural continuity in rural areas and perhaps smoothed the transition to independent government. But the introduction of Western types of law created a huge disturbance in traditional life. It has been argued, with much force, that this imported legal system was responsible for breaking down the disciplines of traditional society and the 'honesty' which corresponded to those disciplines, introducing in their place a multitude of regulations, a multitude of lawyers, and the growth both of crime and of corruption. There are questions of definition here. Many of the sanctions approved in traditional systems (such as the punishments for witchcraft) were crimes in the European calendar; many of the gifts to traditional chiefs and rulers were 'corruption'.

But the argument is not to be waved aside so easily. The introduction of a mass of legal rules, often at variance with local custom and the local sense of justice, administered in a foreign language through interpreters, tied to rules of procedure which might easily overrule the obvious equities, was bound to have many ill results. It gave an open opportunity for the bribing of witnesses and the corruption of judges and created a class of native lawyers at worst unscrupulous and at best a waste of educated talent so urgently needed in other fields. In Burma, says Harvey,[9] seven Burmese took legal training for one who learned medicine. In the Punjab the Finance Commissioner, Thorburn, wrote in 1899: '. . . the country was deluged with a flow of intricate, technical and even mischievous acts, the want of which had never been felt and the meaning of which is a frequent subject of remunerative dispute for those who live by the law.'[10] If the best of the judges were incorruptible, many of the juniors in small courts lived by bribery. Harvey's final comment, which has a wider significance, is worth quoting in full: 'We imposed a modern administration, a good and progressive administration, but it required an ever-increasing variety of departmental subordinates who applied modern rules, rules unintelligible to the simpler public, and applied them largely for purposes of extortion. We ourselves were inaccessible to bribes, but we were also inaccessible to the people, partly because we were so few, partly by the mere fact of race.'[11]

No doubt the transition to a modern, uniform, and exact legal system is a necessary step on the road to modernization. No doubt the Europeans themselves, whose intentions were, in the main, palpably

[9] G. E. Harvey, *British Rule in Burma, 1824–1942*, London, 1946.
[10] Quoted by Harvey, op. cit. [11] ibid.

honest, were forgiven for the surprising foolishness of their law. Perhaps in some parts of Africa, where the magistrates remained British much longer for lack of a sophisticated immigrant lawyer class, the abuses were less great. But certainly the legacy in Burma and Malaya,[12] taken over by independent governments, was one so lawyer-ridden, so repugnant to a traditional sense of natural justice, so weighted against the poor, that it vastly increased the difficulty of building confidence between government and people. Moreover, because so many of the lawyers were immigrants—mainly Indian—it created yet another focus for racial hostility against privileged and parasitic aliens.

It was, however, in the economic field that colonial policy had its widest effect, with its three-tier structure of Europeans, immigrants, and native peoples and its emphasis on commerce and export. The development of this sytem and the problems which it left to the succession states deserve a separate chapter. It is enough here to stress how deeply it had penetrated and divided national structure and how bitter were the tensions it engendered. For the effect of creating a virtual monopoly of key functions—commercial, financial, industrial—in the hands of immigrant groups must be seen through the eyes of young nationals who have often completed their higher education overseas and become passionately nationalist. Those who went to Europe, who had absorbed the ideas of the London School of Economics in the 1930s, for instance, often returned critical of capitalism itself, critical of 'colonial exploitation', inclined to see Chinese or Indian merchants as the protected agents of white exploitation, or as profiteers and grasping landlords preying upon an innocent rural people. Thus, with their socialism, racial hostility was only too likely to go hand in hand.

Moreover, it is hard for Englishmen to imagine the strains and jealousies which can arise when even humble occupations are monopolized by a closed, alien group. If all tobacconists in England were Yorkshiremen, there might be trouble; if all tobacconists were West Indians and they could run every competitor out of business, there would certainly be trouble. It is a tendency of all immigrants to cluster by occupation. The vast expansion of the exchange economy brought by colonialism opened the doors wide for immigrant clustering in just the new commercial and technical skills which provided new opportunities for better livelihood and for which the indigenous peoples were,

[12] Victor Purcell, in his memoirs, gives a light-hearted but in fact horrifying account of the amateurishness, the mistakes, the mistranslations and the underlying corruption of the courts in Malaya in which he served (*Memoirs of a Malayan Official*, London, 1965).

at first, less well equipped. 'Job reservation'[13] aimed against Chinese has been frequently imposed by legislation (Thailand, Viet-Nam, Cambodia, Burma, Indonesia), but it is a sign of anxiety rather than a cure for these bitter jealousies.

The result of these colonial policies and attitudes—political, administrative, legal, ethnic, economic—was to leave to the successor states problems far more difficult than the colonial rulers had had to face. The boundaries they had drawn enclosed a number of unfused cultures. As a third party, with no local electorate to obey, the colonial government could administer each section by expediency—'excepted districts' and sometimes a measure of local autonomy for dissident minorities were a commonplace of British administration. The Chins were ruled by the British, not by the Burmese; and in a dozen similar cases communal or ethnic violence could be thus forestalled. 'Divide and Rule' does not describe this policy—the danger was not combination against the ruler but communal revolt if cultural separation was ignored. Yet the rulers did not fully grasp that their very creation of a unified economy and a central administration—both great virtues in their eyes—was forcing these unfused elements increasingly into a single ecology while doing little to modify their deep mutual suspicions.

When to this heritage of unfused cultures, now to be bound into a modern independent state, are added both the importation of immigrants and the distortions of the economy just described, there can only be sympathy for the post-war nation-builders. A comparison of uncolonized Thailand with Burma or Malaya will make this contrast more vivid. The Thais have learned to live with their Chinese minority over centuries, controlling its growth sharply from time to time. They have accepted, eclectically, some parts of European education and commercial enterprise, but always as masters in their house; they have learned a tolerant compromise with their Malay minority in the south. Their Civil Service is indigenous, interwoven with the prestige system of Thai culture as a whole, keeping in step with its political masters in a gradual modernizing movement. In contrast, consider Burma. In Rangoon, an untrained revolutionary party was confronted by a large British-trained bureaucracy, unsympathetic to upstart rulers, heavily coloured by the tradition of the Indian service. The rice trade, import-export, banking, industry, were wholly in the hands of white men or

[13] e.g. taxi-driving, hairdressing, retailing, and twenty or more other occupations have been prohibited to non-indigenous people by various governments at various times. In Malaya road transport is now reserved to Malay operators.

Indians. The retail trade was Indian or Chinese. Outside Burma itself, five major cultural minorities, whose individualism had been in no small measure recognized by the British, were refusing Burmese domination. From this the new nation was to be made.

In Viet-Nam the greater French cultural proselytizing emphasized the European factor; French Catholicism jostled against Buddhism, the French language against Vietnamese. French-educated Civil Servants filled the government posts in French Saigon, while across the river in Cholon a huge Chinese community found its commercial opportunity in the new French and American exchange economy.

Malaya is obviously the most startling example of the immigrant problem largely created by the colonial system. It is understandable that the British should have allowed Singapore's virtually empty island to become a huge Chinese city; it could be regarded as a separate homogeneous entity. But it is almost incredible that any responsible government should have countenanced the wholesale penetration of the Malayan mainland by Chinese. It is not as though they were concentrated at a few points or segregated into two or three massive industries. Along the whole west coast the Chinese are widely spread, in hundreds of occupations.

TABLE 10

PERCENTAGE OF CHINESE TO TOTAL POPULATION IN CERTAIN STATES (1957 Census)

	Malaysian	*Chinese*
Federation of Malaya	49.8	37.2
Penang	28.8	57.2
Selangor	23.1	48.2 (Indians 20.1)
Perak	39.7	44.2 (Indians 14.9)
Johore	48.0	42.4
Malacca	49.1	41.5
Negri Sembilan	39.5	41.2 (Indians 15.1)
	(*For Comparison*)	
Kelantan	91.6	5.7
Trengganu	92.1	6.6

Figures for a few selected occupations, by race, show how the Chinese, and, considering their lower numbers, the Indians, have penetrated the 'modern' occupations disproportionately to the Malays (Table II).

The addition of Sabah and Sarawak, each dominated in numbers by indigenous ethnic groups who feel far apart from Malays, and each with a quarter or more of their population consisting of Chinese, adds to the immigrant problem an ethnic minority problem which may prove of

TABLE 11

SELECTED OCCUPATIONS, BY RACE (1957 Census)

Occupation	*Malaysian*	*Chinese*	*Indians*
Total Economically Active:	1,023,729	771,963	312,956
'Agricultural occupations'	744,788	291,047	154,091
Administrative, executive, managerial	4,290	15,275	3,014
Clerical	16,695	28,446	12,215
Sales	28,981	120,382	30,629
Craftsmen, production workers	77,708	182,975	64,686

considerable importance, even without the interference of Indonesia. It must be admitted that, but for the accident of colonial rule, the rulers of Malaya would scarcely have been likely to include these two areas of Borneo into a unified state; indeed, Brunei, a Malay sultanate, would have been a more natural addition, and it was Brunei which did not join.

Finally, one resultant from the colonial period has been even more disturbing in South-East Asia than in most other areas—its sudden and chaotic end. Indian independence was decades in the making: only in Africa is the speed at all comparable with that of South-East Asia. Yet Ghana, the first in Tropical Africa to emerge, won independence only after twelve years of postwar colonial rule; Tanganyika after sixteen; Kenya after eighteen. These years were very different from the decades 1920–40. They were years of conscious preparation for independence by the colonial power. Certainly this effort was imperfect, slow at first, hasty and agitated later. But some effort to train successors was made; there was still some time to consider the probable future of minorities—in Nigeria the Minorities Commission reported before the final hand-over, and in Uganda the whole negotiation for independence was centred on this issue. Although many of the plans were swept away (regional government in Ghana was an immediate casualty, and it barely lasted a year in Kenya), yet at least the alternatives were tried. Above all, there was time for the new political parties to test their strength, to combine and recombine, before external control was wholly gone. The Congo shows what could happen in Africa when this period was missing or not used.

Save in Malaya and the Philippines, it was missing in South-East Asia. Burma and Indonesia plunged straight into independence and civil war; Viet-Nam into civil war, partition and independence; Cambodia had a rather smoother passage, though with the slenderest human resources with which to shoulder the task of government. The Philippines moved straight to independence after the war, but in accordance with long-declared plans and with a larger, better-educated and more sophisticated leadership, for which the Americans must take credit. Malaya's future was consciously hammered out in twelve years of discussion and planning and, even there, against a background of terrorist revolt.

The shattering of European prestige by Japanese invasion and the abrupt end to colonial governments gave most of South-East Asia a sudden and violent start in the new world of independence. It is not surprising that the unfinished business of colonial rule should have set worse problems there. Before turning to the detail of these national problems—economic, administrative, educational, cultural—it is necessary to put a prior question—how were unified nations to be founded from the broken fragments of the past?

V

VARIANTS IN THE NATIONALIST IDEA

TWENTY years have passed since South-East Asia emerged from Japanese occupation. It is a long time for memories outside Asia to be fresh; and the Western world had other preoccupations at the time. It is even longer, not merely in time but in changes of outlook, since 1939; yet 1939 or 1940 are the last years in which the old pattern of colonial rule existed effectively in South-East Asia, save in modern Malaysia and Singapore and, for a few very troubled years, in Indo-China. The colonial rulers had been moving gently along with education and training, preparing for some distant day when a native administration, as large as their own and of the same standard, would be ready to take over full responsibility. They would assuredly have said that this time was still two decades or more away. It is doubtful if the Dutch in Indonesia even considered the idea of leaving. Only in neighbouring India was there a real sense of urgency, spurred on by far older Indian political forces.

It is hard to realize at all vividly the economic and political chaos, the lack of trained staff, the confusion of local and national aims which beset Burma or Indonesia in the turbulent cross-waves of politics and rebellion following the war. To say that the transfer of power was disorderly and hurried is a huge understatement; there was barely a transfer at all. Burma broke with the Commonwealth in 1947 and plunged into civil war; in Indonesia the Dutch fought the nationalists and split the empire's loyalties before they yielded independence. The French managed to hand over to the King of Cambodia, but Viet-Nam and Laos were left in a raging civil war. In Malaya there were the long years of Emergency against the Communists in the forest; in Borneo a huge task of reconstruction after the Japanese devastation.

Old nations with a settled political unity and fixed boundaries are apt to think of the problems of new countries in Civil Servants' terms. There are, they observe, the problems of building an economy, of creating an effective administration and managerial system, of designing and financing an educational structure. All these tasks faced the new rulers of South-East Asia; all of them were complicated by racial and cultural diversity: they are the subject of later chapters in this book. But for the new countries there is a prior problem, far more pressing. It is the political problem—how to create a nation at all; who shall rule it; how it shall be ruled. The first tasks are, quite simply, peace (to avoid a civil war or win it); security; a constitution and some agreed way to make it work; a sense of nationhood.

Nationalism is often described as a kind of disease which has afflicted humanity in the last 150 years—a disease because it has led to wars, to the oppression of minorities, discrimination, irrational hatreds between man and man. Such comments come noticeably often from the established nations who are no longer acutely concerned for their own identity. If it is a disease, it is certainly hard to find in past history a state of human affairs which was not suffering from far worse disorders. Vague contrasts with a non-nationalist 'Christendom' in Europe do not make a convincing story, when Europe was so torn with religious and dynastic wars and tyrannies. Farther back into medieval Europe, in the centuries of illiterate local peasant life, when minorities were smaller but no less oppressed, and 'nationalism' was on the scale of clans or cities or a ruling court, there is no delightful contrast to be found. Perhaps in nineteenth- and twentieth-century empires there has been a natural backward glance to the Roman Empire as a model system covering the Mediterranean basin, under which a diversity of peoples and cultures, once conquered, developed in widely different ways under the protection of Roman power. There were times when a man could have walked from Lisbon to the Caspian through a host of different peoples and cultures, without leaving the range of Roman law and the enforcement of order. Indeed, there were periods in colonial India and places in Africa when this parallel was felt and admitted. But the imperial power failed, and the peoples exposed to the rough world by its failure have to make their own protective shell. They find it in nationalism.

For at midnight on Independence Day the old order which held society together vanished. For an instant of time, until a new order appeared, society reverted to the disparate small groups which had composed it before the colonial conquest. Nationalism, as the counterpart of new independence, is a vision of this new order; an attempt to impose upon the welter of events and human groupings disclosed by the failure of authority some new protecting framework within which a unitary social organism can take shape. For areas composed of far smaller tribal organisms—as were many of the colonial divisions of

Tropical Africa—this constitutes an evolutionary leap,[1] the formation of a larger entity capable of independent survival in a world of rival entities far exceeding tribal size. There must be exclusion of elements too unassimilable to use; and there must be inclusion of enough to reach critical size. When there is so much to create, any element of unity already given will be valuable—boundaries, culture, common history. In this task it is natural to feel that one dominant cultural group, within already recognized boundaries, might be able to create an order within which human development could take place in relative security. This has been conceived as the all-important aim. If such an aim contains the possibility of oppression, political, economic or cultural, these risks are in contrast to a state of free co-operation between a multiplicity of small units which exists solely as a possible vision of the future; such a state has never been achieved in the past.

The men who emerged as leaders were nationalists by definition. In conceiving of a society freed from colonial rule, what other picture could they have had but that of the nation-state? In many senses their country had been treated as such by the colonial power. From the many elements which may be thought to constitute nationhood, they emphasized the most obvious—a fixed geographical area, ruled by a homogeneous cultural group, using a common language, and big enough to be viable as an economic unit in the modern world. Only exceptionally have they insisted upon common religion to buttress cultural unity. They and their immediate followers were, in effect, the only 'nationals'; they had grasped the idea of nationhood, which was largely outside the horizon of the mass of peasants; the legitimacy of their position as rulers depended upon it. It may be remarked that, in delimiting the nation, they were quite clear in their choice between cultural and ethnic homogeneity and the boundaries which they inherited. About some religious differences they might be fairly tolerant; about language rather less, though some concessions to cultural minorities might be discussed. But the given frontiers were invoilable.

Thus nationalism in plural societies necessarily has two faces. For the dominant majority, it is self-determination as against a foreign ruler. But for the same majority it is also the right to include minorities, whether racially or culturally related or wholly alien, inside a nation-state large enough to build a modern, diversified economy and to make

[1] This is not a very good biological metaphor, save at a rather low level of evolution. Some 'animals', such as medusoids, are, in fact, a mass of separate organisms which have been combined, in the course of evolution, so that the mass operates in certain ways as a single unit.

the greatest possible show of international influence and status. In Africa, the leaders in Accra were determined to include the Ashanti Kingdom in the new Ghana. In Kenya, the new African Government has no patience with Somali self-determination in the north. In Zambia, the claim of Barotseland for separate government got short shrift from the African leaders in Lusaka. So, too, in Asia, the Nagas cannot escape from the grip of New Delhi, nor the Chins or Karens from the ruling Burmese. Malays in southern Thailand are firmly clasped to Buddhist Bangkok rather than to their Muslim cousins across the border in Malaya. Every inch of the Dutch Empire is firmly claimed by the rulers in Djakarta including even the wholly different Papuans of West Irian. Self-determination is for majorities; nationhood drags ethnic minorities in its train. The only unassimilables who could readily be dispensed with were the immigrants of alien race.

Common thinking today throughout the world has so much accepted the 'national idea' that its contrast with one element in the past—the imperial idea—and with Soviet Communism in the present is rarely mentioned. Rome and many other empires included vast areas and great diversities within an outer ring of military protection, relying upon an army, the benefits of security and law, and a myth of grandeur to hold its parts together. Communism in Soviet Asia has relied upon the Party and its policing sanctions and a myth of political philosophy to achieve a like inclusiveness. Rome, the British Empire, and Communism could include the greatest cultural diversities outside their heartland, and could even allow their central capital, as a symbol of unity in diversity, to become polyglot and polyracial. But in each case the heartland had first to be consolidated. The stages of growth are from Rome to Italy to the Empire; from White Russia to Russia to the northern half of Asia. It is in this stage of first consolidation that an ethnic nationalism is strongest, and least tolerant.[2]

It is thus unreasonable to suppose that, at the very moment of nationalist fusion, the type of racial or ethnic tolerance could exist which can and does exist at the imperial stage. Where fusion can be mainly ethnic, the case is fairly simple. The harder issue comes where it cannot. Burma shares with much of Tropical Africa this problem at the ethnic level—for the racial immigrant diversity has been sharply

[2] One may remark in passing that, while the concept of military empires has been abandoned by the non-Communist powers, the concept of ideological empires on the Communist side has not. One of their claims is the ability to include diversities, long since achieved by Rome or Britain. But while the colonial empires have given a total political independence to their old possessions, the ideological empire is, by its very theory, all-embracing and, by its practice, centralized.

reduced and controlled. The projection of 'Burma', 'Ghana', 'Kenya' has to be beyond ethnicity ('tribalism'), relying on a myth of nationhood which, in origin and emphasis, is primarily economic and political. The trouble here may come when the national image is used to support special advantage for one leading group—Burmese, Kikuyu, Hausa, Creole. Harder still is the case of Malaysia, where the myth of nation has to cover a political and administrative balance between two grossly unlike peoples, closely matched in numbers, where even the geographical perimeter is new and subject to political attack. Nationhood here has been stripped of common culture, common language, common history, geographical continuity, assured boundaries. Perhaps it is a sign of the times that economic potential and a liberal ideology, from British democratic and free-enterprise traditions, was felt strong enough to hold. For if Versailles 'balkanized' Europe—the phrase implies a sinister comment on the quarrels of succession states—it did so mainly on ethnic grounds. More modern nation-making policies would be more anxious to stress the economic or ideological unit, particularly where ethnic groupings are too small for the modern world. The number of independent states in the United Nations, some with less than one million inhabitants, shows how little headway this ideal has been able to make.

South-East Asia offers some interesting variants on the approach to this psychology of nationhood. First, as we have seen, the immigrants are likely to get short shrift, unless they have outside political protection. For a year or two the absorption of their jobs and the spending of their stolen savings form a bone to throw to citizens whose discontent might turn against the Government. President Sukarno, needing friends in the Peking camp to play off against the United States and even Russia, has kept the persecution of Chinese within limits, although the expulsions and riots of 1953[3] were serious enough. The Burmese tolerated both Indians and Chinese while their energies were mainly engaged in the civil war. But now, without apparent protest from an India preoccupied with her own problems, the Indians have been expropriated and have left Burma, with no more property than their suitcases. Their hardship has been little heeded by the outside world. The Chinese, probably for reasons similar to Sukarno's, have been more gently handled.

Rangoon and Djakarta, however, move apart in their handling of the more subtle ethnic issues. The Burmese, hard-pressed and almost besieged at times, have attempted a federal unity, based on the colonial

[3] There were serious anti-Chinese movements in 1960 and 1963.

boundaries. Despite great concessions offered to the minorities, they have never fully convinced them that, as partners in Burma, they would be equal partners with the Burmese. Federal nationalism is always weaker at birth and slower to coalesce. At present, the military Government is turning more firmly to the ideological approach, seeking to project 'the Burmese way to socialism' past the Shan or Karen leadership to the peasants underneath.

The Indonesian policy is far harder to define. Distances, and the cumulative local differences—from Sumatra to Java, Java to Bali, Bali to Borneo or the Celebes or the Sunda Islands—created the greatest difficulty. There were strong relics of independence in Macassar, long left virtually on its own by the Dutch; a marked individuality in Bali; old resentments between Javanese and Sumatrans. But there were, perhaps, two advantages denied to Burma. Dutch influence was still there for twelve years after the War and provided a focus for nationalist hostility and a chance to hold together the unity of an independence crusade—while the British rulers had disappeared from Burma like a vanished dream. Secondly, although the ethnic differences existed, they were perhaps less sharply felt than those in Burma, less aggravated by different attitudes towards the occupying Japanese, geographically isolated by sea straits and poor communications, farther from the central seat of power.

It was natural, then, for Sukarno to adopt almost the imperial rather than the unitary nationalist approach. He has been able, at a stretch, to hold a military perimeter round the Dutch empire, and to suppress minor nationalisms by military means; the army therefore counts heavily at the centre of power. He has been able, with a fine imperial tolerance, to contain Islamic theocratic tendencies (such as Dar ul-Islam) by implying that, as in Rome, the empire is big enough for many creeds; by invoking, as from a proud tradition, the ancient empires of Java and Sumatra, which were not Muslim but Hindu; and by countering with an ideological movement which is in essence secular. By this immensely skilful balancing of the imperial army, the socialist or Communist ideology and the religious fanaticism, none of which are geographically compact or immune from penetration by each other, he has contrived to project 'the grandeur which is Indonesia'—a concept of a vast empire (and it has passed 100 million people now), a Malay empire in an ancient historical sense, and a 'new emerging' empire embattled against the 'old established' villainy of foreign oppressors and their puppets. If Sukarno's empire were to fail, it would be because, in his concentration on politics, the need for successful economic nationhood has been dangerously neglected; and because the unity of Indonesia still depends so much upon the President himself.

Viet-Nam provides another contrast. There was considerable racial and cultural unity in Viet-Nam as a whole, a colonial boundary, a university at Hanoi for the whole country, a common language and common economy. All these elements of possible nationhood have been sacrificed to the ideological difference between North and South. The South, without a genuinely popular government, indebted for its very existence to American economic and military power, is left with no nationalist rallying cry other than 'Freedom from Communism!'—a freedom it already possesses and which may seem to have done it little good. Its enemies, the Viet-Cong, can cry: 'Freedom from foreign colonialists!' 'Popular government!' 'One people, one language, one faith!' It is a strong combination in these days.

The situation of Malaysia has already been described in racial terms. But there are two elements in it which belong to the post-colonial rationalist era and require some further notice. First, there is a purely political division which tends to break on racial lines. The Malay rulers represent an aristocratic, pre-independence régime which could be paralleled by some sultanates of Indonesia or, in Africa, by the North Nigerian emirs. But, wherever it has come, the struggle for independence has contained within itself the stirrings of a social revolution hostile to aristocracies and always able to find an ally in the socialist camp. In Indonesia the leftist revolution is felt to have been achieved, although Sukarno himself and some other leaders belong, in fact, to an older *élite*. But in Malaya no revolution within the Malay world took place. Dignified, sanctioned by religion, mildly repressive of 'new ideas', it might well satisfy Malay traditions for long enough. But Malays are little over half the electorate. The Chinese certainly have no reverence either for Malay aristocracy or for Islam. On the contrary, many of their young men, able, impatient, are far to the left. In Singapore they see the conservatives defeated and the People's Action Party in full command, successful, democratic, modern. Although Singapore is no longer in the Federation, the pulling power of her example on young Malaysian Chinese remains. Thus, through colonial lack of care and foresight, a major danger of politics on racial lines, between two evenly balanced adversaries, has arisen. The history of British Guiana is a gloomy warning of what results could follow if the leaders lose their balance in this dangerous game.

Second, the inclusion of Sabah and Sarawak in Malaysia (1963) has added a racial problem of special complexity. The populations of these two were divided as follows:

TABLE 12

POPULATIONS OF SABAH AND SARAWAK, BY RACE

Sabah (1960 Census)		%
Indigenous	306,498	67.5
	(Dusuns	32.0)
Chinese	104,542	23.0
Others*	41,485	9.1
Europeans	1,896	0.4
Total	454,421	100

Sarawak (1960 Census)		%
Indigenous	387,672	49.9
	(Sea Dyaks	31.1)
Chinese	244,435	31.5
Malays	136,232	17.5
Europeans and others	8,651	1.1
	776,990	100

Note: * 'Others' in Sabah would include some Malays, but a majority of miscellaneous groups from the eastern islands and the Philippines. It is interesting that the Malays, having come mainly from Sumatra, were not treated as 'indigenous' in either census, although established for some centuries in Borneo. There is a higher concentration of them in Brunei, which remains a Malay sultanate under British protection.

In sheer weight of numbers, the indigenous peoples of Sabah have a comfortable majority; in Sarawak they are exactly balanced against a combination of Chinese and Malay. But a glance at educational levels reveals a more significant pattern:

TABLE 13

SABAH, 1960

Population 10 years old and over—Educational Attainment

Completed:	*Primary*	*Form 3*	*Full Secondary*	*Training College*	*University*
Indigenous	3,264	262	92	113	2
Chinese	9,004	3,353	1,178	101	115
Europeans	57	222	521	57	125
'Other'	2,017	1,007	527	46	62

SARAWAK, 1960

Population 10 years old and over—Educational Attainment

	Primary	*Form 3*	*Full Secondary*	*Training College*	*University*
Indigenous	2,970	637	71	82	2
Chinese	18,406	9,325	2,107	184	205
Malay	3,141	775	104	64	7
European	35	183	417	58	279
'Other'	163	153	130	6	55

These figures, of course, relate to years of schooling earlier than 1960. Since then great strides have been made in extending Secondary education to indigenous peoples. Enrolments in Secondary schools by 'race' in 1962 were:

	Indigenous	*Chinese*	*Malay*	*'Other'*
Sarawak	1,381	11,877	1,328	193
Sabah	1,050	4,465	—	—

Although Sabah in particular is now catching up, there were still over four times as many Chinese as indigenous children in her Secondary schools; in Sarawak, four and a half times as many Chinese as indigenous and Malay put together. In terms of educated *adults*, the 1960 figures of attainment are, of course, the most relevant, and here the Chinese lead is far greater.

Thus, when independence and Federation with Malaya came in 1963, virtually the whole top layer of administration and management was held by British expatriates and Chinese, with some Malays in Sarawak. Indigenous ministers were elected, supported by a British and Chinese/Malay Civil Service. The private sector of commerce was almost wholly Chinese; plantation agriculture largely expatriate and Chinese; the great bulk of indigenous people were still in subsistence agriculture in the hills or fishermen on the coast.

Moreover, despite the undoubted majority in favour of the Malaysian link, it was for the indigenous people at best the lesser evil. Malay rulers in past history had not been loved; in contrast, the British had strongly favoured the indigenous groups, and had latterly developed a typical prejudice against the Chinese men of commerce. Moreover the Chinese, clinging to their own schools, infected with Communism, were not easily absorbed into a local patriotism although, as Tom Harrisson has shown, they had a good record of loyalty against the occupying Japanese.[4] When confrontation started, a section (mainly from Sarawak) defected to the Indonesian enemy.

After Malaysia was founded, when senior Malay administrators came from Kuala Lumpur, seeking to integrate development policies and bring the new-comers into a wider and richer world, they had a hard reception. They met among ministers a coolness towards Malays; among the senior British Civil Servants a passionate local patriotism, born of fifteen years of service to their local parish; and they found at almost every point in the economy Chinese or British in command. Moreover, there was no quick way to alter this. There were some hundreds of local citizens training in universities overseas, soon to return with full administrative and professional qualifications—but 80 per cent of them Chinese. To the Federal Government in Kuala Lumpur this presented an awkward dilemma. To leave the British administrators largely in command embarrassed them when Sukarno claimed that Malaysia was a British puppet; moreover, some at least of the senior British had been too long used to their own way and to purely local patriotism. To replace them by mainland Malays might

[4] T. Harrisson in Wang Gungwu (ed.), *Malaysia: A Survey*, London, 1964.

well be unacceptable, and in any case would greatly strain the new Civil Service in Kuala Lumpur, much extended already with new responsibilities and large development plans. To allow young Chinese to enter almost all the senior posts would create difficulties for many years, since the indigenous peoples, the electoral majority, would surely come forward later with full educational attainments and a demand for government jobs.

This vignette of the detailed problems faced by Malaysian rulers in a small area will perhaps illuminate more sharply the general issue facing Malaysian nationalism—the backwardness of the peoples in whose name the state is founded, the penetration of Chinese, and the vacuum left by the departing British.

Thus a glance at four countries—Burma, Indonesia, Viet-Nam, and Malaysia—shows that, perhaps surprisingly, total ethnic solidarity has not, in fact, played a decisive role in the projection of the nationalist idea. Burma has been forced into a federal structure which recognizes cultural diversity and has used economic and ideological factors for a unifying myth. Indonesia, taking the imperial standpoint, has used the army, historical myth, and ideology. In Viet-Nam a pre-existing ethnic unity has been broken by an ideological conflict imported and fiercely sustained from the outside world. In Malaysia great and largely irreducible cultural differences have led to a supra-ethnic appeal. The emotional dynamics of this projection of Malaysian nationhood are not simply identifiable. 'Confrontation' has provided a windfall external enemy as a unifying factor. But apart from that, the appeal is sophisticated. It calls upon all citizens to rally to a modern democratic state, to value the solid benefits of sane and progressive economic planning rather than the delusive excitements of racial nationalism, anti-colonialism, left-wing ideology. It appeals to reason, co-operation, modernity, growing wealth, a measure of cultural freedom (more emphasized for Malays than Chinese). It enshrines an economic freedom which, for the older and more prosperous Chinese at least, contrasts most significantly with the alternative of Peking Communism. In Borneo it offers both the Chinese and the indigenous peoples a more peaceful haven than they could find in the rough winds of Communism or of Sukarno's Indonesia. The fear of these alternatives, negative as it may seem, may be, in fact, the strongest bond. It remains a tremendous question whether these liberal ideas, aided by the fear of alternatives, can hold the remains of Malaysia together in the absence of almost all the older 'natural' sources of emotional unity.

Firm frontiers, a common ideology, and where possible ethnic and cultural unity, are prime factors in the nation-making process. But we must also consider the role of special institutions and special interest groups within the national structure. These may have a strengthening or divisive effect. One such group is the central Civil Service in these new states. The first few years are the years of the politicians. It is they who fill the skies with the new ideas, like the rockets on Independence Night, to which the nation's eyes are to be turned. They are, in the main, incompetent by themselves to match ideas with performance. Save for a very few, the politicians often do not come from the background of the Civil Servants or share their training. They load them with impossible tasks, overriding their technical and financial objections with the primacy of politics—be it education, prestige, anti-colonialism, racial or ethnic policy.

As time passes, however, and as the demand for performance grows, a point is reached where the central Civil Service may be of crucial importance. It may be that the politicians continue the barrage of exhortations, diverting attention from the present to a yet more highly coloured future. The consequence is a Civil Service discouraged, insecure and ineffective. But it may be that a different balance grows, with ministers leaning more heavily on an increasingly stable and competent official cadre. If this does happen—it is perhaps more likely where the leaders have traditionally been rulers—the Civil Service, with a growing group of managers and technicians, begins to form an *élite*. From its very training—often foreign—and outlook, it is less concerned with racial or ethnic differences; it is 'detribalized', internationalist in some degree. The growth of this group and its influence on events may well be one measure of the tolerance in racial and cultural policy which the new countries can achieve.

The omens in Asia, on this issue, are widely different. In Burma, Viet-Nam, and Indonesia politics still rule. In the Philippines, at first sight, the same seems true: but below the surface of Filipino politics, a group of economists, university professors, high-grade journalists, and businessmen are beginning to counterbalance politics with an impatient and hard-hitting professionalism which has begun to take effect. In Thailand and Malaysia, both traditional, though in different ways, this group of planners, educationists, economists, and businessmen is growing. The transition from nationalist utopianism to national achievement and stability hangs mainly upon these men.

Two other groups may play a significant part in the early years of nationalism. One is the large and growing number of young men who have received some schooling but not enough to ensure them paid work outside traditional village life. There is a critical phase, between the era when education is rare and the era when it is universal, in which this young generation is dangerous in any country. Their expectations are likely to be higher than any possible fulfilment, and they become the natural recruits for extremist politicians. Always willing to upset the order which seems to block their hopes, they are especially dangerous when racial issues are involved. The Youth Wings and the 'have-nots', who help to put the leaders in power, will see an obvious opportunity for spoil among the immigrants and foreigners who hold much-envied jobs.

The other group consists of the religious leaders and the priesthood. In Buddhist countries, where the priests are immensely numerous, they are still honoured and provided for even by the poorest. In some degree the opportunity to put on the yellow robe for a time, which is open to all who will accept its disciplines, blunts the edge of unemployment for the young men just mentioned. Indeed, the religious order, still most necessary for rural culture, acts as a quieter backwater alongside the rushing stream of change. Its relation to the more vigorous nationalist movement is as yet ambiguous. Prime Minister U Nu in Burma, a traditionalist and a fervent Buddhist, saw the Buddhist culture of his country as a positive and strong value in the future national personality, and one which could be contrasted with the alien materialism of the colonial era. In Thailand, and probably in Cambodia, religion can be thought to give a useful element of stability to modernizing monarchies. But where nationalism is more fiercely allied with a leftish ideology, the outcome is much more in doubt. There are strong signs of tension in revolutionary Burma, and a confusion of political and religious alignment in South Viet-Nam which may well result in major trouble. These sharper tensions in Burma and Viet-Nam point to the more general conclusions that Buddhism in South-East Asia (like Christianity in Europe) will have to establish afresh its relevance to the needs of modern times, if it is to avoid condemnation as reactionary and parasitic. A priesthood fed daily by the poor will need a good answer to this criticism.

The style of religious influence in Islamic countries is much different. Some Muslim energy—in some places a great part—is absorbed in rivalry between internal sects. But Islam, far more than Buddhism, is a political religion, apt to expect its rulers to be theocrats. They could not expect the British or the Dutch to fill this role. But, with them removed, the more dedicated Muslims, whether in Malaya or Indonesia, were bound by the very tradition of the faith to raise the issue of a Muslim state. The threat of Chinese domination in Malaya, and the secular philosophy of Communism in Indonesia, are a direct challenge to Muslim Malays not only in the political but also in the religious field. The history of the Marabouts in West Africa, the history of the whole Middle East and of Pakistan cannot be neglected. While it may be that in the huge spaces and diluted religious atmosphere of Indonesia Muslim imperialism is too weak to make a national effect, the same could not be said of Malaya, where in both area and population there are pure Muslim concentrations which are large in relation to the whole. There are, indeed, in Malaya evidences of apparent tolerance which may strike the passing observer as an assurance of peaceful coexistence. The Chinese feasting and fire-crackers of New Year resound through Kuala Lumpur (as they do in Djakarta), even during the Muslim fast. But long experience has shown how illusory the signs may be. In India, despite periods of seeming tolerance, the knives could suddenly flash out between Muslim and Hindu. In Malaya, with racial and political differences thrown in, the danger must be rated high. While in Indonesia a Muslim theocracy might even become established in some part of the empire without endangering the whole, for Malaya even the attempt to reach it would be fatal.

Independence thus raises afresh fundamental problems, some of which were thrust into the subconscious under colonial rule, some settled by the mere existence of authority—until authority was withdrawn. Nationalism, as it succeeds to power, is in essence an appeal for unity. If it cannot use an external threat, or an internal racial enemy, it cannot avoid the question: unity on what terms? What main ideology, what rights for minorities, what relation to the religious order, what privileges for groups—the Civil Service, the educated, the well-born, the peasant—what economic justice? Out of their history and present circumstances the countries of South-East Asia have given very varied answers.

VI

ECONOMY AND ADMINISTRATION

THE vast majority of the population of South-East Asia—from 70 per cent to 80 per cent—are described in the Censuses as engaged in agriculture, hunting, fishing, and related occupations. Only a relatively small section—the most 'backward'—are still in the stage of true subsistence agriculture and barter. The sale of crops for cash and the use of cash to buy trade goods is the general rule, even in the Borneo mountains or the Himalayan foothills, though in large areas the main crop is consumed for food and cash is earned by small additions—the sale of fruit or handicrafts. Further, land has not been short, save in a few areas, of which Java is the most important. The easiest and richest land is, of course, thickly settled. But in the hilly country, in areas far from roads or towns, there is still land which could carry a far heavier population. In terms of food supply, yields even from good land could be increased so greatly that food, for the area as a whole, should be no problem. Thai rice production, one of the highest, was about 215 kg. per *rai* in 1962, against 709 in Japan or 467 in Taiwan.[1]

Over wider areas of these peasant lands a way of life was evolved which had great stability. In the rice areas of Thailand or Burma once-a-year crops come fairly easily, there are materials for cottage industry and barter, there is time to take life easily; and much of life and of wealth, in Buddhist countries, was used in religious observance and local festivals, in building pagodas and in serving the Buddhist priests. The pagoda school transmitted culture from generation to generation and gave a simple literacy, said to be 75 per cent in prewar Burma. In harsher conditions—in the hills of northern Thailand or Burma, or the mountain ranges of Borneo—life was more primitive, depending often on a poor crop of hill-paddy, laboriously gained by burning forest and shifting cultivation; and here an animist religion and a culture based on the extended family may often be found.

One main effect of the incoming Europeans was to add plantation agriculture to the older pattern—spices, sugar, tea and coffee, cotton, abaca, and rubber—and also to tempt the rice-grower to produce an export surplus for cash payment. There was parallel development of

[1] The Japan and Taiwan figures are for 1957. 10 *rai* = 4 acres.

mining for precious metals and (on a larger scale) for tin in Malaya, and there was considerable commercial forestry.

Where this development was based on surpluses from peasant-grown crops the social effects were not at first revolutionary, save where crop-loans from merchants drove the grower into debt and loss of land; this was especially serious in the Irrawaddy delta, where the Indian Chettiars operated. But massive innovation, particularly with plantation crops, involved the introduction both of foreign management and often of foreign labour. The classical cases are in Burma and Malaysia, in the recruitment of Indonesian labour for Dutch plantations in the East Indies, and in the growth of large landlordism in the sugar, coconut and abaca plantations of the Philippines.

The second main effect of European enterprise was to orientate the economies of South-East Asia decisively to commercial export. The introduction of the immigrant 'third force' and the export orientation are separate factors but fused into a single process. It was naturally the object of the Europeans to fit the resources of South-East Asia into an existing pattern of world or imperial trade. There were markets in the outside world for precious metals, for silks, for the wide range of tropical crops and fibres, for tea and later rubber, spices, copra and teak. In return, there were local markets for some manufactures. In an ironical way perhaps this was the best policy which could have been followed. It achieved almost automatically what new nations often find so difficult—to find markets, to fit themselves into a world economy already in a fixed pattern and strongly resistant to the new-comer. An Indian Finance Minister was heard to remark, a year or two ago: 'In the past the British used to exploit India by taking her products to sell in their own markets: I wish they would come here and do the same again!'

It would be absurd to deny the immense benefit which European enterprise brought to South-East Asia. But the evolution of this pattern of trade had other consequences, largely unnoticed at the time. The whole pattern of economic activity was built round import-export trade—a highly skilled trade to manage, with specialized markets for two hundred grades of rice, fluctuating prices, competitive skills. Commercial life was therefore centred on the ports—Rangoon, Bangkok, Penang, Singapore, Saigon, Djakarta, Manila—which rapidly developed a Westernized character wholly alien in techniques and standards from the inland rural areas. More important, while the top levels of trade remained under European direction, the middle and lower levels, needing clerks and accountants, middlemen, wholesalers, retailers out in the distant villages, fell into the hands of men from already developed commercial systems. These were largely Indians and Chinese, since neither Burmese, nor Malays, nor Cambodians, nor Javanese were by then as highly skilled in the monetary exchange economy.

The immigrants spread very fast. For while the Tamil indentured labour or the Chinese market-gardeners in Malaya might remain as a relatively enclosed group, the merchants and moneylenders, cotton-ginners and contractors were highly mobile and adventurous. There was a living to be made richer than the life of Kwantung or South India, and for some there were fortunes to be found. Like a plant or an animal introduced into a new environment, with less competitive check upon its way of life, the merchants and traders found a foothold in the ports, and in the great towns which grew around the ports, and then spread out along lines of trade and communication to provincial centres and finally to the village store. As the money economy grew and was more emphasized, unquestionably they gave a service to the cultivator, in finding him a market and cash loans to tide him over from crop to crop. They might remain as merchants, or, in due course, become the effective owner-managers of groups of cultivators who were by then irretrievably indebted.

Professor Raymond Firth has emphasized the remarkable achievement of the Chinese in particular.

> Colonialism may have set the modern structure of South-East Asian society, but the patterns will persist when the colonial Powers have withdrawn. To this new society the Chinese above all have the economic key. In Indo-China, Siam, Malaya, the Philippines, and Java, the Chinese have penetrated the economic system and taken over crucial functions. They have shared in much of the wholesale import trade, they have attained pre-eminence in retailing vital imported goods to the peasant, and they act as middlemen for the collection, storage, and processing of peasant export products. As part of this process they often finance the peasant producer by advances on his crop, gaining a double profit by giving part of these advances in goods, not cash. The Chinese achievement has been remarkable. They have been kept on the margin both of the peasant society with which they deal, and of the European society with which at a later stage their growing wealth would allow them to associate. Though lacking any formal political power, which in the Orient as elsewhere is so often the passport to success, they have built up a trading structure of extraordinary toughness, elasticity, and elaboration.[2]

All through the last fifty years of the colonial period—in some places much earlier—this world-wide problem of the impact of commercial values on a traditional peasant society was growing. The trader, the

[2] R. Firth, 'The Peasantry of South-East Asia', *International Affairs*, Vol. XXVI, No. 4, Oct. 1950.

shopkeeper, the moneylender, who frequently became landlords, were aliens. Intermarriage and the close pressures of common village life might help assimilation in the rural areas; the lack of serious competition and to some extent protection by the ruling Europeans in some countries might prevent violent revolt in the large towns. But resentment, jealousy and cultural friction were there. An occasional riot or massacre or a clamour to expel aliens were the signs of mounting resentment in colonial times. Yet these were, in all, few and scattered. It would have been hard to judge how strong was the pressure from below, since it was so closely controlled and repressed.

When independence came this whole economic pattern was bitterly criticized. First, it appeared to leave the new nations wholly dependent upon the fluctuations of world trade, over which they had no control. That they were fortunate to have such markets was far less considered than that the markets appeared to be managed—if managed at all—by more powerful foreign nations in their own interest. This dependence strikes far more painfully upon a small nation with no leverage in the markets. Price fluctuations can reduce whole regions to sudden poverty, with no redress, with no representation on the councils of world trade, if such exist, no powerful means of retaliation.

Second, the internal pattern of production and distribution was lopsided, concerned with export only. If there were roads or railways, they led from the crops or mines to the ports; if there were resources which could have been used to save imported manufactures, they were not developed. The skills of industrial countries were not taught—why should they be?—and the trading skills had been largely monopolized by aliens. Labourers in the mines, labourers in the fields and plantations, in the forests and coconut groves, hewers of wood and drawers of water—these seemed to be the roles for which the indigenous peoples were cast.

Third, the capital accumulated by the export trade went back to shareholders overseas. It might, indeed, be reinvested in yet more plantations, but little of it, if any, was available to diversify one-crop economies, to develop local manufactures however obvious the opportunity, to build up a local infrastructure larger than the export trade required or to develop social services. In more modern times, as indigenous politicians became more sophisticated, the fact that so much wealth was remitted back to India or China was felt to impoverish the host country. Further, the immigrants' international connexions (between, say, the Cambodian Chinese and their relations in Hong Kong or Singapore or Bangkok) were said to be used to defeat trade and currency regulations and maintain a privileged trading position against local competition.

In the narrowest economic sense the system implies an under-development both of resources for local use and of human skills. There are a thousand instances of raw materials exported unprocessed when a small investment of capital and skill would have established a local industry; to quote but one, timber from the great forests of Sabah was shipped abroad as logs from the east coast while Jesselton on the west coast imported sawn planks for building. The system seems infinitely more objectionable if the local control of the trading economy itself is in the hands of foreigners and aliens.

In summary, the total effect of all these attitudes and policies was to build up an economic and administrative system which was perfectly viable as long as the colonial power was there to run it. The central administration was run at the top by expatriates, with a few of the most highly educated local peoples in the middle and lower ranks, in which also a proportion of Chinese or Indians might figure, particularly in technical or accounting posts. The business system was again headed by expatriates, but a large share of merchanting and wholesaling, and often almost all retailing, was left to aliens with a commercial tradition. From the same source the Europeans found a great range of services—pharmacists, some Indian doctors, restaurant-keepers, middlemen of many kinds both in business and in support of a transplanted European way of life.[3] The plantations and mines, run by expatriate managers, might be able to draw upon indigenous labour. But (for example, in Malaya) where labour could not be attracted out of the indigenous subsistence economy, the answer was found in importing Chinese or Tamils, and by tens of thousands. These coalesced into isolated blocks of foreign culture, under plantation conditions, wholly unintegrated into the wider society.

It was the natural assumption of all these men of commerce that by their development of trade national wealth would grow; no doubt some of it, though a small share, would flow back to the 'changeless' rural communities from which the raw materials came. Malaya grew richer on tin and rubber, the Chinese flourished in Penang and Singapore; but life continued much the same in the Malay *kampongs* by river and sea-shore. Bangkok grew wealthy, but little changed in the quiet Thailand countryside; even today the second city of Thailand after the $2\frac{1}{2}$ millions of Bangkok/Chonburi is a little market town of less than

[3] Both the French and the Dutch brought out more '*petits blancs*' (as did the French in Senegal) to occupy rather lower rungs in the social ladder.

60,000 people, Chiengmai. Manila flourished and the great plantations and estates spread out in certain islands; but neither in the Philippine *barrios* nor outside the French *boulevards* of Saigon or Phnom-Penh, nor outside Batavia[4] and the great Dutch estates, was there any sign of radical change in the villages and rice-fields, save for a steady alienation of land to the big plantation-owners and a steady creeping forward of the Chinese trader.

Thus, two worlds were created: the world of cities and commerce, mainly European and immigrant, and the world of peasants. They were far apart, and the link between them was the Chinese village merchant. Even today in some small village almost anywhere in South-East Asia this picture to a casual onlooker might seem much the same. Yet, in fact, the postwar situation is radically different. For the fundamental assumption of the stability of rural life is no longer tenable; the weight of economic emphasis is changing from commerce towards industry and peasant agriculture; the holders of economic power and initiative are changing, and the governments of Asia themselves, no longer concerned only to establish order and hold the ring for commerce, are throwing themselves into the economic process with all their force.

The new influences which are reaching down into the very roots of Asian life are various in name and description, but all tending to the same direction—to 'development' and, as Edward Shils has put it, to 'modernity': ' "Modern" means dynamic, concerned with the people, democratic and equalitarian, scientific, economically advanced, sovereign and influential.'[5]

In the first place, pressure of population growth is beginning to be felt. Medical provision will grow and its effects will intensify. Population growth is already well up to 2½ per cent per annum in most of South-East Asia, and over 3 per cent in Thailand, Singapore, and the Philippines. Although there is land to spare, it is being eaten up fairly fast. Higher productivity from existing land has become a government objective, not only to provide food, but especially to provide the export surpluses upon which industry and modernity can be founded. Hence, the peasant cannot be left to his placid and old-fashioned life—he must be taught and cajoled and tempted and if necessary forced to learn new ways. New faces come to the village—extension officers, co-operative organizers, leaders for community development, men with films and demonstrations, offers of credit from an agricultural bank, politicians speaking of a new life. Often enough there are tacit or open suggestions that the merchant who has given credit in the past—an alien—is a

[4] Now Djakarta. [5] E. Shils, *Political Development in the New States*, The Hague, 1962.

robber in disguise. Once all this happens, peasant attitudes will never be the same again.

From the peasants' viewpoint, population pressure is felt in a different way. If there is no more land to be had, he, or at least his sons, must go to the town and seek a wage; the self-sufficiency of rural life begins to be broken, the rush to towns begins, 'unemployment' is heard of for the first time. The towns themselves are unsettling. They offer, as they have in Africa or in England, temptations and illusions which gain a deep hold. Thousands of young men from rural Thailand, from Java or from Philippine villages have trekked to the city to ply for hire with *samlors*,[6] *betjaks*, *jeepneys*, a modern Japanese three-wheeler or a Datsun taxi. In the city they see modernity. Not only do they send the news back to the villages, but together they become a city proletariat, perhaps in trade unions, at least a mass following for politicians. Mostly they become unemployed, and naturally they look enviously at Indians or Chinese: it is a short step from envy to a demand for their expulsion. The young countryman-come-to-town, when competition hits him, becomes a racial nationalist very fast.

Education, in its modern sense, adds to the disturbance. Pagoda schools or Koranic schools were not 'modern'. They taught adaption to a way of life which Asian governments, consciously or not, are in fact destroying. State Primary schools, with state-trained teachers, begin to appear in the villages, with a U.N.E.S.C.O.-set target of 'universal Primary education by 1980'. More will be said of these schools in the next chapter; enough to say here that they spring from a different philosophy. The Primary course is not an education in itself, but designed to prepare for the Secondary; and the Secondary leads not to the old village life but to an examination and a claim to a paid job; and the job is likely to be an urban job. The teacher himself brings a new set of values into the village—he has travelled farther to get his training, and seen more, and talked to urban people with their new ideas. He will speak a new language, and, at a later stage, will introduce the most disturbing of all subjects—science.

The doctor or nurse will likewise upset many old beliefs and practices, some with a quasi-religious basis. The community development worker, with perhaps a woman to alter women's idea of themselves and their life, will stir up new controversies. The agricultural officer will alter the rhythm of the working year with double-cropping or new crops. He will preach a doctrine of higher yields, greater money-

[6] Tricycle rickshaws (now banned) in Bangkok; *betjaks* operate in Djakarta and *jeepneys* (jeeps converted to small buses) in the Philippines.

earnings from cash crops, savings to form farm capital—a doctrine of individualism and materialism wholly untraditional. He will deplore—though he may not say so—that savings in earlier times went to build a temple or deck a marriage feast.

Wisely, skilfully, thoroughly taught, followed by small example and local achievement, these ideas could be the salvation of the rural world. But, alas, the tens of thousands of simple village teachers seldom have the chance or the knowledge to reach this ideal. More often what they can give will be scraps of strange knowledge and rumours of a better world, reference to the towns where 'progress' seems to live, disturbing hints of a life which the great majority of rural pupils will never lead—a life which has not yet been made ready to receive them.

The first factor in the economic scene in South-East Asia is the progressive uprooting of village life, through population pressure, the influence of towns, the effect of education, and the impact of modernizing ideas spread through the agencies of government itself. Unspectacular though it is, it is fundamental.

If we turn now to the other end of the scale, to the central government and its plans, we see throughout South-East Asia a switch of emphasis from commerce to production. The reasons have been sketched already. It is a movement away from the export of raw materials organized by foreign firms, obedient to a fluctuating world market, handled in the middle ranks by Chinese or Indian immigrants. In general (again with some exceptions in the Philippines) it is in government that people of the ruling majority race have found places of power, not at first in commerce and industry. By taking a strong hand as government officials in the management of industrial production they hope to achieve two objects. First, the dependence on foreign markets can be reduced, while local resources are more fully developed; second, the native majority can occupy the positions of power and control from the very start, building a productive system, manned by nationals, which will first balance and later overshadow the commercial system monopolized by foreigners and immigrants.

Hostility to commerce thus has triple support—ethnic feeling, the animosity of peasant producers towards all middlemen, and often a doctrinaire socialism which is always hostile to commerce as the very citadel of private enterprise—and always weak in providing any good alternative.

In Asia, as in Africa, the first emphasis was put on industry, on large buildings, and on major schemes for power supply, irrigation, and trunk roads. Simultaneously, under encouragement both from educationists and manpower planners, a great expansion of education was put in hand, to provide the modern skills which the industrial plan would soon be needing. Much could be said about these projects; for the present purpose it is enough to fasten on one special difficulty. Most of the plans were not based on the development of existing skills, in cottage industry and processing; they were concerned with modern mechanized factories and highly technical construction work. Certainly, the need for foreign experts was foreseen for the construction stages; they in turn would train up local engineers to carry on. It was not foreseen so clearly that industry is not only production and technology but also economic business—it must pay its way, under guidance of men who count costs and markets: not only technical but management skills would be needed. While technical theory can be taught in technical colleges, neither business sense nor management skills are easily or well taught in these academic surroundings.

This problem of launching an industrial programme in a society which lacked an existing pool of native managerial and business skills has forced the rulers of developing countries into different plans of action. In South-East Asia three quite distinct patterns have emerged, with many minor variants; and these approaches greatly influence the race relationships involved.

At one extreme, the case of Burma's development is a clear example; in certain ways there are parallels with Indonesia. In the early 1950s the Government of U Nu called in American consultants to prepare an Eight-Year Plan of industrial development. The plan was made and costed, and in due course projects began to show on the ground. But by 1958 it was at least partially in ruins. The story is long and complex;[7] but it is possible in retrospect to summarize the major causes of trouble. First, the plan involved major and complex financial planning by the Burmese Government—the handling of loans and internal accumulation of capital and control of the whole economy to prevent inflation or the squandering of foreign exchange reserves. It fairly soon became clear—and it is not in the least surprising—that a Government engaged in civil war, supported by a Civil Service well trained in procedures but inexperienced in policy decisions, could not achieve this complex task. It did not, in fact, control the economy. The large (and largely foreign) commercial private sector, operating for profit, drove a coach and

[7] A detailed account has been published by L. J. Walinsky, *Economic Development in Burma, 1951–1960*, New York, 1962.

horses through the financial planning, not from ill will but simply by making normal business choices—to expand, to contract, to invest, to hoard, to export capital, to import goods, in fact to play the market regardless of the plan.

Secondly, it became clear that reliance on foreign contractors, who were risking not their own but their governments' money, or were working under 'Aid' arrangements, could go badly astray. The new airport, under Scandinavian contractors, went wildly beyond the estimates; the new steel works (West German) made the wrong products and ran out of scrap; Chinese cement proved faulty and had to be broken up and replaced; the gunnybag factory at first made few bags and large losses. In a word, the very shortage of knowledge which made it necessary to hire foreigners made it impossible to check and control their work.[8]

Thirdly, there was a dearth, not so much of local graduate engineers, but of good technicians and of managerial skills. In short, administratively, technically and managerially, the programme put far too high a strain on the society it was designed to enrich.

The reaction of the military Revolutionary Government, which took over from U Nu for the second time in 1962, was uncompromising. First, it decided to take the whole economy under its own direct control. During 1963 and 1964 a series of nationalizing measures gradually took over both the major foreign enterprises and the banks and finally the whole import–export trade and retail distribution in Rangoon. There was in future to be no sabotage, nor even complication of the Government's planning effort by unregulated free enterprise.

The second decision was to exclude foreign private enterprise investment. The third was to place army officers alongside the senior Civil Servants, to ensure speedy execution of government intentions without niggling bureaucratic procedures. The fourth was to deal severely with the university students and to announce that the Government in future would value practical rather than academic training—the arts faculties in particular were temporarily closed down. The fifth was to switch the planning emphasis away from industrialization and redirect it towards peasant agriculture. The Government took over the purchase of the whole Burmese rice crop and the financing of the farmer by seed and fertilizer loans, which were lavishly increased. Thus, in little over eighteen months, Burma moved to the full Communist planning methods (without adopting Communism), based on government control

[8] The British Government seems to have found it equally difficult to control the highly technical work of Ferranti, largely for the same reasons.

of the whole system of production, distribution and finance, save that the peasant farmer remained a peasant owner—he was not collectivized. The 'Bolsheviks' of this revolution, providing the drive and idealism, were the army officers, using the old Civil Service as a tool and with scant respect for its dignity.[9]

It is easy to see that this policy, partly a reaction from earlier mistakes, partly the result of a strong socialist philosophy, partly a resurgence of Burmese xenophobia, would have a devastating effect, not merely on European enterprise but on the other immigrant minorities, both Indian and Chinese. Their occupation as city merchants and retailers was swept away with one hand; their position in the villages as distributors, moneylenders, crop-purchasers and cotton-ginners was destroyed with the other. The whole private sector was virtually eliminated, except for the farmers themselves; and even in the Civil Service, Indians, Anglo-Indians and Anglo-Burmans felt their position suddenly grow highly insecure. This type of planning, emanating from a highly nationalist Government, is naturally staffed and controlled by the racial majority in political power, and leaves almost no safe niche either for European firms or for immigrant Asians. It may appear in other countries, of which Cambodia could well be one.

It is interesting that Indonesia, also Communist-influenced, went far in the Burma direction, but has slightly drawn back. Nationalization of Dutch and other foreign enterprises has gone far, though not to the full limit. Government trading and industrial enterprises have been created, but not to cover the whole field. The Indonesian Government is still seeking to attract Japanese and other firms from overseas (even from Holland) under arrangements of various kinds by which the Government retains a measure of control. It was probably because President Sukarno realized, after fifteen years of experience, that nationalist enthusiasm and a crop of new universities still do not produce entrepreneurial and managerial skill, and because Indonesia was so large to administer and in such desperate economic straits, that the Government stopped short of a total take-over. In consequence, a private sector remains, and within it the Chinese trader can still find a place, though no security.

The second main development strategy, the 'middle road' policy of a mixed economy, is typical of Malaysia and Thailand, with Thailand

[9] While we were in Burma it was announced that the partitions would be removed in Government offices, so that the 'bureaucrats' could not hide behind closed doors.

leaning to free enterprise and Malaysia to government initiative and control. This policy accepts that foreign investment in industrial enterprise is necessary and desirable, both for itself and because it provides a training-ground to teach practical managerial and business skills. In both countries the policy has met with great success. Although Thailand's heavy industry is chiefly in foreign ownership and control, quite large numbers of Thai businessmen (and businesswomen) are beginning to appear, sometimes in partnership with expatriates, often with Chinese, sometimes on their own. Simultaneously, it has given the considerable Chinese element in Bangkok a chance to share richly in the boom conditions, in wholesale and retail trade, in contracting, and in service enterprises.

In Malaysia the effect is the same, save that the Chinese element is far more pronounced. The European firms on the mainland tended to settle in Kuala Lumpur or Petaling Jaya (the local industrial estate) and to recruit and train a maximum of Malay employees, in order to stand well with the Malay Government. But the Chinese Government of Singapore has been far less inhibited. It has attracted to Jurong, which must now be one of the most quickly successful industrial estates in the world, not only European and American capital but significant large-scale Japanese enterprise, as well as interests from Hong Kong. Here there is no question of preference to Malay employees; industry is growing up Chinese from top to bottom. Singapore, with its great commercial empire, its newly planned shipyard with floating, dry and building docks, its steelworks, oil-blending plant, tyre and engineering factories and a growing host of smaller industries, is on the way to building one of the great industrial complexes of South-East Asia. With two universities, a vigorous political life, a great reserve of commercial skills at all levels, a free welcome to capital and a remarkably efficient administration, it could begin to show the extraordinary dynamism of Hong Kong. Chinese all over South-East Asia look with pride towards it and many go there for higher education or economic opportunity. Its population, about 1,714,000 in 1962, is conservatively estimated to pass two million before 1970.

Thus in Malaya and Singapore the open-door policy to private enterprise is greatly developing the Chinese element, while Malays pre-empt most of the administration in Kuala Lumpur and, in small numbers, learn to be managers in businesses which will be mainly European-owned. To offset this industrial picture, the Malaysian Government is spending lavishly on settling Malays on newly cleared land, planted with high-yielding rubber, and on a widespread and energetic programme of improving rural facilities (roads, water, buildings, irrigation, health) and Secondary education in the rural (i.e. Malay) provinces. Malays will dominate in agriculture (save a strong Chinese element in rubber) and in government; Chinese in industry and commerce, and, for many years to come, in higher education.

Clearly, the balance has advantages. Much will depend on whether the Malay Civil Service can maintain control and impetus in the complex planning machine of the Federal Government in Kuala Lumpur. Under largely British and American guidance it has been set a task, in complexity and detail of control, which would daunt a much more experienced service. If it should crack under the strain, or fail in the huge agricultural plans now maturing, the whole concept of Malay rule might be endangered, with disastrous consequences. At present the plans are going ahead with remarkable drive and considerable success.

The third pattern of development is shown by the Philippines—a full-blooded, *laissez-faire* capitalism, supplemented by government enterprise. There is a large apparatus of planning which provides much employment in the central departments in Manila and gives a modern look; but it has little effect on the real investment decisions. Nationalism has its say, particularly in laws decreeing the Filipinization of retail trade—a move aimed primarily at the Chinese middlemen, but causing much embarrassment to European firms. Both Chinese and Europeans, while enterprise remains free and the economy buoyant, will no doubt find ways of continuing their business within the law. Indeed, the chief effect has been to give a considerable competitive advantage to Americans, who are treated as Filipinos under the Laurel-Langley Agreement[10] up to 1974. There are, however, signs of considerable nationalist restlessness at the privileged American position.

This raw capitalist system, in which great and ostentatious wealth is matched by acute poverty in the towns, large landlordism in the country, and heavy unemployment everywhere, may have social repercussions in the future. This would only take a racial flavour if revolt fastened upon the dominance of American and possibly Spanish interests in the plutocracy. Attempts to divert feeling against the

[10] The Agreement, signed at independence, treats American individuals and firms as Filipino—an example of the frequent compromise between trade interests and idealist anti-colonialism in American foreign policy. It covers only 100 per cent American or Filipino firms; those with some shareholders of other nationalities may not escape the clause.

relatively few Chinese are not likely to succeed indefinitely, once the part they play has been yet further reduced.

Of the three approaches—extreme socialism, the mixed economy, and extreme capitalism—the socialist in the short run is likely to lead to most racial hardship. The attempt to build direct partnership between government and 'workers and peasants', and to stimulate national unity and enthusiasm, invariably demands some enemies and scapegoats, a role for which racial minorities are ideally cast; and as traders and middlemen in private enterprise the Chinese and Indians are in a specially exposed position in a socialist state. But in the longer run it could be the far more wealthy group, including many Chinese and foreigners, in the mixed and capitalist régimes, against whom the wrath of the indigenous peoples is turned as a result of inequality and the failure to provide paid employment for the uprooted rural populations.

For most areas of South-East Asia have not managed to avoid the pitfall into which so many hastily changing countries have slipped. While on the one hand the mass of peasant population is being disturbed, on the other hand the investment in high-technology industrialization does not absorb more than a small fraction of the labour which is emotionally displaced from rural life and streams towards the towns. The figures in Table 1 (p. 14 above), show the extraordinarily small numbers, compared to the total population, who are employed in organized industry in any country of South-East Asia. The significant comparison is between the total employed and the numbers who emerge every year from a completed Primary education, who might be thought fitted to enter the work-force of modern industry. In East Africa this comparison has recently been made. The Kenya Education Commission (1964), taking one year's output from the final form of Primary schools, concluded that, from 103,000 school-leavers there would be 67,000 for whom (in the words of the Report) 'there is no prospect of further education or paid employment'. An exactly similar situation has arisen in South-East Asia. Even where young people have had a technical and vocational education, employment is still hard to find; in Thailand in 1961 an inquiry revealed that 40 per cent of the graduates of technical and vocational schools were unemployed and looking for work.[11]

Even where the industrial programme is most successful—and it is successful in Manila, Bangkok and Singapore—the wealth created tends to widen rather than narrow the gap between rich and poor. The acute

[11] Labour Division, Ministry of Public Welfare, Thailand, 1961.

anxiety on this score felt now in East Africa, which is poor in minerals and short of well-watered soils, is not yet felt so strongly in much of Asia where life is easier from the monsoon rainfall and richer resources. But, with some exceptions, really effective effort to start economic growth from the agricultural sector and to design and provide both education and health services suited to its needs is still rarely to be found. In general, over the whole area, agricultural services are understaffed, underequipped, and often trained in urban surroundings in quite unrealistic programmes. Even in Malaya the remarkable settlement schemes will deal with only the natural increase in population; basic agricultural advance on existing holdings outside the rubber plantations has been, until the last year or two, of low priority and greatly understaffed.[12] In Indonesia the obsession with political crises has left no time to build an agricultural service—a minor peasants' revolt in central Java at the end of 1964 is a small sign of the times. In the Philippines conflicting government agencies, corruption and landlords' pressures have vitiated most projects, despite major legislation designed to reduce and reform the old tenant system; in Thailand things have been easy, and for the moment remain so; in Cambodia there is indeed a start, but most development effort has been centred round Phnom-Penh and Sihanoukville.

A few years ago all this might have been said of Burma. A flow of agricultural graduates, badly supported by transport or equipment, were making little headway, and the research stations, without strong direction, made little contribution. It is, however, interesting that perhaps the greatest vigour in all South-East Asia, outside Malaya, is now being shown by the Revolutionary Government of Burma in a direct and wholesale effort to tackle rural advance and to make a bridge between the powerful and rich and the village cultivator. Technically, this effort may be poorly supported, possibly misdirected, possibly unwise in its concentration on massive outpouring of cash loans to farmers. But politically there is little doubt that an effect is being made. There are appalling difficulties to be faced as untrained army officers attempt to handle the buying of a huge rice crop; there may well be a large 'loss' of public funds in unrecovered loans; there will still be a long delay before major irrigation pays a dividend; there have been mistakes in tractor policy and in commodity distribution; there has been gross hardship in the expulsion of many useful merchants and great difficulty

[12] 'Research in agriculture in Malaysia is in its infancy': K. T. Joseph, in Wang Gungwu (ed.), *Malaysia: A Survey*.

in replacing their commercial skills. But while the Government remains of the same mind there is and will be progress, however expensive in technical or administrative mistakes; and this progress is headed towards a more unified nation, a more balanced economy and a lessening pressure of social dissatisfaction at inequalities of wealth and the dominance of the city. There might even be a real solution of the ethnic minority issues, if the weight of government effort is aimed at betterment of their real conditions. Burma has settled the problem of immigrants in the brutal way; there could be more excuse for this if, in the final reckoning, national unity on the basis of a prosperous indigenous rural culture were achieved.

Such an account of Burmese policy may seem far too generous. Those who have suffered from it might well say it has been brutal, xenophobic, grossly misguided in its belief that Government can run the whole economy; that it has antagonized the whole educated group and led the peasantry into great dangers. Certainly the human cost of this ideological ruthlessness has been high, as it was in Russia or China. But certain fundamental values contained within it must not be denied; for it is these values which have given the Communist revolutions their first attractiveness. If this attraction has often been followed by disillusion (why is a Berlin Wall so necessary?), it may be the political methods rather than the social and economic objectives which are at fault. If in one sense the current history of Burma is an awful warning, in another it is a criticism of other systems which have failed to include more than a fraction of the people in the benefits of advance.

In the first nationalist phase, when the middle class (particularly the private sector) is composed mainly of 'left-over' colonials and Asian immigrants, there is a natural logic in the alliance between the new leaders and the peasant masses. The peasants are the 'sons of the soil', the nation of which nationalism speaks. And—ironically in view of the usual sequel—this alliance, if it had been effectively pursued, might well have proved the best long-term policy both in social and in economic terms. Tolerance of a largely alien private sector which provided its own skills, matched by vigorous government effort in aid and development of agriculture and of the mass of farmers, might have made good economic sense. Only in Malaya was this policy pursued, partly for racial reasons. The most usual sequel, in China as in Africa, was a gradually mounting attack on the foreign or immigrant private sector leading eventually to expulsion, and an attempt to replace it with new industries manned by nationals unskilled in management. Meanwhile, the rural sector, low in prestige, starved of trained men, was largely unreformed. The Revolutionary Government of Burma, after the fiasco of industrialization, has turned back to the land and its people, but only after virtually destroying foreign industry and commerce and losing fifteen years.

The Burmese case, as it now stands, is exceptional; so also is the Malayan drive for rural development. In the rest of South-East Asia both the economic and the administrative development is of a type likely to need, and to emphasize and favour, an urban *élite*. It emphasizes investment in undertakings modelled on those of developed countries, which require a high proportion of university-educated staff and a low proportion of labour; and it involves a large development of central agencies for planning and administration with relatively little attention to the quality of provincial and rural administration. The educational system, considered in the next chapter, has been shaped in a corresponding pattern, with the greatest emphasis on the university level, which is the springboard for jobs and prestige. The result has been to create a swollen central Government, already in some cases too big and complex to control its own limbs, increasingly staffed by university graduates trained in a highly academic tradition.

Thus the gap between 'two nations', created by the colonial economy, remains. If it is economically not much wider, it is psychologically far more dangerous. While the rich 'nation' was led by Europeans, the enemy was external and opposition could be a unifying nationalism, with some side-hitting against the Europeans' minions, mainly Indian or Chinese. In this stage, the peasants were not greatly disturbed by new visions or promises; they were governed by a colonial Civil Service which was in certain ways impartial and often more sympathetic to the indigenous than to the immigrant peoples. But independence replaced the Europeans by men of local nationality; the potential object of resentment becomes internal, and the form of economic development chosen is a form tailored for city men and university graduates and foreign or immigrant skills. If it is rather more energetic than colonial rule, it is usually less efficient, and certainly more corrupt. Where it is capitalist (Thailand, Malaya, Philippines), the foreigners remain and even increase. Where it is Socialist (Burma, Indonesia), a horde of small officials replace the immigrant trader. In neither case, save perhaps in the rural development programmes of Malaya, is there real opportunity for growth from below, from existing crafts and local shrewdness, or for the Primary school-leaver, who is tempted from the village and rejected by the town.

Not only the economy but also the administration has become more centralized. Where the colonial régime was represented by planters and administrators, both were in the rural area. Certainly the British District Officer, who was given a great degree of freedom and responsibility, considered his district work as the cream of his career; Headquarters was regarded by many as a penal posting. But after independence things looked very different. For Thai or Malay, Indonesian or Filipino, the prizes are all in the city. Government is not primarily local administration but central economic planning, and it is central Government and the Westernized city surrounding it which has the jobs and the power and the prospects. Thus life tends to drain away from the provinces. They get fleeting visits from experts; their most able young men are pulled away to the towns; their officials gaze anxiously back to the city for the chance to return. Even university lecturers, provided with fine houses in the new University of Chiengmai, used packing-cases instead of furniture, in the hope of a short exile.

VII

EDUCATION AND SOCIETY

NOTHING will so deeply colour the quality of life in South-East Asia as the style of education which is chosen; nothing is more difficult to assess in its manifold relationships with the structure and the modes of action and the temper of society. Bare lists of schools and teachers, numbers enrolled, or examinations passed, tell very little of significance. Asian societies have plunged into radical change and wish to use education as a chief tool in achieving it. But upon education also falls much of the task of retaining continuity within change, so that society itself does not lose that sense of shared values which gives it character and cohesion.

In the period before the main impact of the Western world, the peasant societies of South-East Asia, as those elsewhere, had fashioned an education full enough to transmit the disciplines and culture of a static world. For daily profane life, society was barely larger than the village and a neighbouring village or two. Within this circle, work and property and marriage were contained, with only the rarest contact with the more distant world. Children were taught the rules of family life and social custom and learned from childhood the skills of farmer, fisherman or hunter. The sailors (and pirates) of the islands moved farther afield, but their home culture was not much wider.

There was one larger contact: this was with the religious world, at least where one of the great religious, Buddhism or Islam, was strong. The Buddhist monk was known to belong to a wider circle, and to deal with knowledge beyond the reach of laymen. In many Buddhist countries every young man might spend some months or longer as a monk, learning the sacred texts and precepts which should guide and sustain his community. Some were given to the temple for life, to the pride of their parents. The monks, and the Koranic teachers, gave in their schools at least a baptism in that wider river of tradition which immersed whole tracts of villages, whole regions and kingdoms in a single cultural element.

Beyond the village there might well be, among the greater peoples, the king or sultan, not merely secular power but a most potent and unifying religious symbol. His great and lesser servants, in descending order from lords to humble tax-collectors, though less revered and sometimes feared or hated, still carried some aura of the king's sacred authority and of his practical power. Not all societies were part of so large a unity; for clans and small hill-tribes or for the dispersed, unstructured subsistence cultures (in Borneo, as one example), society stretched barely beyond a chief or clan-head near at hand.

Thus, for the village child, to be educated was to be 'socialized' within the family and village, to learn the crafts of livelihood and to share in the greater circle of religion. For the great rulers it was clearly more. It included first and foremost the religious duties of the ruler, Buddhist king or Muslim sultan. It included certainly much history of his line and kingdom. It might well include a literature, mainly sacred and historical. It included the law, and it included an aesthetic education in fine workmanship, weapons, buildings, dance and music. It included a concern with economic works—the control of rivers, the planting of forests, the construction of cities and reservoirs and fortifications. For rulers in the last two centuries at least it included some knowledge of the outer world, perhaps a foreign education; a growing interest in the knowledge and techniques which foreigners brought to the ruler's court, or which he might see in travel.

Between rulers and villagers lay only a small official hierarchy; to this day the Malayan sultans are, in certain circumstances, easy of access to their humblest subjects and direct in decision. In the towns there were merchants, educated in money and trade, perhaps more widely travelled, but in other ways little more learned than the villager himself.

If we draw a double line here and add up these elements of society, the total, with a common language added, is a culture at once religious and aristocratic, passing on at each level the education necessary for that level and drawing from the priesthood, which linked the humblest village to the ruler, much of its common nourishment. Despite vast differences in wealth, there was no abrupt qualitative cultural break between rulers and ruled.

When the colonial rulers came (Thailand excepted) there were somewhat different attitudes to the cultures which they found. The British, by the nineteenth century at least, had perhaps the widest and most varied experience as colonial administrators. They had a vigorous if naïve morality, sometimes coupled with religious faith, sometimes resting mainly on an assurance of their rightness which sprang from their success. They responded to Burmese or Malays or Dyaks by respecting, within the limits of control, their political and social organization, though amending their administration; by a romantic or even poetic interest in their religious and aesthetic culture; by moral disapproval of many elements in both administrative and religious practice. They were inclined to leave society as they found it, but improved by British standards, in eliminating as far as possible cruelty, inefficiency and those social or religious customs which offended their moral sense or grossly hindered economic progress. Administrators deplored and suppressed religious enthusiasm if it led to riots or ritual deaths; agriculturalists battled against customary practices which destroyed fertility or caused erosion; Residents restrained the more arbitrary acts of tyranny or corruption if they could. But on the whole the British were inclined to accept and protect Asian cultures, and in some degree to admire them. Indeed, they were more sympathetic to the Buddhist and Muslim cultures of South-East Asia than to the Hinduism of India with its undercurrents of sexuality and violence.

It followed that, in education, the British were inclined to accept that Malay, or Burman, or Chinese, or Tamil, or even the lesser groups or tribes should continue the basic education already developed for their culture, under their own teachers, in their own language, but more organized, with some additional money and facilities. Hand-in-hand with the missions they helped also to organize a higher education, in the modern style and in the English language, which would train some local people to help with administration and, in due course, be fused (at least in office hours, but seldom in social contact) with the ruling class. This was a practical and empirical policy, arising from the necessities of circumstance. If Englishmen made little Englands for their private lives in Asia, it scarcely occurred to them to try to make Asians into Englishmen, too; they were constantly surprised when this occurred.

Indeed, it was with these educated Asians that the English (as compared with French or Americans) mainly failed. It is usual to call the English reserved, and not without reason; in fact this is often a reserve based on minute conventions of social and personal behaviour which govern admission to unreserved familiarity—in effect, conventions of class. The English were apt to be embarrassed by trivial and unwitting breaches of their code, and found it hard to unbend; no doubt, too, they were half-consciously anxious at the underlying challenge to their own position. They were far more happy and at ease with the unsophisticated, and often gained not only their respect but their devotion. But it is not the unsophisticated who take over power.

Despite differences in personal style between British and Dutch (about which both sides would no doubt be self-righteous), there was no radical difference in their impact which is relevant here. The French, more self-confident if not egotistical in the aesthetic elements of culture, politically more Roman, morally more tolerant, established a decisive French administration and a French education for a small minority firmly modelled on French standards and curricula. They then selected among the most able of their colonial subjects a few to whom a full French education was offered. These they accepted socially to a far greater degree; and to them they gave, often through many years in France, the full gift of French culture, from cookery to the opera. Archaeologically and scientifically interested in local culture, they never for an instant considered this as potentially surviving in competition with the superior and modern civilization into which France would generously embrace them.

The strongest contrast to British, Dutch, or French is found in the Philippines. There, the Spanish Catholics, nearer to the French, imposed their own civilization. But the Americans brought a totally fresh attitude, wholly unlike that of European colonial powers. Perhaps the most anti-traditional people in the world, still intent on 'strangling the last King with the entrails of the last priest', the Americans saw the 'backward' societies much more in black and white. Ignorance and superstistition, undemocratic govenment, poverty of technique were the enemies. To combat these, they brought an uncomplicated idealism and common sense. Education, Protestant morality, technical advance, and commercial enterprise would bring the peoples into the daylight of a free progressive world, as it had brought America.[1] Thus long before the Second World War the Philippines were moving fast into the attitudes of modern commercial democracy, modified only by the strong persistence of Spanish Catholic culture. In this they were, and are today, unlike any other nation of the region.

These differences in colonial style have left their marks. In the ex-British Burma and Malaysia, and in Thailand, where British influence has been strong, traditional political and social structures and many languages and cultures continued in considerable strength. In Indonesia, where the Dutch made no political provision for an independence which they did not expect, their defeat left a political vacuum, with a small *élite* of administrators highly educated in Holland. In Indo-

[1] Professor Tinker points out that 'almost as soon as Dewey's guns had stopped firing the transport *George Thomas* dropped anchor in Manila harbour, with a boatload of Grade-School teachers, male and female. The "Thomasites" did not come to the Philippines to create an *élite*, but to educate a whole people to democracy' (Personal communication).

China, the French had scarcely attempted to bridge the huge gap between peasantry on one side and on the other an *élite* group so deeply tempted by French culture as to find readjustment to Asia hard. In the Philippines, the Americans left a world nearer to Latin America than to its South-East Asian neighbours.

After the War any thought of cultural and political continuity was at first submerged in the rush of simple, powerful new ideals which swept over the ex-colonial world and was reinforced by the developed countries. In Africa, traditional peasant cultures were seen as relics of ignorance, superstition, poverty of technique, unwarranted submission to unenlightened rulers, neglect by the colonial powers. The two cardinal remedies would be massive modern education and capital investment. The main ideal would be the open, technical, individualist society, socialist in philosophy, democratic in government, materialist in values, with economic growth as its overriding mission. In South-East Asia there was no open attack upon Buddhism or Islam—quite the reverse; they were praised as part of Asian personality, part of freedom from colonialism. It was simply that the new dominant values became irrelevant or incompatible with a religious or an aristocratic culture. Nehru in India preached the secular state; U Nu in Burma tried and failed to combine a Buddhist philosophy with the driving materialist energy needed for modern enterprise and the planning of economic growth.

In terms of education, the new ideals implied a secular system of state education in the usual Western forms—Primary, Secondary, technical, or university. As a tool of progress it must be primarily instructional; and the instructors would be trained by the state to pass on the foundations of useful modern knowledge. If it had any function to socialize the child, it would be to prepare him, not for his traditional world, but for a new world of hygiene and scientific agriculture, commerce and democracy. Religion would be a subject among other subjects where required. Behind this concept lay the weight of example in the secular and successful West, and the urging of international educationalists. It was necessary to catch up with the West; it was necessary to provide a modern ruling group able to handle the technical elements of economic planning; it was necessary to teach science and the new politics of nationalism to whole peoples. U.N.E.S.C.O., not always mindful of its cultural responsibility, flew the banners of education and science, and helped to plan the programmes.

South-East Asia, as it adopted this new philosophy, was already well advanced, compared to Africa, in the higher realms of education. There had been access to Western universities over a long period for a small *élite*; and universities had grown up in Rangoon, Bangkok, Singapore, Hanoi, Manila. But these few peaks of attainment had been reached largely through mission schools and special foundations, wholly in an international language, framed on the model of Western universities and tied to their attitude to learning. There had been little impact lower down. Those who attended them were, to a large extent, carried outside the boundaries of their culture and assimilated to the ruling colonial group. Perhaps Thailand (as might be expected) retained a university system most nearly matched to the traditional hierarchy of Thai society.

Thus the target became universal education, and as soon as possible, and an immense expansion was set on foot. Table 14 below gives some figures of expansion of enrolments over various periods in the last ten years.

TABLE 14

INCREASE IN TOTAL ENROLMENTS (1950–61)

	Primary Education		*Secondary Education*	
	1950	*1961–2*	*1950*	*1961*
Burma (state schools)	387,500	1,546,900	50,639	240,484
Thailand	3,116,800 (1954)	4,086,100	82,919 (1954)	270,700
Malaya	599,400	1,133,300 (1962)	34,686	202,368 (1962)
Indonesia	5,000,000 (approx.)	9,600,000 (1962)	352,431 (1956–7)	585,300
Cambodia	182,200	590,400	4,296 (1952–3)	40,923
South Viet-Nam	400,900 (1953–4)	1,361,400	43,000 (1953–4)	228,495
Philippines*	4,083,000	4,438,900	483,933	663,500

Note: * The main Philippine expansion of Primary education took place earlier.

These are formidable figures, and they were not achieved without paying a price. Vast numbers of teachers were required. Hurriedly trained, from an educational background which was itself inadequate, they could not hope to maintain the standards set, often by expatriates, in the few older Secondary schools. To expand the universities when the level of Secondary education was thus falling implied inevitably lower standards of entry. Even at that, in Burma, Dr Hla Myint has pointed out, in 1960 97 per cent of candidates failed their matriculation. In Thailand, in 1963, a large proportion of candidates entering the universities did not, in fact, meet the formal entrance requirements.[2] In Indonesia the President has announced a target of 1,000,000 university students (1 per cent of population) by 1970, and twenty-four new universities have been set up within a decade. In the Philippines the growth

[2] 700 out of 933 entrants to Thammasart University in 1963 failed the entrance examination.

of colleges, mainly provided by private enterprise, has reached an enrolment of over 300,000 — 1 per cent of population, higher than the United Kingdom ratio. The University of Saigon was working double shifts to fit in its science students. Only in Malaya and Singapore were the old restrictions on quality and entry firmly maintained in the English-language University, though it was supplemented in Singapore by the more open, privately financed, Chinese University of Nanyang.

Meanwhile, at the lower end, huge additional numbers of children were flowing into the Primary schools. Where the growth was fastest and the teaching force least trained, few lasted more than the first years of the six-year course. Table 15 (p. 111)[3] shows the percentage of enrolment in the last year (usually the sixth) of Primary education compared to Year 1 and the similar percentage for the last year of Secondary education compared to the first. These figures are not, of course, survival rates,[4] and the contrast is exaggerated somewhat by the constant growth of numbers at the point of entry; but the calculated survival rates of a single age-group are almost as striking (Table 16).

The pyramid of education which these figures disclose has some very strange features. Naturally, the number who survive from the first grade of Primary education to the final year of Secondary, where the matriculation examination is taken, is extremely low. If the percentages in Table 16 are accumulated, the result is that, for every 1,000 children entering Standard I of Primary, the following numbers reach the final form of Secondary: in Burma, thirty children; in Malaya, fifty; in Thailand, twenty-five; in Indonesia, twenty; and in Cambodia, nine.

There is the hurdle of matriculation itself to pass. A slightly different calculation, for boys only, records that from 1,000 boys entering Primary in Thailand in 1950, it was reckoned that four would matriculate in 1962 and probably two would graduate in 1965 or 1966. In Burma the figure is even lower. In Malaya, out of 1,000 boys entering Primary, about 150 might enter the university at current survival rates.[5]

[3] U.N.E.S.C.O.–I.A.U. Manpower Report (South-East Asia), 1964.

[4] i.e., the Year 6 pupils are a proportion of the *current* Year 1 pupils.

[5] This is a considerable improvement on the success rate if it were taken back to the starting-point of 1950 upon which Table 16 was based. What is more startling is the very high rate of loss after the first year of Primary (in Burma about two-thirds fall out), and the fact that only in Malaya do more than 50 per cent survive the whole Primary course, or more than 30 per cent survive the Secondary course as far as university entrance. Yet a surprising number of those who do survive Primary enter Secondary—figures are in most cases nearly 50 per cent—in Thailand apparently 80 per cent. This compares with figures of 10 per cent or less gaining Secondary places in East Africa.

TABLE 15*

PRIMARY AND SECONDARY ENROLMENTS (1961–2)

	Primary Enrolments Standard VI or VII as % of Standard I	*Secondary Enrolments Final Form (Matriculation Level) as % of Form 1*
Burma	2.6 (Year 7)†	18.0 (Year 10)
Thailand	8.5 (Year 7)	25.0 (Year 12)
Malaysia	73.2 (Year 6)	2.6 (Year 13)‡
Indonesia	45.0 (Year 6)	19.0 (Year 12)
Cambodia	27.0 (Year 6)	3.0 (Year 13)§
South Viet-Nam	35.0 (Year 5)	11.4 (Year 12)
Philippines	38.7 (Year 6)	(Not comparable)

In some cases, actual survival rates have been worked out:

TABLE 16

PERCENTAGES OF SURVIVAL THROUGH SCHOOL GRADES||
(1950–62)

	Primary Education % Surviving Standard I–VI	*% Surviving from Primary VI to Secondary*	*Secondary Education % Surviving from Form 1 to—*	
			(a) Form 4	*(b) Form 6*
Burma	12.0	51.4	51.0 (Form 3)	— (No Form 6)
Thailand	13.6	80.0	81.5 (Form 3)	18.0
Malaya	56.4	35.0	59.0 (Form 5)	32.3
Indonesia	45.0	21.0	77.0 (Form 3)	20.0
Cambodia	40.0	48.0	37.5	3.5
South Viet-Nam	51.0	50.0	—	—
Philippines	43.0	63.0	63.0	— (No Form 6)

Notes: * U.N.E.S.C.O.–I.A.U. Manpower Report (South-East Asia), 1964.
† This very low figure is due to an immense congestion of 'repeating' pupils in Standard I.
‡ This very low figure is due to the extremely limited provision of 6th forms.
§ Cambodia has only very recently provided for the 2nd *Baccalauréat*.
|| I am indebted to my colleagues on the research staff of the U.N.E.S.C.O.–I.A.U. Research Programme in Kuala Lumpur for the following figures.

The difference between the survival rates and the present proportion between the lowest and the highest forms in both Primary and Secondary schools shows the mounting rate of new enrolments, and casts a warning shadow of the huge demand for Secondary education which will arise when the present Primary entrants reach the end of their course. Further, the survival rates will no doubt improve, and this will add yet more to the pressure.

In the light of the earlier cultural system which I have tried to describe, it is easy to see what is happening. First, the effort to replace the old Pagoda or Koranic schools with a new, secular Primary education, carried out at extreme speed, with half-trained teachers, and with little clear definition of its objective, is at first partly rejected and partly unsuccessful. It is rejected by many village parents, who withdraw their children in favour of the older cultural pattern, in which the child, from an early age, took part in family work, while the parents taught him custom and the Pagoda or Koranic school taught him some letters and the rules of religion. It is unsuccessful because, without first-rate teaching, this form of literary education, with its tendency to abstraction, is at first too strange and difficult. The result for the 50 per cent or 60 per cent of children who never complete the Primary course is that they gain a smattering of knowledge of a new kind which is almost useless to them and is rapidly forgotten.[6]

Secondly, the equation between education and salaried work becomes more and more heavily emphasized. At first, the opportunity to get Secondary education is all-important; then, as jobs fill up, a university degree is needed. Pressure mounts to expand the Secondary schools (whether there are teachers or not). Standards fall; then there is pressure to reduce the level of entrance to the university, which is now too high for the Secondary pupils. Both to win votes and because more university graduates are needed for the new economic and administrative plans, the standards are duly dropped. More B.A.s appear; but then, as competition starts at this higher level, something more is needed—perhaps a doctorate, or (because the local degree is losing prestige) a foreign degree from England or America or France. The late T. S. Eliot remarked, as long ago as 1947:

> Any educational system aiming at a complete adjustment between education and society will tend both to restrict education to what will lead to success in the world and to restrict success in the world to those who have been good pupils of the system . . . Furthermore, the ideal of a uniform system such that no one capable of receiving higher education could fail to get it leads imperceptibly to the attempt to educate too many people, and consequently to the lowering of standards to whatever this swollen number of candidates is able to reach.[7]

The warning has certainly been justified in many countries. Rangoon University has gone sadly downhill; students who have completed a

[6] The Beecher Commission observed this situation in East Africa and concluded that less than four completed years of Primary education of this type was almost totally forgotten and totally wasted.

[7] T. S. Eliot, *Notes towards a Definition of Culture*, London, 1947.

B.Sc. at Chulalongkorn University in Thailand are willing—and eager—to start the B.Sc. course again in a New Zealand university; many of the private colleges, with university status, in the Philippines are stigmatized as 'diploma mills'; Indonesia is expanding universities at a rate which makes high standards inconceivable in more than a very few of them. Malaya and Saigon are desperately holding firm to their British and French standards against the mounting pressure of politics and student ambition. Meanwhile, international aid (and the competition between donors) helps to swell the ranks of higher degree-holders by offering M.A. and Ph.D. courses (not always of good quality) and thus sharpening competition; and it encourages yet further local expansion, far beyond what the indigenous economy could finance, by sponsoring yet more institutions of higher education.

Educational inflation has other effects. The overwhelming prestige of the university downgrades the status of technical education at post-Secondary level. Moreover, it makes the Secondary course itself entirely geared to university entrance, never a terminal course in its own right—though at most 20 per cent and in many cases far fewer Secondary entrants actually reach the university. It emphasizes the academic degree—still on the old lines, but watered down—as against practical training and novitiate. In consequence, throughout the area a shortage of technicians and of practical engineers or agriculturalists can coexist (as it does both in Burma and Thailand) with a surplus of university degrees in agriculture or engineering.

This state of affairs in fact reflects the style of economic planning which has been adopted, and adopted largely under the guidance of foreign experts from developed countries whose advice is coloured by the model of their home society. They are urban and technological in outlook; the factories, steelworks, dams and city-developments which they plan reflect societies rich in technologists and in all the host of university disciplines which developed societies need for their large units of capital and organization, for planning, co-ordination, analysis, control, research, finance. They look around for the same resources in a developing country and mark down their absence as a critical bottle-neck in human resources. It is this style of planning, aided and abetted by ambitious governments, which demands so many sophisticated skills, and results in a 'manpower' policy in which the emphasis is on the top level.

This philosophy and its educational results reinforce the emphasis on urbanism and centralization. The capital cities grow and grow, the graduates flock to them and learn there a style of living which, for the successful, quickly rises to the international luxury scale. A job in the provinces, without air-conditioning or tarmac roads or good restaurants or the chance of quick promotion, seems infinitely unattractive. Thus the gap between bureaucracy and peasantry, between rich and poor, between town and country, between university graduates and those who failed, grows wider and makes a mockery of the egalitarian, socialist philosophy which inspired the educational expansion. The gap in attitudes grows wider as the urban educated lose touch increasingly with the real problems which the vast majority of their own people face. Some awareness of this problem is indeed growing. It may be evidenced in the Philippines by the desperate experiments of encouraging young college graduates to live and work for a year in the villages and at village standards. That such a scheme—artificial if meritorious—should be thought necessary underlines the seriousness of cultural disintegration.

It is interesting that the reversal of policy and revulsion of feeling which has taken place in Burma, described in Chapter VI, is in part a reaction against the results of this top-heavy style of education and social structure. The Burmese Army rulers have singled out for reproof not merely foreign capitalists and Indian shopkeepers but the educated bureaucracy and the academic university students. They are making a desperate effort to close the gap between Government and peasants (senior Cabinet Ministers have been holding mass 'seminars' with peasant farmers) and educational policy is being revised towards a more 'practical' aim, with greater emphasis on the lower levels and upon agriculture. How far this effort can be carried remains to be seen; but it is a notable example in South-East Asia of a genuine attempt to re-fashion education in conformity with a wider social ideal.

Two further influences are helping to keep the educational inflation going. In many cases, manpower planning, based almost invariably on optimistic estimates of growth in the modern sector and of the employment opportunities which it will create, encourages governments to believe in the shortage of university graduates—though failing to suggest any remedy for the alarming growth of urban unemployment among uprooted country people and the leavers from Primary schools. Since survival rates through the educational system are so low, a huge volume of additional pupils must be poured into the lower levels in order to obtain a handful of graduates. This not only defeats any effort at qualitative improvement; it keeps the emphasis on academic attainment while uprooting a hundred times more children than can hope for its rewards. Meanwhile, U.N.E.S.C.O. targets, from the 1962 Addis Ababa Conference and subsequent meetings, are set for further vast expansion at the Primary level, and this maintains the pattern of high input, high wastage and low output in the whole system.

There may well be a heavy price to pay. For the moment the very fact of high fall-out in schools is keeping down the numbers who complete a cycle and expect a wage-paid job. But if the situation in Africa is any guide, this will not continue long. Parents even in remotest villages eventually learn that school success means everything for their children; and even a small improvement in teaching leads to a higher rate of success. Within another five years a deluge of children will complete Primary school, and a flood, smaller but more vocal, will complete Secondary; and all will be determined not to live, as 70 per cent of the population must none the less live, in agricultural occupations. The oil refineries and steelworks and even the already swollen governments will not have jobs for them. It is in this sense that the new educational systems in South-East Asia are preparing the young for a way of life which cannot be provided. Many have discovered this already; many more will soon find out.

Perhaps the shortest way of describing what is happening is to say that education has been assumed to be a total substitute for culture; or—and this is to say much the same in other terms—that material and economic aims have been taken as a substitute for a total social philosophy. Let us hear T. S. Eliot again:

> In earlier ages the majority could not be said to have been 'half-educated' or less: people had the education necessary for the functions they were called upon to perform. It would be incorrect to refer to a member of a primitive society, or to a skilled agricultural labourer in any age, as 'half-educated' or 'quarter-educated' or educated to any smaller fraction. *Education*, in the modern sense, implies a disintegrated society, in which it has come to be assumed that there must be one measure of education according to which everyone is simply educated more or less. . . . Error creeps in again and again through our tendency to think of a culture as group culture exclusively, the culture of the 'cultured' classes and *élites*. We then proceed to think of the humbler part of society as having culture only in so far as it participates in this superior and more conscious culture. To treat the 'uneducated' mass of the population as we might treat some innocent tribe of savages to whom we are impelled to deliver the true faith, is to encourage them to neglect or despise the culture which they should possess, and from which the more conscious part of culture draws its vitality; and to aim to make everyone share in the appreciation of the fruits of this more conscious part of culture is to adulterate and cheapen what you give.[8]

[8] Op. cit.

At the beginning of this chapter I sketched—in a much oversimplified way—the relation of education to culture in the old régime. It is surely true that the application of the new philosophy—that education (one might add, economics) is the measure of all men—will teach simple people to neglect or despise their own—Buddhist or Islamic or Hindu—cultures; that the drive towards universal 'education' will adulterate and cheapen what is given. Both are happening already. It is also surely true that in the drive towards material economic progress few have been interested even to ask the questions of political philosophy—how does a society hold together? What are the roots of its unity or its shared values? If these questions had been asked, the West would hardly have pressed so hard upon the developing nations the adoption of an educational style suited to democratic, sceptical and highly technical societies. In fact, both this educational philosophy and the democratic system are being applied to societies which only yesterday were religious and aristocratic, without any allowance for the transition in cultural, social or political terms.

The development of an Asian culture is a declared object of the Asian governments. Yet neither they, nor U.N.E.S.C.O., nor the World Bank, nor the other foreign advisers seem to have given great thought to it. Present policies are more likely to turn Asia into a latter-day replica of the civilization of the West. Naturally the period of transition is full of imbalances and strains. So, indeed, it must be, if it is moving towards this particular end-product—'The Managerial Society', 'The Affluent Society', 'Organization Man', 'The Lonely Crowd'.[9] It is probably true that this is, in fact, the destination, with its disadvantages subconsciously suppressed; and its chief advocates would be impatient of criticism of the present stage, when the full daylight of general education and democracy is still only a lightening of the Eastern sky. What is ironic in this situation is that the group who will take most slowly to this change will be the indigenous majorities of South-East Asia—the Burmese and the Thais, the Cambodians and the Malays. The group which will take most eagerly, swiftly and successfully to it will be the immigrant Chinese.

The advocates of rapid change to a new secular training for Asian peoples have much right on their side—and I believe, much illusion. A few years ago U.N.E.S.C.O.—to give it its due!—asked the Institute of Traditional Cultures in Madras to carry out a study of *Traditional*

[9] I have chosen titles which reveal some self-criticism of the social and cultural pattern into which the West has stumbled while its eyes were firmly glued to economic and technical progress.

Cultures in South-East Asia, and the result was duly published under that title. Within it come some sentences by an Andra journalist, Narla Venkatesvara Rao, which put with splendid clarity exactly the attitude which supports the modernist view:

> While valuing our traditional culture as a great heritage of which we could be proud, I stand for the modern culture of the common man, based on freedom and equality, on education and enlightenment, on scientific truth as against religious faith; in short, the culture of the new age of freedom and peace. I am against any attempt to go back to a supposedly golden age . . . If we take care of our future, traditional culture can take care of itself. Those parts of it which have vitality would certainly survive, as they already constitute a part of our being, while the rest are bound to disappear in spite of any attempt on our part to breathe new life into them. Talk of reviving a culture betrays ignorance of its very nature.[10]

'The modern culture of the common man', 'the new age of freedom and peace'—it is easy to be sceptical about these phrases. But they stand for great human ideals which may not be blasphemed against. What seems so doubtful is whether the right means of achieving them—of achieving a real culture for the common man, of achieving equality, of achieving peace—are the means which are being chosen. Certainly equality and peace are not very evident in the early pages of the new national histories which we see unfolding day by day.

Perhaps the possibilities seem to have been put in a negative way in this chapter—a false contrast between remaining in an old culture which excludes scientific and democratic advance, and losing native culture completely in favour of the full Western materialism. This is far from my intention. There are, I believe, very considerable possibilities of retaining essential cultural continuity while accepting wider and more accurate knowledge in every field of thought. Nor are the social and cultural perplexities of the Western world incapable of more attractive and valuable resolutions than have yet been found. Some far more positive suggestions are made later in this book, after a closer look at the cultural situation in South-East Asia. But it is necessary to insist that a thoughtless and brutal break with cultural tradition, in pursuit of purely economic goals and with equally abrupt political innovation, can do irreparable damage and lead to exactly the situation which genuine nationalism and a pride in the rich traditions of Asian civilization would most wish to avoid.

[10] *Traditional Cultures in South-East Asia*, Madras, Institute of Traditional Cultures for U.N.E.S.C.O., 1958. This publication was reviewed by Morris E. Opler, *Journal of Asian Studies*, Vol. XIX, No. 3, May 1959. I am indebted to Mr Opler for this quotation.

It is surely symptomatic that an attempt to suggest an alternative educational policy raises a series of questions which have barely been properly formulated, let alone answered by research and experiment. In societies where at least 70 per cent of total population are going to be in rural occupations for the next two decades—and few would deny this—what is, in fact, the right educational policy? It is useless for education to attempt to prepare children for an unchanged rural life, when their parents are demanding an escape from it, at least for the children. 'The schools alone are helpless in effecting any dramatic change in rural life. They can be effective only if they are part of an economic and social plan which both makes farming more economically attractive and creates a sympathetic youth and adult opinion to back the progressive aims of the school.'[11] Nor is it sensible simply to hope that education by itself will create jobs: 'To educate regardless of employment opportunity may work in a society which is fluid and where individual initiative is prized. It is not effective where society is only just emerging from a static and authoritarian stage.'[12]

If, in fact, economic policy were to change, to lay an emphasis on widespread rural development, what then should education do? We can paint a word picture of a Primary system far more closely related to real conditions and far more sensitive to the valuable elements of tradition, followed by a Secondary system of county colleges deliberately designed to serve a modernizing rural economy. But to translate these phrases into a syllabus, a structure, a system of values and prestige, an altered balance of monetary and social rewards between rural and urban life—this is to demand answers which have not been worked out either in developing or developed countries. When the Burma Government altered its economic and social policy there was no precedent or guidance to suggest a policy for education which would match it.

[11] V. L. Griffiths, 'The Contribution of General Education to Agricultural Development, primarily in Africa', paper prepared for the Agricultural Development Council, Inc. (unpublished), 1965.

[12] ibid.

VIII

EDUCATION—LANGUAGE AND MINORITIES

THUS far, in speaking of the major direction and philosophy of educational change, and of its relation to the majority cultures in South-East Asia, nothing has been said of the minorities, nor of the critical issue of language: these two issues cannot be separated.

In the whole of the area there is a triple language problem. First, the use of the language of the dominant indigenous people; second, the use of an international language—English, French, Spanish or Dutch; third, the use of minority languages, and here there are slight but important differences in attitudes towards the languages of indigenous minorities and those of the immigrant Chinese and Indians. This chapter will mention briefly the situation as it existed in the colonial period, examine the present problem country by country, and finally consider some more general policies and choices which must be settled for the future.

In general it was colonial policy to use the dominant local vernacular for Primary education and an international language for Secondary and higher education; to allow some indigenous minorities and the immigrant groups to use their own vernaculars at the Primary stage, and not to prevent the immigrants even from establishing Secondary schools of their own.

The reasons for this policy are straightforward. The international language was used because it was the language of government, and the best educated must both understand and use it as they increasingly entered government service. Again, it made it possible to send the best local students to the metropolitan country for higher education, and later to staff a local university temporarily with expatriate teachers. In plural societies an international language thus provided a lingua franca capable of use at the level of national politics and administration, and in higher education, and this was useful even where a major local language, let alone a limited and often corrupted lingua franca, was available for the daily contact between races.

Finally, no doubt the colonial Government had it in mind that the growing use of English or French or Dutch would bring the Asian countries into the orbit of international civilization, and thereby help to close the gap between nations in the world. The British Commonwealth would have been impossible without the use of English in all its parts.

The reasons for continuing with local and immigrant languages were equally forceful. Some schools already existed, as a foundation; teachers in large numbers would have to be local; financial economy was essential. In any case, probably no one in those days, except possibly the French, conceived of a total 'take-over' of local culture including the universal adoption of a foreign tongue. In the case of the immigrants, they themselves usually provided their own schools and teachers, and the colonial Government was faced only with arranging some transition from immigrant schools to official higher education for a small proportion of pupils who desired and merited it.

Thus, in Burma, English was the official language for Secondary and higher education and Burmese for Primary in the main Burmese area. But local languages were also used among some indigenous minorities, and Chinese and Indian languages (mainly Tamil, Telegu and Hindustani, but also others) by the immigrant groups. Hindustani became the popular lingua franca of Rangoon, with English as the government language, so that the Burmese in Rangoon were sandwiched between two foreign languages and had to learn both. A similar situation existed in Malaya (English, Malay, Tamil and Chinese); in Indonesia (Dutch, Malay, and Chinese) with no official teaching in the indigenous tribal languages; in Indo-China (French, Vietnamese or Cambodian, and Chinese); in the Philippines (English, one of the main local dominants, some Spanish and Chinese). Thailand was far more widely dominated by the Thai language, but English became fairly extensively learnt in higher education and, as always, the Chinese established their own schools.

I. THE LANGUAGE SITUATION IN INDEPENDENT STATES

The main effect of independence was naturally to upgrade the language of the dominant group which came to power. Burmese, Thai, Malay, Bahasa Indonesia[1], Cambodian, Vietnamese and, in the Philippines, Tagalog, the main language of central Luzon, have all become official languages and all are backed by some degree of nationalist enthusiasm.

[1] A manufactured form of romanized Malay with European additions. See R. B. Le Page, *The National Language Question*, London, 1964. See below, p. 126.

They are all mutually unintelligible, save for the links between mainland Malay and Bahasa Indonesia.

Burmese, Thai, and Bahasa Indonesia are the only official languages of their country; English or Dutch become simply foreign languages taught as such. In Malaysia English is also a national language, officially only until 1967 (except for Sabah and Sarawak, where there is an extension to 1973); in Viet-Nam and Cambodia the situation is more confused, since French persists widely in official use and in South Viet-Nam the American influx has increased the use of English very rapidly. In the Philippines, Tagalog in some degree is treated as a lingua franca in private life, but English remains dominant in all public affairs.

The first problem of this major change was to make some compromise in higher education and official life between the official local language and the international language. The second problem was to decide upon the future status of minority languages, whether indigenous or immigrant, in the school system. It is easiest to deal with these two issues country by country before attempting any general comment.

In BURMA,[2] Burmese itself, a Sino-Tibetan language with no affiliates in the other South-East Asian countries, is spoken by about fifteen to sixteen million people, if Arakanese is included: that is, about two-thirds of the population. Karen is one of the same subfamily of languages, with about two million speakers, as are Chin and Kachin (half a million each). Thus over eighteen million out of twenty-two and a half million in Burma are within the same language group; but Burmese and Karen are not mutually intelligible. Easily the next biggest is the Shan language, of about one and a half million speakers; this is a language of the Thai group and there are perhaps another 200,000 Thai-group speakers. The third main group is the Mon-Khmer family of languages, including about half a million in the Wa group. The Mons are much assimilated to the Burmese and probably an extremely high proportion speak Burmese. The remaining main languages are Chinese and Indian languages, and English.[3]

The decision on the use of English in Burma is clear. First Burmese Secondary education and then the universities were changed over to

[2] The details in this paragraph are from R. B. Noss, 'Language Policy and Higher Education in South-East Asia', Consultant's Report, U.N.E.S.C.O.–I.A.U. Joint Research Programme in Higher Education, Kuala Lumpur, 1965.

[3] See also Table 2 in Chapter II, where the figures for minorities are based mainly on language groups.

Burmese as the language of examination, with English taught, from Middle School upwards, as first foreign language. Inevitably, there have been great difficulties. The English-medium mission Secondary schools, which were obtaining the best results, had great difficulty in switching their teaching staff to Burmese. All mission schools have now been taken over by the Government. It was even more difficult (at first, virtually impossible) to adapt university work. Most of the university staff after the war were English-speaking, and in subsequent years other foreigners, including Russians, have come in. Almost all the university textbooks were in English. Even now, where Burmese-speaking staff cannot be found, English is used. The drag on student performance is extremely heavy. Classical Burmese itself is an extremely difficult language, known to perfection only by the more scholarly Burmese; and it is full of ambiguity unless used with unusual accuracy. Where English has still to be used, either orally (which is becoming more rare) or in textbooks, which are still mainly English, the students have a slow and imperfect comprehension. In the technological subjects —such as medicine, engineering, physics—this difficulty is acute; it is certainly gravely delaying an urgently needed supply of doctors. In extreme cases (for example where Russian physicists, lecturing in Russian, are translated into English by an interpreter to Burmese students who know English only as a foreign language) the handicap and the expense of time can be imagined.

There is no short way round this difficulty. University staff are busy translating textbooks, and the supply of Burmese university teachers will slowly increase. Meanwhile, the teaching of English—which is Burma's only link with her Asian neighbours, let alone the outside world—is hampered in many ways by the difficulty which the Burmese Government feels in allowing English tutors—along with any other foreigners—to enter and work in Burma. All foreign-language teaching has now been forbidden, except in the Government Foreign Languages School, which is quite inadequate. If, as is deeply to be hoped, the Government gains confidence in the final success of the nationalist movement which it leads, it may well be that Burma will feel able to re-enter more fully the international companionship of learning for which an international language is a first necessity.

The Burmese policy on minority languages is more simple. The Union of Burma consists of five states and one 'special division', and in theory education was listed as a state responsibility. In the general confusion of civil war and insecurity during the 1950s an extremely mixed situation continued with mission schools, government schools,

Pagoda schools and a considerable number of private schools scattered through the country, with no common doctrine as to language. From 1955 onwards the central Government, largely by decreeing that the matriculation examination must be written in Burmese, forced the Secondary schools into the use of Burmese. At the same time it was stated that all government schools should use Burmese as the language of instruction. However, not only does this appear to conflict with the state responsibility (as well as with the colonial pattern where local vernaculars were used in Primary schools) but the Government has not had full control over the areas concerned, and it appears that a concession was made to the states for the use of local vernaculars in Primary 'for a reasonable period'. While at present the use of Burmese is no doubt spreading into the state Primaries, it appears that vernaculars are still in use quite widely in local schools, though no quantitative estimates are available.

As to Indians and Chinese, the Government has had no truck with separate provision. Indian Primary schools, provided by the various Indian communities, existed in large numbers before the war and continued after independence, though in reduced numbers. They included some Muslim Indian schools teaching in Urdu as well as the Hindustani, Telegu, and Tamil schools. It appears that the same concession as to Primary schools given to the national minorities was offered to the Indians. In 1948 an Indian Education Society was formed which ran a central school for some Indian higher education (not all schools were affiliated) and arranged for them to take the university entrance examination of the University of Calcutta. However, all government aid has been removed from the Indian schools, and as government pressure on the Indians continues—and particularly on those who have not taken out Burmese citizenship—it seems likely that separate Indian schools, even at Primary level, will be further and further reduced, until the last of the Indian community is absorbed almost entirely into Burmese life.

The Chinese were in the past a smaller minority than the Indians in Burma, and have therefore attracted less hostility or nationalist opposition. However, if the present estimate of their strength—possibly 350,000—is at all accurate they must be approaching closely the much-reduced total of Indians. As in every other country in South-East Asia, the Chinese have insisted upon providing Chinese schools and teachers; but they cannot, of course, enter Burmese higher education without learning Burmese, and only a small proportion in fact enter the university.

In THAILAND the whole situation is far simpler. The Thai language is virtually universal (90 per cent of the population over five years old speak it)[4] and all Thai citizens must be able to speak it. The small hill-tribes and other minorities do not really contest this linguistic dominance, although in the Malay areas of the Kra Peninsula, with nearly 750,000 Malay Muslims, Malay is generally used and Thai administrators or businessmen in the area have to learn it. Moreover, because Thailand was never colonized, there is no nationalist fear of using an international language. As far back as the nineteenth century it became a tradition for the wealthier classes to learn English and to send their sons to English schools, and sometimes to English universities. This involved a long stay in England, and a very high proportion of educated Thais speak English with idiomatic fluency. Many public reports and official documents are printed in both languages, and this is likely to continue in view of the presence of the United Nations Economic Commission for Asia and the Far East (E.C.A.F.E.) in Bangkok and the manifold ties with other United Nations and American agencies. The use of British universities is, however, likely to decline, because their standards are so exacting. Many Thai students find it more profitable in prestige to take a first degree in Thailand and then a 'soft-option' Master's degree or doctorate in one of the more easygoing American universities. Salaries in many official posts are graded by educational attainment, so that a higher degree has a cash as well as a prestige value.[5]

There are, certainly, some disadvantages in using Thai for the more advanced university work because of some shortage of textbooks in Thai. However, since English is widely learned as a second language, Thai students, in fact, can probably use texts and periodicals in English with adequate ease and speed—certainly better than comparable students in Burma.

Thailand has always been determined to absorb Chinese immigrants into the Thai way of life. Soon after the war Chinese schools were very numerous, and there were about 175,000 Chinese children on the rolls, in both Primary and Secondary schools. But in 1948 the Government closed all Chinese Secondary schools and limited the amount of time given to Chinese teaching in the Primary schools. Ability to speak Thai was made a condition of citizenship, and non-citizens were banned from a considerable number of occupations and suffered other

[4] 1960 Census.

[5] Several Thais asked us to persuade the English universities to be more reasonable, as they would have liked to have an English degree.

forms of discrimination. As a result of these measures, Chinese schools declined fast, and by 1956 there were fewer than 50,000 pupils on the rolls. No exact figures are available for the numbers today.

In SOUTH VIET-NAM language problems are again much more troublesome. Vietnamese covers probably 80–85 per cent of the population (the minorities are Mon-Khmer or Chinese-speakers) and does provide a lingua franca for daily life; but in government and most of higher education French or English is still essential. There is no immediate prospect of an adequate supply either of Vietnamese texts or of university teachers using Vietnamese. Moreover, English is beginning to compete with French, particularly in the Saigon Government and in the army with its huge American contingent. Much of the teaching in the University of Saigon, notably in the Science Faculty, is now in English, though some other faculties use French. There is a good deal of evidence that half the trouble met by students in the University of Saigon lies in poor comprehension of the language of instruction. In Dalat, a French Catholic University, French is more fluently used, and in Hué Vietnamese is used for teaching wherever possible.

As elsewhere, the large Chinese population (about 800,000) has its own schools. These were closed briefly in 1956, when the Viet-Nam Government offered citizenship to all locally born Chinese; but they were quickly reopened, with the proviso that the headmaster must be locally born.

In CAMBODIA the complication of the use of English is absent,[6] but the Khmer language, which covers over 90 per cent of the total population, has made little headway against French in the schools. The Pagoda schools, which as late as 1950 accounted for half the Primary enrolment and were conducted in Khmer, now include only about 12 per cent of pupils, the remainder being Franco-Khmer state Primaries in which Khmer is used at the 'infant' stages while French is introduced in the elementary and all higher stages, with examinations conducted in French. French is the language of all Secondary schools and of all post-Secondary education. The minorities—Vietnamese, Chinese and Malay—maintain their own private schools at the Primary level.

In the PHILIPPINES the choice of a national language has been made more difficult by the existence of several major vernaculars of the basic

[6] Though a surprising number of officials could speak it, as a result of scholarships to America.

Malayo-Polynesian language group which is spoken by 95 per cent of Filipinos. The four largest of these vernaculars, which are mutually unintelligible, are: Cebuano, 7 million speakers; Tagalog, 6 million; Ilocano, 5 million; and Hiligaynon, 4 million speakers. Tagalog, the language of Central Luzon, was chosen as a 'national' language, now known as Pilipino. A fairly effective compromise has been reached in the use of Tagalog, other Philippine vernaculars and English. Tagalog, as the national language, is the medium of instruction in Primary schools in Tagalog-speaking areas; in areas where the local language is Ilocano, Cebuano or another vernacular, Tagalog is taught, as a matter of national policy, to ensure that all Filipinos have some medium of common communication. It is not, however, the language of higher education or official life; English takes this place, being taught as a second language in Primary schools and used for instruction in Secondary and higher education. Spanish is also a compulsory subject for two years at the university level; and this requirement is insisted upon by the powerful Spanish element in ruling circles. In general, the dominance of English at higher levels seems assured; although Tagalog may continue as a demotic lingua franca, it is not very effectively taught outside its own area,[7] and might give way to English as higher education spreads more widely. It is a sobering thought that any child from outside the Tagalog-speaking zone must learn three new languages (Tagalog, English and Spanish) in order to complete his education.

In INDONESIA the advantages of using Bahasa Indonesia, which was invented in 1928[8] for nationalist purposes, have already been enough to ensure its success. It avoids the adoption of Javanese, which would have been unacceptable in other islands,[9] and it is being rigorously used for all official purposes and rapidly coining new words when they are needed.[10] It has become the medium for higher education (local languages still being used in Primary) and more and more books are now being published in it. However, it is still necessary for students in higher education to be able to read English texts—English replaced

[7] It appears to be taught mainly to enable students to read the works of the national hero, Rizal, in the original.

[8] It is based on a Malay dialect widely used as a lingua franca from much earlier times.

[9] R. B. Noss (op. cit.) gives the following figures for the main Indonesian (Malay-Polynesian) language speakers:

Javanese	45,000,000	Minangkabau	3,500,000
Sundanese	15,000,000	Balinese	2,500,000
Madinese	8,000,000	Batak	2,500,000
Indonesian/Malay	7,500,000	Makassar	2,500,000

[10] e.g. *Kudeta* = *coup d'état.*

Dutch as the first foreign language after independence—and this involves a serious difficulty in finding teachers of English for Secondary schools. In the various universities there are a number of foreign (largely American) teachers using English. In fact, the Indonesians have shown surprising energy in learning English, which was certainly spoken, and fluently, by all the central Government officials and university staff whom we met in 1963. Confrontation, and the ejection of the British Council in the summer of 1964, may make it impossible to continue widespread English teaching.

The Chinese in Indonesia (estimated at about 2½ million in 1960) have become in certain respects well integrated, but have retained, as always, a cultural separateness which even after generations of intermarriage with Indonesians renders them identifiable and therefore liable to nationalist attack. According to preference and tradition some Chinese in colonial times sent children to Chinese schools, some to Indonesian and some to Dutch schools. While it is difficult to generalize, it is probably true that Chinese insistence on the maintenance of Chinese culture, at least in the home, and on knowledge of a Chinese language, will ensure the continuance of at least some separate Chinese schools in Indonesia for as long as they may be permitted to operate by the Indonesian Government.

Finally, in MALAYSIA we reach by far the most complex and anxious problem. In the Malay peninsula the establishment of Malay as the national language was part of the bargain upon which the relation with the Chinese was founded, and it is deeply valued by Malay nationalists. It is a way of insisting that the Malayan mainland is Malay, whatever the population figures may become. It is the Malay homeland now, even if the Malays were immigrants themselves, and even though full citizenship and voting rights have been given to Chinese and Indians who quite soon will outnumber the Malays themselves. In theory, by 1967 Malay becomes the only official language, all government communications will be in Malay, and all higher education, including the university, will be in Malay. The State of Kelantan published an ordinance in the summer of 1964 decreeing punishment for any Civil Servant not using Malay in government documents.

In fact, in higher education this wholesale adoption of Malay would be unworkable. Wisely, the decision is not challenged frontally, but in practice the empirical difficulties will presumably force some compromise decision.

Malay is, indeed, a lingua franca for minor contacts, particularly in the shops and markets, and members of all races in the Peninsula pick up the minimum competence which they may need.

However, in education the situation left from the past is certainly difficult and complex. In 1962 the following numbers of pupils were enrolled in schools of various language media in Malaya:

	Malay	*English*	*Chinese*	*Indian*	*Total*
Primary	489,246	229,339	354,366	62,318	1,133,269
Secondary	14,534	156,463	31,371	—	202,368

The annual growth rate, during rapid expansion in 1955–60, was 4.7 per cent for Malay-medium Primary schools, 9.8 per cent for English-medium, 7.9 per cent for Chinese, 4.7 per cent for Indian. Interestingly, in 1960–2 the Malay rate is 2.2 per cent, English 6.4 per cent, Chinese —2.7 per cent (fall in numbers), Indian 3.7 per cent. Probably the Chinese were increasingly moving into English-medium schools.

Malay-medium Secondary schools are now being fairly rapidly increased, but up to now by far the best hope, not only of getting a Secondary education but of entering the university, was to join an English-stream school; university work, except in the Department of Malay Studies, was and still is virtually exclusively carried out in English under English and Chinese teachers. The English-stream schools contain some Malays and Indians, but the majority of pupils are Chinese. Thus, if the English and Chinese Secondary streams are added together they reflect the dominance of the Chinese in Secondary education.

In the university the racial distribution of the first-year students in 1962–3 and 1963–4 was as follows:[11]

	Malay	*Chinese*	*Indian*	*Others*	*Total*	(*Malay* %;	*Chinese* %)
1962–3	114	290	102	10	516	22	58
1963–4	158	398	123	16	695	22.7	57.3

Of the 114 Malay students in 1962, 108 were in Arts; of the 158 in 1963, 141 were in Arts. In contrast, of the 398 Chinese students in 1963, 178 were in Science and Engineering, with 48 in Medicine and Agriculture, against 172 in Arts. The Malay students were, in fact, bound for government or for teaching, the Chinese for the professions and business. More than double the number of Chinese graduates, compared to Malays, will appear in 1966–7.

It is not necessary to comment on these figures, since the implications are clear enough, except to say that the existing *stock* of Secondary

[11] U.N.E.S.C.O.–I.A.U. Research Programme. Population figures (see Chapter I) were (mid-1961)—Malays 50.1 per cent, Chinese 36.9 per cent, Indian/Pakistani 11.2 per cent, Other 1.8 per cent.

or university graduates, arising from past educational attainment, is far more heavily weighted in favour of the Chinese and includes, within the Peninsula, Chinese educated in the University of Singapore (1949) and, even older, the Medical College (1905) and Raffles College (1928), both of which served the mainland as well as Singapore itself.

The comparable language-medium breakdown for schools in Singapore in 1961 is as follows:

	Malay	*English*	*Chinese*	*Indian*	*Total*
Primary	20,018	148,029	127,606	1,243	302,070
Secondary	1,774	40,038	21,981	91	66,478

While under the old system the Chinese students from Chinese-medium Secondary schools had to take a pre-university course (mainly to strengthen their English) before entering Singapore University, the Chinese Secondary system is being reorganized to correspond with the English-stream system, leading to an examination which gives direct access to the University (it is comparable to the Cambridge Higher School Certificate), and this, from 1964, has resulted in a rapid increase in Chinese enrolments from the Chinese-medium schools. The university student body in Singapore, numbering 2,149 in 1962, is, of course, overwhelmingly Chinese.[12]

In addition, the Chinese-medium University of Nanyang in Singapore had a student enrolment of just over 2,000 in 1962, and this is growing.

Thus, the total university population in Malaya and Singapore consisted, in 1962, of 4,260 in Singapore and Nanyang, of whom probably nearly 4,000 were Chinese; and 1,430 in Kuala Lumpur, of whom again 60 per cent would be Chinese and not much over 20 per cent—say 400—Malays, giving to Malays a total of perhaps 500 out of 5,700. There were, however, some hundreds of Malays (as well as Chinese) studying abroad, and preference in granting scholarships is another advantage which has been conceded to Malays.

The situation in Sabah and Sarawak has already been briefly mentioned. The Chinese population represents only 23.3 per cent (Sabah) and 31 per cent (Sarawak) of the total, against indigenous populations of 67.2 per cent (Sabah) and 50.3 per cent (Sarawak, where Malays account for 17.5 per cent). But educationally the Chinese are vastly ahead, both in accumulated stock, current output and numbers studying abroad.

[12] Population figures (see Chapter I) are: Malays 14 per cent, Chinese 75.2 per cent, Indian/Pakistani 8.3 per cent, Other 2.5 per cent.

Enrolments by Race—Secondary Schools, 1962

	Chinese	*Indigenous*	*Malay*
Sarawak	11,877	1,381	1,328
Sabah	3,750 approx.	1,050	—

In both Sarawak and Sabah strong pressure has been exerted by the Governments on the Chinese-medium Secondary schools to convert to English-medium and, although one or two may stand out against this (involving loss of government aid), the transition is being fairly quickly achieved. It will ultimately, no doubt, result in a larger proportion of Chinese students qualifying for admission to English-medium higher technical and university education, and will tend to increase the Chinese lead in qualified manpower.

In this situation the language policy of the British colonial Government in the past has been somewhat strange. Possibly with some idea of a future link with Malaya, and no doubt considering that Borneo was in any case a part of 'the Malay world', Malay was chosen as the first language of instruction in Primary schools for the indigenous people, each of whom had, of course, their own language. The Sarawak vernaculars are, indeed, related to Malay; but those in Sabah bear little sign of consanguinity.[13] In consequence, quite large numbers of teachers were trained in Malay, and taught Malay to the pupils entering Standard I. At a later stage in Primary, English was introduced and English became the medium for Secondary education, except for those Chinese—the majority at that time—who preferred to continue in Chinese Secondary schools. By 1963 the indigenous peoples were objecting to this 'false start' in Malay, as they were unlikely to use it at home (particularly in Sabah, where the Malay population is negligible) and in any case had to learn English for Secondary education. They demanded English from Standard I. This request coincided with the success being achieved in East Africa in the teaching of English from Standard I to Africans, and in consequence the Colonial Government responded with some sympathy. A few Primary schools are already moving over to this system. Simultaneously, virtually all Chinese Secondary education will be in the English stream.

It is thus clear that, unless there is a change in policy, both the Borneo territories—now Eastern Malaysia—will become more and more English-speaking, with Malay used in Sarawak as a lingua franca for parts of daily life, mainly in the towns. They each have access to the English-speaking University of Singapore, in a Chinese environment, but they would not be able to enter the University in Kuala Lumpur, if

[13] Professor Le Page suggests a relation with Philippine languages—see below.

nationalist feeling there were to be successful in insisting that the University should use Malay exclusively by 1967.

Thus in Malaysia as a whole the Chinese have a strong educational lead in each of the constituent states of the Federation. Moreover, the population figures for Malaysia[14] show that only if the indigenous peoples of eastern Malaysia were to be counted as Malay-speaking would there be any majority of the natural Malay-speakers to the Chinese or English sector. In fact, most of the Chinese, with the indigenous peoples of eastern Malaysia and the Indians, are all likely to be in English Secondary and higher educational streams and will thus outnumber the natural Malay-speakers by about six to four. By numbers at present enrolled in Secondary or in university courses this proportion would rise to more than ten to one.

It is necessary to add that there is a distinction between those who are naturally (by current cultural origin) Malay-speakers and the much larger group who can speak some sort of Malay when needed in contact with Malay-only-speakers. Those who can use Malay if necessary include a very high proportion of all races in the Malay Peninsula (and this alone means a majority in Malaysia), a small proportion in Singapore, and a fairly large number in Sarawak, where, according to Professor Le Page, whose book[15] on the language problem is far fuller and admirably clear, Malay is the largest single lingua franca.

2. SOME GENERAL CONSIDERATIONS

This general review of the language situation in seven South-East Asian countries brings out some facts and problems which can now be more clearly summarized.

First, at the present moment the most educated group in Burma, Thailand, Malaya, Singapore, Sarawak, Sabah, the Philippines, and (increasingly) Indonesia can speak English. In Malaysia and the Philippines it will have been the main language of higher education; in Burma, Thailand, and Indonesia, the first foreign language. In South Viet-Nam English is increasingly spoken among the educated; only in Cambodia is it relatively very rare. English clearly has a long lead over any other language as an international link in South-East Asia, and there are reasons why it may remain dominant. First and foremost, it is the only common language in which all the countries of South-East Asia can communicate with each other. It is also the language of Australia and New Zealand, who are playing an increasing part in

[14] Before the secession of Singapore. [15] Le Page, *The National Language Question.*

South-East Asia, through the Colombo Plan and in other ways. It is also the language of America and a principal language of the United Nations, through which the great bulk of financial aid comes. Nor does it seem probable that any local language can provide an alternative. Some form of Malay has easily the largest second claim, in terms of population covered, as a lingua franca, covering potentially the whole of Malaysia and Indonesia for simple uses; but it is useless for the Buddhist world and for the Philippines.

Second, no country in South-East Asia has prevented the immigrant Chinese from setting up their own schools, although all, save Singapore, have insisted that Secondary and higher education should be either in an international or in a local national language. There seems to me little doubt that the British in particular were thoughtless in countenancing the growth of Secondary education, throughout Malaysia and in Burma, in Chinese or Indian languages. The result was to emphasize a cultural separatism which has been extremely hard to cure. In Burma, owing to the historic link with India, the Indians were allowed to establish themselves as a kingdom within a kingdom; after independence the problem was dealt with by the virtual suppression of Indian culture. But in Malaya much the same separatism almost happened with the Chinese, though checked by the fact of indirect rule through Malay sultans and a tendency for the British to favour the Malay peoples. In Singapore the whole commercial prosperity of a port of world importance was frankly built upon Chinese labour and Chinese commercial skill long before the political implications of the future had been considered. Chinese culture remains lively and buoyant throughout Malaysia. Elsewhere it holds a clearly inferior position, which is not likely to be altered.

Third, the adoption of a national language is causing much trouble in the development of higher education. In Burma this is acute, almost disastrous. It is somewhat troublesome in Thailand, and in Indonesia, but the national language is so well established in both that this may be overcome. In South Viet-Nam and Cambodia, French remains dominant, but undoubtedly South Viet-Nam in particular is held back by the mounting confusion between Vietnamese, French, and English. In the Philippines an objective observer might question whether the teaching of Tagalog outside its own area is worth the educational cost to the children, since English has gained ground so fast inside the whole of a very comprehensive educational system. Finally, in Malaya difficulties in linguistic transition from Malay, Chinese, and Indian streams have certainly been at the root of much educational drag, and explain some of the low rates of survival through the educational system. They also cause considerable expense and waste of personnel in training teachers for so many different streams and phases. The natural language to adopt for higher education would undoubtedly be English, supplemented in certain departments by an all-Malay stream—for example, in Malay Studies and possibly in part of the Education Faculty. Serious difficulty and delay in educational advance would only be caused if Malay nationalism insisted upon rapid and complete Malayanization of higher education as early as 1967. In the Philippines there is no serious threat of insistence on Tagalog as a university language.

Finally, linguistic policy is now released from the stark alternatives which at one time were suggested as the only possible choices. There is much evidence that in polyglot societies children are able to learn three or four languages *for different purposes and contexts* without serious handicap to their ability to use one effectively as the medium of higher education. As Professor Le Page has observed, a Chinese child in Malaya may use one Chinese dialect to one parent, a second to the other, English when speaking of school subjects, and pidgin Malay when buying in the market; in addition the child will probably have learnt Mandarin Chinese as the medium of Primary school. It may well be that, in the early stages, the child is not conscious of using several different languages, but simply of using the form of words suited to the occasion—speaking to mother, buying vegetables, learning at school. East Africans are certainly capable of speaking a vernacular at home, Swahili for certain intertribal purposes, and English as their educationally developed language. The technical problem lies in the method of teaching and the moment at which the main educational language is introduced to the child. This flexibility (which is perhaps surprising to the extremely monoglot English) gives a far more hopeful vision of the possibility of maintaining both cultural identity and modern international learning in the mixed societies of South-East Asia.

PART THREE

IX

THE IMPACT OF MODERNITY

I. THE TRANSFER OF INSTITUTIONS

MOST of this book has been concerned with the immediate past, and with the new situations and ideas which appeared in Asia when colonial power was withdrawn. It remains in these closing chapters to make some estimate of how the future may develop.

The driving force of change lies in the realm of ideas. But ideas are dangerous to handle without constant reference to the background of technical facts and political feelings upon which they act. The ideas of nationalism and progress, freedom and equality in the new states of South-East Asia have still to come to terms with the hard facts of Asian economies and cultures.

In most of the region, economic development has been approached by adopting both the technologies and the institutions of the developed countries. By 'institutions' I mean a wide variety of forms of organization. They would include the large industrial or commercial corporation, the factory and its type of management, banks and a credit system, trade unions and co-operatives, industrial agriculture; they would include also a complex system of government, concerned not merely with maintaining order and justice but with the direction of economic affairs; and they would include a large, state-controlled system of education, culminating in universities.

How far these institutions grew up in the West as the product of technical and scientific advances made in the last two centuries, and how far technical advance has itself been made possible by them, is an immensely complex question: technical and institutional change provoke each other in a very subtle alternation. Certainly the universities of nineteenth-century England (or France or Germany) did not create the Industrial Revolution—in the early stages they played scarcely any practical part in it. Yet technical progress would have been unthinkable without the prior growth of learning and experiment, inside and outside the universities. Today, fundamental university research is a condition precedent to further industrial advance.

Institutions and techniques in different fields of national life are mutually dependent. Shell International or Imperial Chemical Industries would not have reached their present complexity without developments in banking, transport, and communication, education and training, in the skills of industrial management and in organized scientific research which were developed by other groups in the surrounding society. They depend also upon moral and behavioural conventions in society—the honesty of managers, the conscience of workmen, the reliability of calculations made by scientists. In turn they made possible new advances in other social organizations by pioneering new methods, which are used by others.

In looking back on our own cultural and technical changes we are thus essentially looking at a process of organic growth, each organ developing as other organs necessary for its supply or control develop alongside it. There is a tacit assumption that by conscious analysis of these sequences and deliberate stimulation of them the whole process can be much accelerated for the developing countries. If it can, at least there must be the most exact analysis of the order of growth, the distinction of cause from effect, the necessary conditions for each phase. To take one of these institutions and establish it in a predominantly peasant society, where the supporting systems which it needs—credit, skills, education, technical services, political morality—are absent or only half developed, seems against all reason. Institutions are organs in the body of society, shaped by its needs and dependent upon the surrounding whole: a man's eye will not work for a lion.

In fact, what happens in developing countries is an attempt to create at least a microcosm of 'developed' functioning, naturally centred on the capital city. Large organizations are set up, possibly by inviting foreign investment, complete with foreign managerial staff. Universities are urged to expand engineering or other faculties in order to produce a supply of nationals with the right academic training. Credit systems are taken over from the colonial régime, and possibly nationalized. Special and often artificial arrangements are made for raw-material supply and marketing.

At the next stage, even where the main modern undertakings are properly staffed—and this is not always easy—the lack of support from the surrounding society begins to be felt. Perhaps the techniques transferred from another continent do not work in Burma or Borneo, and there are no local scientists to consult. Perhaps the trade union is irresponsible; perhaps politicians demand too much; perhaps the planning departments are out of step, and irrigation is started before soil survey is complete or the peasant farmers educated to use it. The natural inclination when these manifold difficulties arise, is to set up further modern institutions to overcome them—a Science Foundation, a School of Management, an Institute of Educational Research, often with the aid of foreign experts who bring with them the assumptions of their home society. Within a few years a little England or America or Russia (in fact, usually a hybrid, which adds to the trouble) has been established—a patch of twentieth-century institutions and technology surrounded by a largely medieval—indeed, sometimes primitive—rural population.

The economic effects of this policy—much oversimplified here—are beyond the main scope of this book;[1] it is the social effects which concern us. For the result is to re-emphasize the dominance of the centre over the provinces, the advantage of the 'educated' over the others, the pre-eminence of officials over private persons, the contrast between the techniques and institutions of traditional life and those which are introduced. Because the centre is emphasized, local administration is neglected; because educational qualifications are emphasized, education loses its cultural content and becomes a struggle for jobs; because officialdom is emphasized, no men of substance grow up in the private sector to balance the policies of government; because modern technology and organization are emphasized, existing skills and organizations are brushed aside. Speaking of the development of modern society in England, Sir Ivor Jennings remarked: 'What, in fact, happened in the Tudor period was that a new middle class, based on the production of cash crops in the rural areas and the consequential increase of trade in the towns, had developed. The "knights of the Shire" had become landowners farming for profit. The "burgesses" were often landowners from the neighbourhood, though some of them were merchants.'[2] In South-East Asian agriculture there are few places where this could happen, partly because socialist policy would not tolerate it but chiefly because agricultural progress, from the lack of an educated and economically independent class in the farming areas, has to be planned from the centre and organized by officials. There is a possible exception in the Philippines.

In the same way in industry, despite some efforts to favour 'cottage industry', the imposed pattern is more often Western—a 'light industry'

[1] See particularly S. H. Frankel, *The Economic Impact on Underdeveloped Societies*, Oxford, 1952.

[2] Sir Ivor Jennings, *The Changing Quality of Political Life*, Oxford, 1956; Vol. II, 1957.

established with a 'manager' and a 'labour force'; and this pattern is quite foreign to the organization of rural production based on the extended family. Each time such an industry is established, with the most modern machinery and an amount of capital far beyond local savings, a manager from the centre has to be imported. Moreover, it puts out of business the cottage weavers, or shoemakers, or metal workers; and often it does so whether it is efficient or not, because its losses can be made good from public funds or by protective import tariffs.

In Chiengmai (North Thailand) there is a 'cottage' lacquer industry. The extended family work together, in their own compound. They know where to get the raw materials—bamboo or wood, clay, lacquer. They rig up the simplest home-made springs and turning-wheels. They know the lorry system which will take the goods to market; the cash return is distributed on a family basis. This family is exercising a simple management skill. But if a 'light industry' is set up it needs machinery, a manager, wages, accounts, and all that goes with a far more complex social and technical system. The family head almost certainly would fail as the 'manager'; someone would have to come from Bangkok; and thus the local initiative would shrink and the profits would go to a limited company in the capital. In this particular case, probably because of the limited market, the cottage industry has survived and was even given expert advice on the quality of the product; but it is exceptional.

It will, of course, be said that all these things have happened in the industrial revolutions in the West; that English handloom weavers were put out of business by the nineteenth-century mill-owners; that this is indeed precisely the pattern and price of progress. But the English case is not on all fours with the Asian. The English mill-owners were local private citizens, not paid managers or government officials; they grew out of local society, gradually extending local skills and patterns of organization; and they themselves would not have claimed to be educated men. They grew out of the ordinary texture of local life, not in tens but in hundreds. They achieved much, and the government and the universities caught up with them later.

The result of the modernizing process in South-East Asia is thus deeply divisive of national unity. It creates a far wider cleavage between government and governed than existed before the colonial period, because it is an abrupt cultural break, a difference not merely of degree but of quality. It also distorts education, so that it points only towards the qualifications needed for a 'modern' job; and it inhibits initiative and the slow but wide diffusion of 'management skills' among private citizens able to make their own experiments and learn from them. Finally, it gives a great advantage to the commercially sophisticated immigrant, who is far quicker to adapt to the new economic pattern and find a way to profit from it. The mill-owners of Burma or Thailand were the Indian and Chinese immigrants. To encourage them may be politically unacceptable; to ban them may be economically disastrous. It was perhaps lucky, in one sense, that Malaya and Singapore had acquired too many Chinese to allow of expulsion—Malaya's wealth, after the European pioneering, is largely due to them. The Burmese are paying the price of expelling the Indian commercial community while trying to build an economy which still needs commercial skills.

If we think of the great bulk of the Malay people, or of the Thais or of the Khmers or of the Burmese, there is a danger that, unable to enter this small world of urban twentieth-century life, they will nevertheless both envy and resent it. Unless their own environment and opportunities are changing fast enough to absorb their energies and ambitions, there is likely to be trouble. It is this danger which the new Burmese and Malayan policies are seeking to avoid.

It would be false to give an impression either that there is no effort to avoid the disadvantages of transferring institutions from developed to developing countries, or that strains and dislocations can be avoided when society is bent upon rapid change. In every country there are some efforts to start development from below, to improve cottage industry, to encourage local self-help, to find leadership in the villages and spread simple education in hygiene and in productive methods among the mass of villagers. The difficulty is that the weight of prestige and emphasis is not really behind these campaigns. For governments they are slow, unspectacular, a low-yielding political investment. For individuals they carry little attraction compared to the opportunities of metropolitan life. Even where the central government has accepted first priority for agriculture, the evidence is more often to be found in large dams and heavy farm machinery, often uneconomic or unsuitable, rather than in the patient unspectacular development of skills and methods which would take the peasant community one step at a time from where it is to where it hopes to be.

There is an economist's argument for deliberately unbalanced development—for creating the microcosm of twentieth-century techniques and institutions, as a stimulant. It is not necessary to enter this controversy; for, in effect, this school of thought has had its way, because its suggestions chime so well with the natural ambitions of new states. Development *is* unbalanced; we are concerned with the cultural and political results.

2. THE EFFECTS OF INDUSTRIALIZATION ON RACE RELATIONS

The growth of industry and commerce in mainly agricultural societies provides, where it takes place, a new set of social relations within which new roles can be played. Both men and, increasingly, women may move out of the world of family employment to become wage-earners in factories and offices where a wholly different hierarchy and social pattern is found. The social effects of this change may be left on one side for a moment. But possibly the relations between races could be much affected by the new environment in which they meet as fellow employees, graded not by the old criteria—family, age, religion, race—but by new criteria of skill, experience, aptitude, long service. In an ideal world the industrial employer would like a labour force not rigidly divided by caste or race or other qualities irrelevant to production, but socially and occupationally mobile, interchangeable, fitted to their work and level of seniority simply by their industrial qualities. If a Malay or Burmese or Indonesian works beside a Chinese at the factory bench, with certain technical interests shared, perhaps with a certain community of feeling as members of the factory social group, it might seem probable that new relations would spring up between them. They are no longer in the fixed traditional role of Malay peasants and Chinese traders, with the stereotyped attitudes developed over decades between the two. In a new situation may they not find a new relationship?

A study of this question has recently appeared,[3] comparing such situations over many areas of the world, including among others South America, South Africa, India, and Malaya. Its conclusions are a disappointment to any hope that such changes in social and technical organization have, by themselves, any powerful effect in tempering racial discrimination where it is politically entrenched. Industry works within the total environment of political and social values, and has to conform closely to them. If, as in South Africa, the policy of the dominant group is to reserve occupations for one race and to prevent social mobility, then industry is both able and likely to organize itself

[3] *Industrialisation and Race Relations: A Symposium*, London, 1965. I was fortunate to have the task of editing this extremely interesting symposium. See especially the essay by Professor Herbert Blumer.

accordingly. If black salesmen are unacceptable to white customers, then the seller must conform or go out of business. 'Industrial imperatives accommodate themselves to the racial mould and continue to operate effectively within it.'[4] Where the political philosophy at the top changes, industry will change. Thus when an African country gains independence, African managers become necessary and acceptable in European firms; and they are at once taken on and trained.

The difficulties are greatest where there is a colour distinction between European and other races. The evidence from some parts of Indian industry[5] does certainly imply that difficulties of language, caste, religion, and local origin in India are less troublesome in the factory setting as between Indians than might have been feared. There is a considerable 'bunching' of particular groups in particular departments or occupations; but almost all groups are represented in almost all departments, and even the necessity for many separate canteens has been largely avoided, provided that a choice of diet is available.

This absence of cultural warfare at the place of work appears to be only an armistice. Indian workers in a Brooke Bond Tea Company factory are said to have remarked: 'We co-operate together at work in the Company's interest, but when we get home we shall probably spit at one another.' Anthropologists could quote many instances where attitudes attached to particular roles or circumstances may be modified or supressed where a new, non-traditional situation is introduced. But this only emphasizes the fact that the special circumstances of modern industrial work may do little or nothing to modify communal hostilities outside the work-place itself.

South-East Asia is nearer to the Indian than to the African experience. A considerable mixture of races has long been accepted in daily contacts, both in society and at work. Moreover, there is a certain balance in racial attitudes. The Chinese, probably more energetic and successful, are supported by their own self-esteem; but they are both a minority and immigrants, so that Burmese or Thais can feel superior to them in numbers and political power. The South Indian labourers in South-East Asia find a standard of living possibly higher than they could expect at home and make no great claim for social advancement in their immigrant position; the Indian merchants are compensated for lack of social esteem by quite high economic success. On the whole, racial feeling in South-East Asia is based on economic jealousy, and

[4] Professor Herbert Blumer in *Industrialisation and Race Relations*.

[5] The Tata steel industry at Jamshedpur and the Bombay cotton industry, studied by Professor Morris David Morris in the above symposium.

political nationalism, and not upon the deep colour[6] prejudices of South America, the Southern United States, the West Indies, or South Africa and Rhodesia.

Industrialization in South-East Asia has therefore less rigid barriers to break down between individuals, though there are bound to be some difficulties where members of different communities, previously insulated from each other, are brought together in an industrial setting. Racial group loyalties could still be strong where there is any cause for economic jealousy—for example, an undue predominance of a minority race in the higher salary ranges. Professor Silcock has pointed out[7] that in 1947 aggregate Chinese income in Malaya/Singapore was about two and a half times aggregate Malay income; average Malay income per head was M$258 against M$656 for Chinese. By 1957 (in Malaya only) the Malay aggregate was about 30 per cent of total income, as against 54 per cent for Chinese. These figures conceal the fact that Malays were mainly in low-earning industries rather than in the lower levels of occupation in industries also employing Chinese. But the quicker adaptation of Chinese to industrial life could easily produce the same contrast within single occupations and firms; and this would certainly lead to racial tension. Further, tensions generated in the political field could easily spill over into purely industrial situations. Similar trouble could easily arise in Thailand.

Thus there is little reason to suppose that industrialization would smooth out racial antagonism within the mass of the labour force; industry is more likely to reflect, in its social structure, the political balance of power and the dominant nationalist and racial philosophy. 'The transformation of race relations in industry is brought about by forces which lie outside the industrial structure and not within it.'[8]

Industrialization does, however, speed up the growth of a middle class in the main urban centres, a class less exclusive and less attached to the old social hierarchy than the middle class of officials who were, in Burma, Thailand, Viet-Nam, and to some extent in Indonesia, a close *élite* either of birth or education or both. This middle class of managers and technicians, accountants and bank managers, scientists and university teachers is likely to be quite tolerant of members of immigrant

[6] Both in South America and the West Indies colour is more a sign of social grading. There is not so much a 'colour bar' as a hierarchy, social and economic, running downwards from light skin to dark. But this is a complex distinction which it is not relevant to pursue here.

[7] *Industrialisation and Race Relations*, and in *The Political Economy of Independent Malaya*, ed. T. H. Silcock and E. K. Fisk, Canberra, 1963.

[8] Professor Herbert Blumer, in *Industrialisation and Race Relations.*

or minority groups who share its standards and skills. Among the younger educated group, including both men and women, this opportunity to gain a good income and standing and to be largely released from the social stranglehold of the old hierarchy comes as a breath of freedom, a vision of new possibilities, an enjoyment of the emancipation of thought and dress and social contact which it brings. This group is the real beneficiary of the new economic development, whatever its other disadvantages may be. They are its advocates and its strength. Their catholicity and tolerance of non-national members in their ranks may be of some importance in the lowering of destructive racial tension. Yet although they are an important minority for both administrative and economic advance, they carry few votes in a democratic system, and their very tolerance is a weakness in face of the passionate feelings of the prejudiced.

3. EDUCATION AND SCIENCE

For the mass of people, education in the schools is not the first modernizing influence. Adults pick up the new ideas from local administrators, from townsmen, from local politicians, from the evidence of their eyes. Contact with Europeans, the radio, new ways of speech and dress, new and strange goods brought by a trader start the process of questioning. It is a little later that the demand to learn the new knowledge comes, and the school will be called upon to give it. Certainly by now in Asia the task of the state schools as the chief modernizing influence is accepted from both sides—parents and governments alike.

The effects are far from simple. In a broad sense 'modernizing' education implies the transfer of those subjects which are governed by natural physical laws out of the realm of magic and religious myth into a neutral zone of science. The mechanical arts—the functioning of a petrol engine—enter this zone at once. Where the aid of 'nature' is still needed, as it is in agriculture or medicine, the change is slower: both myth and science are invoked simultaneously.[9] Social organization and personal morality are the last to be affected by new concepts, the least amenable to science, the most emotionally charged.

In the African or Asian village the schools are bound to start this process, cutting away great areas of traditional belief and custom, sometimes against resistance. The farther education is carried, the greater is the clash. Naturally, at first the effects are mainly in new

[9] In England tractors are still blessed on Plough Sunday.

skills and tools—literacy or a better plough. But change cannot be halted at this level. Systems of land tenure, systems of clan organization, systems of authority next become involved, as the implications of new technique and knowledge begin to be seen. Demonstrable success with the new knowledge at some critical point—the growing of crops, the cure of disease—may begin to cast doubts on the validity of tradition in other, wider fields, extending in the end to ultimate religious beliefs.

This role of education in substituting a scientific approach for cultural custom or religious-magical belief is not in itself destructive of cultural continuity, except in small, usually primitive, and specialized cultures which may be totally extinguished. A major culture incapable of incorporating both technical and social change would be dead. The danger to continuity comes at two points. First, there must be no break in the sense of history. The monuments of the past, the reverence for ancestors, a certain Vergilian piety towards the founders and forebears is of the essence of strong cultures. Even the agnostic in England, brought up within tradition, will not enter the parish church and see the tombstones in old script, the record of parish priests, the list of local men killed in battle, without this sense of a continuing unity with the past. To create this sense of historical unity is the duty of the Primary school and of parents. In a real sense, social ontology must recapitulate phylogeny; the child must live through and feel the virtues of his forebears even though his life may be so widely different from theirs.

This at once shows how adult and sophisticated the concept of a tolerant plural society must be. For Indian or Chinese children, when they grow up abroad as immigrants, cannot in one generation become Burmese or Malay. It is at least strongly arguable that their first schools and their parents should hand on to them their own traditions and pieties. The capacity to live with aliens can only be the product of a longer, liberalizing training. The United States, with the advantage of its great wealth and prestige, has taken enormous pains to instil a sense of common nationhood among immigrants, yet there are still considerable gaps between communities of different origins.

The second danger lies at a much later stage, when advanced education leads to a questioning of ultimate values, including any one form of religious belief. Because the progress of knowledge has thrust this question on the scientific nations of the West, it must also, unavoidably, be passed on to Africa and the East. There is no reason why Islam or Buddhism at their highest levels, should not remain as the ultimate background for the Asian educated man, as Christianity—but only at the highest levels—has for many sophisticated Westerners. But this implies a refining process (as animism, magic, idolatry of many kinds are melted away) and a clarity of definition which the West itself has not achieved. Without this process, there will not be Buddhist or Islamic or Hindu or Christian cultures for very long. The challenge of science will relegate any religion to the status of a superstition unless it is met with equal rigour and ability at the highest level.

In fact, in the present situation, whether in Africa or Asia, this final stage of education is largely left to chance. There are most evident clashes between Muslim or Buddhist tradition and the incoming culture from developed countries. The young man who perceives these contradictions has little to guide his choices—the most powerful argument may well be the evidence of economic backwardness in his own culture and the promise of economic success which the 'modern' ideology offers.

Thus the young generation may become denatured, picking up bits and pieces of post-Christian scientific culture while still surrounded by a society in which a major, non-Christian religion is officially practised and in which 'superstition'—primitive animism and magic—is still surviving. They learn the art of living in two worlds, as the Africans have so quickly learned it. Nowhere is this more true than among the overseas Chinese, whose children are busily striving to pass the Cambridge Higher School Certificate or the *Baccalauréat.* Among the followers of a Chinese funeral, battling their way with swaying effigies and loud music between the Chevrolets and taxis of a modern Asian city, there may well be a Chinese science student. He will no doubt cling to his modern knowledge in fields where it applies; but at present the values of the culture which produced it will be hazy in his mind, and the claims of family, tradition, and solidarity with his community will be strong. In the future this balance may be reversed.

The graduates of South-East Asian education will, in fact, face an even wider and more terrifying choice of values than the younger generations of the West, who themselves have been growing up in an apparently disintegrating Christian culture. The most sophisticated will certainly cling to the natural sciences and economics as reliable sheet-anchors, where they can be applied; but in the confusion of choices between nationalism, democracy, Islam, Communism, Buddhist non-attachment, the Confucian family order, the Cold War, they will be sorely tried. It may be reasonable to suppose that the more intelligent among them will reject racialist prejudices, partly because they have shared studies and perplexities with fellow students of many races and religions; and that this group will come to form a middle class with a tendency to make social rather than racial distinctions. In this there is hope for the plural societies of the region.

But at the lower levels, among those who achieve only a Primary or an incomplete Secondary course, confusion is at present the general rule. This half-completed education is not enough to give a vocational skill, even if there were jobs where such a skill was needed; but it may be enough to unsettle outlooks and values. Great words—democracy, progress, freedom, science—are picked up, like hand-grenades in the hands of a child, to be thrown just as ignorantly and dangerously in the political skirmishes of the future. If the young are uprooted from the culture of generations and then spewed out of the new training before they have had time to understand it or profit from it, these young citizens of the coming generation could indeed be hard to manage. If there have not been worse results by now it is probably because the educational system has been too ineffective to uproot completely, so that the great majority of children have fallen back into traditional life; but this will not continue. Education is a powerful medicine and it will produce dire fevers if its purpose and content are not more thoughtfully prescribed.

4. SCIENCE AND INTERNATIONAL AID

It is in the application of quite simple science to the material problems of Asian life that the greatest and most immediate gains of modernity will be found. It is easy to be cynical or despairing in watching the impact of Westernization and modernity at the political level and in the more spectacular and expensive economic projects. But in far less publicized and humble ways, and often without much cultural disturbance, agricultural and medical science in particular are gaining small areas of ground; and what is gained is held. All over the region, mainly through the loan of foreign experts—Indian and Russian, Chinese and Japanese as well as those from the Western powers—there are small projects quietly going on which will leave a mark long after the present politicians have disappeared. The list is endless—malaria eradication, plant-breeding, forestry, pesticides, soil survey, the use of chemical fertilizers. The observant traveller in South-East Asia will find such points of growth in each country. Here, in a hot Malayan rice-field, are two Japanese plant-geneticists breeding a new rice for double-cropping; here, three Englishmen, hundreds of miles from the capital, working on Thai cotton cultivation; here, a campaign against filaria-infestation in a group of Luzon villages; a 'Colombo Plan' New

Zealander reorganizing the teaching in a Singapore Trade School; the World Health Organization deeply involved in leprosy control; a Japanese craftsman improving the quality of lacquer in a Thai cottage industry; a Swedish U.N.E.S.C.O. expert teaching fine mechanics in Rangoon—so that the microscopes which foreign aid has given can be maintained; a team from an American university staffing a new Indonesian medical school; a London pathologist and a retired British geologist teaching students in Mandalay. Technical aid, from the United Nations, from individual governments and from the great foundations, is perhaps less often misapplied than the far larger sums of government economic aid, and some at least of it is going into just these smaller projects which are little known but of lasting value. This is to mention mainly foreign aid; but in most cases local men and women are learning the job and sharing the devotion without which the job will not be finished.

This is indeed an impact of modernity, and one instinctively recognized as good. It is one in which the growing middle class of South-East Asia, native and immigrant alike, can find an increasing part and an increasing satisfaction in the common disciplines of science. If one asks why this type of modernization raises fewer doubts than the multi-million dollar projects, it is because the smaller projects involve no great cultural revolution, give few opportunities for corruption, do not depend upon scarce managerial skills, are within the reach of local savings and local personnel, and involve the personal example and devotion of a few people whose attitude is as educative as their skills. They are directly and closely in touch with the life and already-felt desires of the peasant people and bring quick and tangible results to them. A man can grow better rice and more of it, see his children grow healthier, cross the new bridge and tend the new cattle, without ceasing to be a Buddhist, a villager, the head of a family who respect him, a man still living within his own Asian world.

5. RELIGION AND SECULARISM

There are religious differences in Asia both between immigrant races and their host societies and between internal groups within both the Malay and the mainland worlds—for example, between Christian and Muslim Indonesians, between Christian, Buddhist, and Muslim groups in Burma, between Christians and Buddhists in Viet-Nam. On the whole, these differences do not appear to have played a vital part in communal animosities. The economic or political strains between ethnic groups have been more important. The Christian Karens or Muslim Arakanese in Burma have demanded a greater self-determination in protest not against Buddhism but against Burmese domination. Catholic-Buddhist hostility in South Viet-Nam has more political than purely religious animus behind it. Malays in Malaya are probably demanding a Muslim state only secondarily for religious reasons; their main objection is to the political and economic power of the Chinese. Hindu festivals and holidays are observed in Malaya, in Singapore, in Djakarta, without evident friction. Moreover, we have seen that the overseas Chinese are extremely tolerant and eclectic in their religious attitudes, and the immigrant Indians, away from the embittered communal environment of India, do not seem to carry the same inflammable feelings with them to South-East Asia. Probably the two most dangerous points, where national unity could be split on religious lines, are in Indonesia, if the Muslim parties should gain ascendancy and attempt coercion of Christian minorities; and in South Viet-Nam, where French-influenced Catholics and anti-French Buddhists have been in conflict.

While therefore there is no especial reason to fear solely religious conflicts in South-East Asia, over and above the strains which already exist on economic and political grounds, it is also necessary to ask whether the advance of modernity and of national independence might not produce a secularist attack on religion itself.

For some developing nations, secularism has a positive, revolutionary value, as indeed it had in some of the earlier European revolutions. It symbolizes to them the prestige of science, since it was the development of science which, in the two centuries from 1700 to 1900, opened up the vast difference in development between two halves of the world. The great objective which new nations set themselves—to catch up with the West, to abolish poverty and ignorance, to gain equality in world affairs—seem to be attainable by secular means; for it is not the religion of the developed countries, nor their art or philosophy, which is to be envied and emulated, but their material, technical, secular achievement. Indeed, there has almost invariably been a failure to recognize how much of Western achievement was, in fact, built upon and sustained by the fundamental religious values of Christendom. Most developing countries have looked to simpler arguments. They perceived not only that progress may be delayed by ignorant superstition, but also that in many countries religion was associated with the old régime, with authority—in some countries the revolution which culminated in independence was a revolution first against the colonial power but thereafter against a feudal or hieratic society.[10] It was felt, not without reason, that in such societies the close association of religious and political rule gave a mystical sanction to conservatism which inhibited the new forces in society and the new, dynamic attitudes of mind which were demanded by the times.

But, outside Communist-influenced territory, an aggressive secularism is rare in Africa, and almost non-existent in South-East Asia. The anti-colonial struggle in South-East Asia was not, in the main, led by intellectuals with strong anti-traditionalist beliefs. U Nu in Burma was a devoted Buddhist, and the present Army régime, though somewhat impatient with the Buddhist priesthood, has other and more pressing social objectives; nor would it wish to challenge religion among its own chief supporters, the peasantry. In Thailand the 1932 Revolution replaced the royal autocracy by forms of dictatorship which yet preserve conservatism, the monarchy and religion. Prince Sihanouk and the Malay ruling houses have accepted more democratic titles without losing either political or religious prestige. Even in Indonesia, where the revolution looks more radical, powerful Muslim elements are still prominent in it, and Sukarno has also adapted elements of Hindu and local tradition to give a traditional and mildly mystical flavour to the nationalist idea. The religious 'establishment' has not been destroyed in South-East Asia—it supported nationalism rather than opposing it.

Secularism was therefore not only unnecessary, since there was no powerful religious establishment in opposition to the emerging rulers;[11] it would have been positively in conflict with an important element of nationalism—the desire to establish an Asian personality based on cultural tradition. This concept is not, as it has been largely in Africa, a myth inspired by poets with the aid of some romanticizing of history and a good deal of borrowing from Mediterranean and Islamic culture. The Asian culture and tradition are there: they are living modern traditions, both within the Buddhist and the Muslim world, and they were emphatically non-European. Although Buddhism, Hinduism and the Chinese religions could claim to be more especially Asian, Islam has been long enough in Asia and has become embedded in so many purely Asian customary systems to count as part of Asian civilization. In contrast to the animist religions of Tropical Africa, which were

[10] See some excellent comments on this subject by Dr Mansur, *Process of Independence*, London, 1962, and also E. Shils, *Political Development in the New States*.

[11] The Filipino revolt against Spain was very largely directed against the Catholic hierarchy in the Philippines. But this is now old history.

bound to fade with the whole way of life which they reflected, the religious systems of Asia are well able to play a continuing and indeed essential part in the marriage of tradition and modernity.

6. THE TEXTURE OF SOCIAL LIFE

From these generalizations on the direction and effects of social change, it may be refreshing to turn back briefly to the local and particular. Do these changes, in fact, happen in rural Thailand; are these attitudes really expressed among the Dyaks of Borneo, or among the Malays of Johore? To prove this would require a review of many detailed sociological studies in each country of South-East Asia, and this cannot be attempted here. Nevertheless, it is perhaps worth while to get a little nearer to real life and to look for a moment through a scholar's microscope at some particular society in the process of change.

Such a study of a single district is that carried out by Dr M. G. Swift in a Malay settlement in the Jelebu district of Negri-Sembilan, Malaya.[12] The Malay settlers here had come originally from Minangkabau in Sumatra, and tradition has it that they married women from the aboriginal races in Jelebu and settled in the valley, while the aboriginal men retreated to the forested hills.[13] Perhaps it was partly at least for this reason that the holding of rice land in this matrilineal Malay society was traditionally through the women.

As in most of the Malay Muslim world, in Indonesia as well as Malaya, the society was primarily regulated by the *'ādat*, usually translated as 'custom'—the system of traditional cultural and kinship rules in part derived from fundamental religious tenets, in part added to by historical founders, by the concord of wise men, and by the growth of habitual usages. The *'ādat* lies within the general Muslim law (*sharī'a*), but is often more specific and detailed in individual societies. The system of administration of the *'ādat* in Negri-Sembilan was through clan chiefs, a district chief advised by a council of clan chiefs and finally by the state ruler (*Yang di Pertuan Besar* or *Yam Tuan*).

It may be valuable to look briefly at the influences of modernity affecting this society under three headings—economic, administrative, and social.

[12] M. G. Swift, *Malay Peasant Society in Jelebu*, L.S.E. Monographs on Social Anthropology, No. 29, London, 1965.

[13] A small illustration of the process of settlement and displacement described in the opening pages of this book.

Rice cultivation was the centre of traditional economic life, and it is through the rules affecting rice land and rice husbandry that the *'ādat* system of control still operates most markedly. Rubber, a new crop, needed new rules. But even before the introduction of rubber, government land legislation, by taking some lands outside *'ādat* control, had started a process of weakening the traditional system. When rubber was widely grown, on the hill slopes above the rice valleys, rubber land became increasingly the object of individual purchase, and escaped from the *'ādat* system of inheritance through the female line. The third main crop was fruit, where 'ownership' often consisted in rights to pick from natural or improved groups of fruit trees growing here and there in the forest. Both fruit and rubber were cash crops, rubber being regarded increasingly as a main source of income, fruit (which might fail in a bad season) as a welcome windfall of cash earnings in a good year.

Over the years the growing importance of rubber and the freer transfer of rubber land has been gradually resulting in a concentration of holdings and wealth among those who grew their rubber well and could add to their holdings. There has been more differentiation between wealthier owners and poorer peasants who may become tenants or merely paid tappers on other land. Further, the cash transactions, both for rubber and fruit, brought in the Chinese merchants as rubber- and fruit-buyers based on the nearest town and as shopkeepers. It is remarkable that the Chinese were not only more successful as shopkeepers—they had better wholesaling links with other Chinese—but in certain ways more popular than Malays, for they were more willing to give credit and accept a proportion of bad debts than the Malay village shopkeeper who was always pursuing his customers (often relatives) for the recovery of small debts. Relations between Malays and Chinese remained fairly easy. Chinese labour for rubber-tapping was generally considered more efficient than Malay,[14] and above all easier to handle, since it was outside the kinship system; an owner always finds it difficult to deal strictly with a poor relative who feels entitled to work (and work badly) on his land.

Thus both in agriculture and petty commerce the transition from a customary, rice-growing, self-enclosed society to a cash economy with urban contact, individual landownership, increasing differentiation in wealth and entrepreneurship, and increasing commerce in consumer goods can be traced. It is significant that the bulk of the Malay villagers

[14] Cf. also Newell, *Treacherous River*, who records the very much higher hourly rate for Chinese as compared with Malay labour in Province Wellesley.

accepted almost fatalistically that the Chinese merchants and shopkeepers were bound to outdo the Malays and largely pre-empt this range of economic opportunity. Interestingly, the extreme development of a pure cash economy is represented in the settlement schemes of the Federal Land Development Authority. Here, Malay settlers, who are married men with children and are selected by the state governments, are allotted a section of rubber land, a section of orchard plantation, and a small garden for growing vegetables. The 'villages' have no kinship relationship, and no rice land. They are wholly part of a modern cash economy, with the usual community centre, school, and clinic as common services. Professor Polyani has pointed out that, in customary societies, '. . . the elements of the economy are embedded in "non-economic" institutions, the economic process itself being instituted through kinship, marriage, age-groups, secret societies, totemic associations and public solemnities. The term "economic life" would here have no meaning.'[15] The process of disentangling the economic from the kinship system, until it is wholly separate, is one way of describing the movement from a customary to a modern market economy, and it is this movement which is half complete in Jelebu and wholly completed in the settlements.

In administration, the weakening of the *'ādat* and of the power of the clan and district chiefs is directly caused by the creation of a parallel system of government officers. Dr Swift found a constant rivalry between the clan chief and the lowest layer of officialdom, the *ketua*, who is an unpaid[16] village head responsible to the next district official up the line and thence to the District Officer. As more and more aspects of life become the subject of governmental interest or even legislation, so does the *ketua* gain in evident prestige and influence, although junior to the clan chief in *'ādat* ranking, and holding no *'ādat* office. Moreover, there are fewer subjects and occasions when the office-bearers in the *'ādat* system can really enforce their decisions (which the government will not do for them), and enforcement is more difficult as the relevance and binding force of *'ādat* is less universally accepted.

For the system of social values is more and more orientated not only towards wealth but towards the holding of a government or salaried job.

[15] K. Polyani, C. M. Arensberg, and H. W. Pearson (eds.), *Trade and Market in the Early Empires*, Glencoe, Ill., 1957.

[16] But he has certain allowances.

It is the district administrative staff, the teacher, the agricultural extension officer—people who are in touch with even more senior officials and the modern world of commerce and government—who now have prestige in the village. These people are carriers of new ideas and attitudes.

The appeal of new ways is enhanced by their identification with wealth and prestige, for the new ways are the criteria which distinguish a member of the modern *élite* class of officials from the peasantry. The villager is aware of the modern influences in the life of the upper class and, though he criticizes them, he himself has an insatiable desire for the products of modern industry. A bicycle, a sewing machine, a radio are common possessions in the village. . . .

The appeal is even greater to the young. For the adventurous few, modern ways suggest really radical notions, such as choosing one's own spouse . . .; for any youth they provide a charter for revolt against the older generation. For the elders have not validated their claim to wisdom with any tangible success, a clear proof that they do not understand the modern world, and should give way to those who do.[17]

I would like to add one more passage, not from Malaya, but from the study of a tribe far out in the French-speaking Sahara:

. . . a tendency for the patriarchal family to weaken and transform itself into a series of conjugal families . . . numerous young people seeking to escape from paternal authority . . . in place of tribal organisation there will be substituted a new structure of social organisation. Officials and public employees and traders are forming little by little a kind of middle class which is perhaps the embryo of the Saharan social system of tomorrow.[18]

I have included this passage only to emphasize how similar is the pattern of change in social attitudes in wholly different parts of the world, once the modernizing influences take a hold.

Among the results of this change in values is a tendency for the sanctions of the *'ādat* system even within the central sphere of its own competence to break down. Dr Swift records the alarm and embarrassment within the kinship system when a marriage between matrilineal cousins was arranged by two modern officials. Such a marriage was punishable by outlawry in the *'ādat* system, although not disallowed by Muslim law. Yet because of the prestige of the parties concerned, it was carried through, and with a large wedding party, although many of the conservative kinsmen stayed away.

While the successful modernists are naturally well content with this direction of social change, the simpler Malay peasantry regard it with a certain regretful fatalism.

[17] M. G. Swift, op. cit. [18] *Les Mekhadma*, Paris, Prohusa, 1960 (trans.).

The villager feels himself threatened and regards new culture patterns as part of that threat. More general than rejection is the notion that adjustments must be made, although what adjustments the village does not know. Many villagers when discussing the future seem sure of only one thing. There will be many more changes, and the Malay will be the loser from them all.[19]

'The Malay will be the loser . . .'—not the Chinese, not the Government and its officials, not the white-collar workers. But if the peasant is resigned now, there will be voices telling him that he need not be the loser; that it is the Government, or the Chinese, who are his enemies; and one day the younger generation, if opportunity does not come their way, will listen.

7. SOME COMMON THEMES

It is impossible to summarize the conclusions of this chapter in a few words without gross distortion. But before attempting a more general evaluation in Chapter X it may be useful to pick out three or four leading themes which run through the whole picture of modernization.

The economic process, in its present form, appears to be widening the gap between rich and poor and between the capital cities and the provinces. It is doing so for many reasons—in part by the adoption of advanced technology and the institutions which correspond to it; in part from the desire for speed, more easily achieved in towns than in rural life; in part by emphasis on centralized socialist planning; in part by a real need for national self-respect and prestige; in part because of the shape of the economy bequeathed by the colonial period. This process would naturally give yet more opportunity to the more sophisticated immigrants, and for this very reason there may well be either deliberate discrimination against them, or greater racial jealousy, or more probably both. There is little hope that the process of industrialization will by itself contribute much to racial integration; history shows that industry will accommodate itself to the dominant political and social atmosphere. The outcome of this type of economic growth may well be to strain social cohesion, to embitter race relationships, and to expose a flank highly vulnerable to Communist criticism.

The same lack of widespread development makes it impossible for the educational system to adapt itself to national needs, even if the will were there to alter its present *élite*-biased structure. Education is bound to disturb customary values, and this is, to some extent, its task. But the result can be only destructive—instead of creative—if the opportunities corresponding to new attitudes and wider horizons are

[19] M. G. Swift, op. cit.

not, in fact, available, either in wage employment or in more productive farming.

In particular, the introduction of science and scientific attitudes, even at the humblest and simplest levels, is socially ambivalent. It has decisive possibilities for good, often exemplified in the attack on productivity or on problems of disease in which international technical aid has played such a large part. But it is also perhaps the strongest solvent of customary values and the traditional order, by contradicting customary beliefs and practices, which are not detachable details but part of a way of life which stands or falls as a whole. To mention only two aspects: it will tend to destroy the respect of the young and educated for the old; and it will attack at first the fringes and later the centre of religious beliefs which are the central expression of a culture. There is no strong reason to believe that major Asian religions will be subjected to direct secularizing attack or form a focus for violent communal disturbance on a large scale; indeed the relative toleration which exists, compared to the violence of political and economic tensions between racial and ethnic groups, may be a sign that modernity places a higher value on wealth and power than upon religious faith. Internal weakening under unchanged conventional forms is a greater danger than fanaticism or secular attack.

Neither the economic process nor the impact of education and science can be taken alone. In real life they come as mutually interacting processes, as the cash economy, the schools, and a new kind of administration and officialdom slowly transform the social texture and its values. In this transformation, it would seem that the beneficiaries of an *élite* educational system and the immigrants with more experience of a cash economy will come off best, and the peasants worst. We thus return to the same point—the narrow concentration of development.

X

CONCLUSION

THE title of this book points to a special phase of history into which the peoples of South-East Asia have entered. It is a phase when many varied peoples are being welded into far fewer modern nations; are seeking a political system for their new national life; and are facing the agonizing transition from a traditional to a modern culture capable of gathering the fruits of modern knowledge from the whole world. Earlier chapters have examined some of their special difficulties; now some attempt—however difficult—must be made to state more simply the broad choices which lie before them and the values upon which these choices rest.

Modern knowledge has everything to offer in material welfare to these peoples: within a single generation it could enrich them in health and livelihood beyond our present imagination. But between now and then lies a long pilgrimage, in the search for ways to graft this knowledge into the living organism of society. It is a road beset by difficulties, and to describe them merely as economic or political or racial would be to conceal how deep they lie; for they reflect a more profound movement of human development.

It is a movement from the shelter into the open; from the shelter of the family and clan and village, in which the individual is held (both restricted and supported) in a network of customary duties and obligations, mutual aid and mutual sacrifice; from the shelter of an unquestioned religious faith, however coloured by superstition and myth; from the shelter of custom and ceremony,[1] familiar ways and tools

[1] I have in mind some passages from O. Mannoni (*Prospero and Caliban*, London, 1956) on the strains of relinquishing 'dependence', whether on parental or colonial or religious authority. 'The occidental has accepted abandonment and learned to live in a kind of emotional vacuum in which yearnings towards perfection . . . can take root and flourish. These yearnings have been at the core of an ideal which the civilisations of the West have cherished, whence are derived alike their success and their discontents' (p. 209). For the nostalgia which many Europeans feel, the wish to return to the shelter of custom, cf. W. B. Yeats ('A Prayer for my Daughter'):

> And let her bridegroom bring her to a house
> Where all's accustomed, ceremonious;
> For arrogance and hatred are the wares
> Peddled in the thoroughfares—
> How but in custom and in ceremony
> Are innocence and beauty born?

and the cycle of work in the fields; from the shelter of authority, however arbitrary, which limits choice and its anxieties; from shelter which is, however, also half-light—poverty, not least of mind, restriction of human skill and imagination and response. The movement from shelter and its shadow into the open and the brighter light is painful—to be self-conscious, self-reliant and self-dependent, educated and rational; to cast away both the superstition and the magic from religious belief; to form a new society, based not mainly upon kinship or race but upon the far more fragile bonds of shared interests among equals; to claim freedom of thought and choice; to reject hereditary authority and assume the restraints of self-government—these are choices which strain human courage to the utmost. They carry formidable dangers of personal loneliness, social disintegration, tyranny unregulated by custom, misery unrelieved by either family or faith.

This transition from dependence—on authority, colonial or national, on unquestioned religion, on the family and on an unconquered natural environment—to independence ('freedom and equality' . . . 'the new era of freedom and peace') is an unavoidable part of the journey into the modern world. It is a world which at the conscious level aims to be rational and scientific, which rejects all authority not based upon either natural science—the facts—or upon human democratic consent, or upon a religious belief which is purged of superstitious or magical elements.

It may seem to the reader premature to be concerned about such a transition for the peasant societies of South-East Asia, which are now only starting on the pilgrimage. Indeed, it is not made in a day, but in decades. The troubles of the transition, however long it is, arise from the emotional strains of leaving so many familiar supports and sheltering places. Dependence on colonial power can easily slip into dependence upon the charismatic leader, with its implications of tyranny; erosion of the family and clan system can produce the anxious insecurity of wage-employment; erosion of religious belief can become a wholly undisciplined materialism with a strong undercurrent of neurosis and despair. The remainder of this chapter will attempt to put in more concrete terms the ways in which difficulty is likely to arise and the influences both of help and temptation which the traveller may meet.

If, in this movement of transition, the aim is to provide, from year to year, a growing betterment and emancipation for those now living—not for some distant generation in the future—then some road must be found to avoid a sudden and brutal break in ways of life and values. For there is a short cut which is always beckoning—the way of Communism. It would be futile to deny the possibility that, by whatever mixture of persuasion, choice and force, some parts at least of South-East Asia will take the Communist road. It offers a radical break with tradition, a frontal attack and total victory over existing authority and privilege. It is addressed to the mass of people, with some hopes of power for the intellectuals who support it; above all, it offers speed. History seems to show that, for this speed, there is a bitter price to pay by those now living—the famines of Russia in the 1930s or of China in recent years meant suffering on a scale which can barely be grasped. But men fired with a new faith do not always count the cost—or hope never to pay it. Certainly in Asia today the speed of change which Communism offers is attractive, and any other choice must at least compare with it. To combine some continuity of culture with an acceptable rate of change is a formidable task. Looking back over the earlier chapters of this book, we must ask what prospects there may be of success.

I. ECONOMIC GROWTH

In physical terms the prospects could be good. South-East Asia is rich in resources; Tropical Africa would indeed be glad to have the potential of Burma, Indonesia or the Philippines. Even in Cambodia, one of the least well endowed, there are great possibilities in forestry, the raising of rice yields, cotton and fibres, fishery, and above all in harnessing the immense potential of the Mekong River. The riches of Sabah's east coast soils and forestry have barely been touched.

The issue lies in finding a social and political approach to the development of these resources which gives real opportunity to the citizen without sweeping away his present life and values.

> The problem is not to wipe the slate clean in undeveloped countries and to write our own technical and economic equations on it, but to recognize that different countries have a different language of social action; and possess, and indeed have long exercised, peculiar aptitudes for solving the problems of their own time and place; aptitudes which must be further developed in the historic setting of their own past to meet the exigencies of the present and the future.[2]

There is no lack of historic tradition. From the great dam of Polonaruya in Ceylon to the irrigation works of Angkor Wat, Asia is strewn with the achievements of its past. The resources of today still lie mainly in land and the potential skills of the mass of people; and advance on a

[2] See Frankel, *The Economic Impact on Underdeveloped Societies*, Oxford, 1952.

broad front must use those skills, and can use them very largely in their own setting. It is for this reason that earlier chapters have so repeatedly emphasized the neglect of the rural sector; the danger of transferring the institutions and outlook of highly industrialized societies; the consequent tendency to stifle initiative at low levels by large state-run and state-assisted enterprises; the movement, in education and metropolitan development, towards a small *élite* ruling a passive mass. For the mass will not remain passive for many more years; the education which is spreading, however poor it may be, will see to that. If opportunity is not more widely spread, the appeal of Communism becomes overwhelming; it would not have to convert a lively and progressive people but simply to replace one centralized bureaucracy with its own.

Clearly, development cannot stop simply at primary production; it must include a far greater and growing commercial and industrial sector. Here the difficulty of promoting organic and widespread growth is more serious. There are economic, political and racial arguments in the way. Economically, the problem of collecting capital for huge enterprises, made possible by modern science, and of handling them when launched, has led to central economic planning and governmental execution. But these arguments have spilled over into a belief that, in far humbler fields, government can use money better than the private citizen.[3] It is a strange belief, since the salaried minor official anywhere in the world will go home early and grumble about his pay, while the Chinese or Indian trader, helped by his family, is working far into the evening for the few extra shillings upon which his livelihood depends. But the belief is supported by a socialism, consciously or unconsciously adopted by so many leaders, which teaches that society must be constructed rather than helped to grow; by a semi-Pelagian belief that the naturally good citizen will be corrupted by motives of private profit but preserved in virtue by the virtuous official; and by a failure to value the accumulated total of small private enterprise, because it is so difficult to measure or control.[4]

Racial jealousy also tells heavily against this type of growth, as it has in East Africa. For the immigrant races have a lead in commercial skills and they might hold or increase it. But this is a negative and short-term argument. The function of commerce and small industry is vital and is matched by the need for widespread rural opportunity. By one

[3] See footnote on p. 163.

[4] Yet sometimes even the planners are surprised—it appears that recently, in the Punjab, there has been a startling growth of small business and manufacture, neither planned nor assisted, under the shadow of great enterprises into which public money has been poured.

means or another it must grow, and to a size far beyond the capacity of a 5 per cent immigrant group to handle. The choice lies between state-organized co-operatives and communes, state credit and state marketing on the one side, and the growth of subsistence peasants into commercial farmers, into traders, into small manufacturers within the texture of largely traditional life. It is here that the economic issue merges into the social. There may well be a possibility of development which does not involve the violent disruption of society to which China —or for that matter Burma—is committed. For the tools and techniques needed for a vast increase in rural production are not too difficult to assimilate if they can be introduced within the context of village life—even the weekly aeroplane can become quite quickly an unremarked part of the scene. In the long run these innovations do bring major cultural change; but they can do so only by putting into the bloodstream of rural life an added nourishment which gives both the energy and the vital cash rewards for changing. The development of some of the most backward areas of Africa has shown that, given the reward, the productive effort and even the business skills are not slow to appear.

The Chinese Communists have made much of their development of rural areas, and they have much to show,[5] though we know little of the social cost and the catastrophes. The South-East Asian governments have the opportunity to show as much energy within their present social structure; if they fail to do so, the writing will be on the wall.

2. THE CONTINUITY OF CULTURE

If we look at the same set of problems from a cultural rather than the economic standpoint, the answer is the same. The kings and sultans of a former age were indeed more widely educated than villagers, and infinitely more rich. Yet the Muslim sultan or Thai king belonged unmistakably to the culture of his people—indeed he focused and symbolized it: their arts and crafts and their religious observance were reproduced at their highest level in his court. To this day, for example, the silk for the Queen of Thailand's dresses is woven on hand-looms in a village weaving industry.[6]

[5] As an example, the development of Communes in Hua Dong (Kwantung Province) (cf. *Far Eastern Economic Review*, Vol. XLVI, No. 12). This is an example of Communist-inspired self-help, based on irrigation, increased crops, the design of simple threshing machinery, the purchase of small diesel plant to run it—i.e. the transformation of subsistence farming into a farm-factory using largely local skills, initiative and commercial sense.

[6] In Lampoon. Sometimes the looms of individual owners have been assembled in a central weaving shed under shared management.

In the modern world there is no longer this continuity. The centralization of power and influence among a group of Westernized officials and entrepreneurs means that new ideas reign in the capital which grows farther and farther apart from the mass of people. The quality of local administration is poorer, and the values it conveys are an uncertain mixture of the old culture and the new. To effect the transition many governments substitute for the old official the party representative who will preach with all the energy of enthusiasm the gospel of the new national ethos and purpose. It is a fairly crude and simplified gospel, quite probably with racialist and anti-foreign verses. Where the natural caution and disbelief of peasant societies is overcome, the result is a political revivalism which can quickly upset the disciplines of customary life and will be gladly used by sectional interests and leaders for their own purposes. If this is true in the rural areas, it is more true of the less rooted towns. Political ferment grows; if it is not contained and educated, it can lead to violence and breakdown of the established order—peasants' revolts, communal rioting, student demonstrations, separatist movements among groups whose self-consciousness has been aroused and whose respect for authority has been broken.

These are the extreme symptoms. More probably the gap between the privileged and educated centre and the rural areas may be felt first in a drift to the towns and an apathy and disillusion in the country. This can lead simply to stagnation, unco-operative refusal to take part in government schemes, possibly to retrogressive religious and cultural revivalism, or, where the time is ripe, to Communist peasant movements.

It is easy, through secular schools and party politics, to break down the older pattern of order and clan and religion in the villages. In much of Africa the chiefs have been broken by the politicians and pushed into a limbo of trivial customary duties. In South-East Asia there has been more effort to use and modernize them. But it is very much harder to provide, both economically and politically, a substitute way of life to the young school-leavers who are the especial victims of uprooting. Youth Brigades and Young Pioneers and the Youth Wings of national parties spring from this situation, and they are the most difficult of all social groups to handle this side of violence.

It may well be true to say that the problem of cultural continuity is largely a problem of rural administration. Unless the process of modernization is stimulated throughout the mass of villages, it will go on (in ways which are unregulated and irrelevant to four-fifths of the population) mainly in the towns. This is partly a question of the school system, but also of the quality and extent of training which is given to rural administrators and leaders (at present far too little), so that the new colours are woven far more directly and skilfully into the pattern of traditional life.[7]

It is perhaps inevitable, in the first generation of widespread education and independence, that the centre should monopolize the able and ambitious. But as the jobs fill up, and as each country begins to settle down to the long haul of the future, a greater share will slowly find its way to the country towns and to the growing points of commercial and industrial life around them. It is urgent that the nature and style of rural education, which could be a chief tool of cultural continuity within change, should be worked out. The teacher-training colleges are, in the modern world, as important as were the monasteries of medieval Europe.

3. RELIGION

In religion we reach at once the most valued shelter for the human spirit and thus, in certain ways, the deepest shade. If, in some senses, it is hard for men to step out from the shelter of political authority and take responsibility upon themselves, it is far harder to face the accidents and suffering of life without recourse to magic or sacrifice to forestall or reverse them. Yet on the road to modernity there may be both individual customs which, though momentarily, block the path, and larger attitudes of mind which sap the travellers' energy and weaken belief that effort is worth while. In some degree the growth of knowledge does reduce the range of misfortune in at least the physical world. There are fewer unnecessary deaths, less unnecessary suffering from curable diseases, fewer floods and famines and crop failures, a sense of greater mastery and security in the world. It does not reduce the sharpness of suffering in the mind, for which some ultimate belief is needed. Thus the effect of growing technical power and knowledge may be to drive religion out of its superstitious role in the mechanics of existence back to its fundamental dialogue with the human spirit on the meaning of life. This, too, can be a gradual process, and it is well that it should be so; there will at first be few with the courage and balance to find comfort

[7] French administration was particularly aware of this. See, for example, the training of rural *animateurs* in Senegal. There was an interesting parallel, established by a Belgian U.N.E.S.C.O. expert, in the *Centre d'éducation de base* outside Saigon at Tan An—which Viet-Cong thought worth while to destroy. British 'community development' methods do not seem to flourish in South-East Asia (except in the Philippines) as much as in Africa.

in it; for the new gods are not easy gods. The majority of pilgrims need some more personal and friendly guidance on their way.

Buddhism, Islam, Chinese religions all provide a sense of order in the community, and a personal discipline which is vital to political and social life. All contain a higher range of thought still valid when the cruder elements are cut away. If for Islam the dangerous counterpart of faith is zealotry, for Buddhism it is withdrawal; and both are equally fatal to the task which lies ahead.

The Chinese attitude poses a more difficult problem. Strongly materialist, it will fit well enough into the economic effort now demanded—perhaps so well that it would arouse both jealousy and persecution in the majority culture. But it is, as Buddhism and Islam are not, cut off from its source. Mainland China is following other gods: the vitality and higher ranges of Confucianism or Taoism are not being renewed. The Nanyang Chinese are, in some senses, already modern men, largely materialist and agnostic; in other ways the humbler mass of their communities are deeply sunk in superstition, magic, multiple gods of household and field quite as primitive as the Buddhist *nats* and less redeemable through any higher central philosophy embodied in a living 'church'. Unless among the Nanyang Chinese themselves a revival of the higher range of traditional Chinese thought can come about, it may well be that Communism will take its place. At least Communism provides a world outlook; at least it is energetic and modern; at least it seems to speak to the condition of the great peasant masses of South-East Asia. Moreover, it is well suited to their energy, appealing to their patriotism, and (with its anti-racial, proletarian philosophy) offering a solution to the dangers of minority status by hoping for a merger of all the dispossessed against traditional authority. The leaders of the Chinese commercial communities, who have so much to lose from Communism, may well be wondering what could be put in its place.

So, in this movement towards 'the modern culture of the common man', I would disagree profoundly with the proposition, either that 'traditional culture can take care of itself' or that it must at once be based 'on scientific truth as against religious faith'.[8] While scientific truth is growing, while vast and sudden changes are happening in traditional life, the shelter of a higher religion will be more anxiously needed than ever—its alternative is the fatal and bloody religion of political power. Nor will traditional culture look after itself. There will be, for sure, violent secularist movements in Asian politics, both attacks on the 'establish-

[8] See Narla Venkatesvara Rao, in *Traditional Cultures in South-East Asia*, cited above, p. 117.

ment' where, as in Malaya, it has a religious basis, and attacks on superstition as an impediment to economic growth. But if, in the immense strains of social and economic transformation which lie before Asia in the next decades, the continuity of a cultural refuge and restraint is deliberately broken, a disintegration of society, with appalling consequences, could follow. The Western world, far farther down the road of science and secularism, has felt bitterly the collapse of values and of spiritual refuge. No one would wish the other peoples of the world to wander in these barren places.

4. POLITICS AND POLICIES

In the short term the shape and role of politics in the first decade or more after independence is largely shaped by the historical accidents of the way in which full self-government was attained; by earlier history and tradition; and by the necessities which each new government faced. This accounts for the extremely varied types of government which are to be found today in South-East Asia.

Burma	Military Dictatorship	Socialist/Revolutionary
Thailand	Monarchy + Dictatorship	Traditional/Conservative
Cambodia	Monarchy + One-Party	Traditional/Reformist
S. Viet-Nam	Military Dictatorship	(Civil War)
Malaysia	Parliamentary Democracy (Monarchy)	Conservative-Reformist
Indonesia	Dictatorship + Modified Democracy	Socialist-Revolutionary
Philippines	Parliamentary Democracy	Conservative.

Indonesia is the hardest of these to define. It is impossible to neglect Sukarno's ascendancy, which in one sense is the most important fact in Indonesia. Yet below him a great deal of the democratic process has continued—major organized parties, of which the Communist, army and Muslim interests are the most important; balancing of interest in a ministerial government, and much popular campaigning. There is also a certain balancing of interests in the transitory civilian governments of Viet-Nam. It is of some interest that the revolutionary governments are in the countries where internal difficulty and economic failure have been greatest; and that even a shadow of the full-blooded African 'one-party' system exists only in one country (Cambodia). There Prince Sihanouk has achieved an act of extraordinary political skill in transferring the traditional prestige of the monarchy to a Prime Ministership held by himself, and in building a coalition of national interests (the *Sancrum*) as his Government. Malaysia and the Philippines, both full democracies, both economically successful, have both built systems on a strongly conservative foundation—the Malay aristocracy *plus* expatriate enterprise, both European and Chinese, in one case; big business, landowning and the Roman Catholic Church in the other.

In the long run, however, politics must aim to provide a framework of stable government based on 'consent' or acceptance. Consent does not necessarily imply Western-type democracy—Prince Sihanouk's Government probably has 80 per cent consent; it is perhaps best inferred by the absence of powerful repressive forces. Traditional authority which is accepted may indeed be well suited to provide just that element of reassurance and continuity which is of some comfort in the transition to the modern world. But in these days consent to traditional systems is a fairly fast-wasting asset. It is almost certainly true that the traditional régimes must either achieve a change to forms in which the newly educated can have more say, or be crushed by the powerful and lasting authoritarianism of Communism. There is no denying that this is the great debate in South-East Asia today.

The pull of Communism is immensely strong—even its most forceful proselytizing could not succeed without a measure of welcome. It is strong because it speaks of the development of the whole people, and means what it says. It is a fierce criticism of the past—of the poverty, disease, and ignorance which remain in Asia even in 1965. The colonial powers must take a share of blame for this lack of development.[9] But the new national governments have to shoulder the task, even if it was not of their making. If, in this book, the need for policies aimed at the whole people—rural people—has been stressed again and again, it is because this is the crucial issue. There is little doubt that, in the longest run, Communism would do the job. But for those who care for the sufferings of the living, there is surely a duty to seek a less brutal way. Russia, after more than forty years, has lately shown many signs of learning from the mistakes of authoritarianism, particularly in the agricultural field and in intellectual life—but only after untold suffering. China is still in the first stage. Even where economic success comes, the struggle for human freedom has still to be fought against the bureaucracy and the arbitrary power which still accompany Communist success.

[9] President Franklin Roosevelt is said to have remarked that France left Indo-China after 100 years no richer than she found it. Although such criticism largely forgets the conditions of 100 years ago in Asia and Africa, and the much poorer means available to combat them, yet some of the blame must stick.

It is on this fundamental value that the democratic world has taken issue. Indeed, it is this long-term view which has twice trapped America into the agonizing paradox of supporting corrupt dictatorships (South Korea; South Viet-Nam) in the desperate hope of gaining time for reform before, in their blindness, they drag down a whole people with them into Communist subjection. The troubles of South Viet-Nam today, and the international intervention, must be largely laid at the door of the Diem régime which failed to gain the support of the mass of people. If British support of Malaysia is less violently criticized, it is because the Malaysian Government has pursued widespread development with far more vigour and far more consent.

There may well be no third chance for any country of South-East Asia which fails in reform. It is under the shadow of this threat that the policies of nationalism in the remaining countries must be seen. This book has endeavoured to present with sympathy the problems which new governments faced—some inherited from colonialism, some part of the very process of creating nationhood from such mixed materials. But sympathy is not enough. Every policy which delays advancement of the mass of rural people while enriching the metropolitan few; every policy which hampers education—as linguistic nationalism does; every policy which destroys economic initiative—as racial policy does; every concession to prejudice and prestige weakens the chance of survival in freedom. Widespread development, education, and the creation of opportunity at lower levels will assuredly help. But whether direct election by universal suffrage must be included in all countries at this moment seems a much more open question. Racial competition and jealousy are strongest among the poorest and least educated in society, whether among whites in Britain, America or Rhodesia, or among Malays. If political power rests unreservedly with them, democratic leaders have extreme difficulty in resisting their demands. Such success as democracy has achieved depends upon those much-neglected factors—the agreement on moral values and the degree of social justice which through time a society has been able to achieve.

Racial attitudes, seen in this grave context, show more and more clearly as a dangerous anachronism: dangerous because they cripple some forms of enterprise and skill—European, Chinese, Indian—which are desperately needed, and encourage governments to enter fields in which they have little experience or skill; dangerous because they open a door to Communist criticism; anachronistic because the pilgrimage is towards a more rational and educated world, capable of rising above the prejudices of colour and local culture. That prejudice will continue for long enough among communities still bound by tight traditional conventions and still near the danger-line in daily livelihood, is inevitable—neither Britain nor America has conquered such prejudice. But that it should be countenanced or still worse encouraged by governments is unworthy. It is here that Malaysia has been forced by circumstances to meet the issue face to face. It may be that such a test should never have been set, and that the facts of human social nature are too heavily weighted against it; but it has been set and cannot now be evaded. If Malaysia could provide one example in Asia of a nation able to maintain democracy and tolerance in the most difficult racial situation in the whole Eastern hemisphere, it would be an achievement of historic significance. Alas, the omens are not good; even the breach with Singapore does not seem to have shocked either side enough to rise above communal attitudes.

5. THE OUTER WORLD

South-East Asia cannot travel the road alone, even if it wished. Help from outside is too valuable to be refused. Yet, in crude or more subtle ways, much outside influence is also a struggle for the soul. The Cold War is only the most evident and damaging sign of this.

Of all the influences, the American is the hardest to assess fairly. It is greatest in sheer wealth; it is the strongest in simple, positive ideals. To disparage these ideals simply because they further the political battle of the American nation against Communism is indeed beside the point. For it is the American vision itself which is bitterly hostile to the values of Communism and it is a vision founded on positive values. Based in history on the revolt against tyranny, on the poor man's escape from privilege and aristocratic power in Europe, it is justified to Americans by the power and personal freedom of their society, founded upon a belief in the individual and a hatred of the tyranny of the State. If these beliefs are true and valid, they must be fought for, and it cannot be helped if less worthy motives—commercial opportunity, national vanity—become attached to them in a wicked world. The American claim to greatness rests upon the values which she has the courage to state and to defend.

Yet, for winning admiration and respect in Asia (or elsewhere), the American image is defaced in two ways. First, by the injustice, racial arrogance, and materialism of some of its home society, where individualism itself has overshot into the very evils of unregulated capitalism which split Europe for a century and provided the fuel for Communism. The impact of President Kennedy—and perhaps of President Johnson in future times—was so marked abroad because it seemed to show an America conscious of this flaw and moving to repair it. Second, because the very vigour and simplicity of the American approach has, as its obverse, a *naïveté* in social and political thinking which can have unfortunate results in old societies moulded by complex histories and values. This is not a brash criticism of American leadership, which is certainly as sophisticated as any in the world. It is because America really is a democracy, in which the actions of government must reflect the broad wishes of the American people and express their values. The American people, suspicious of the sophistication of Europe, inexperienced in the complex process of colonial rule, are sorely tempted to drive a bulldozer of money and technology through the complications and perversities of the societies which they seek to help or win as allies. Throughout South-East Asia thousands of Americans, as individuals, fight devotedly alongside the nationals of many countries in the battle against poverty, disease, and ignorance. American treasure is poured out to aid them. But the value and gratitude for this unexampled effort is largely lost by too great political pressure on nations hypersensitive in their pride, and by too little awareness of the growing points, the style of action, the political and social necessities of very un-American societies. While in one mood they are anxious to democratize and are embarrassed by the dictatorships they may be forced to support, in another—and ultimately stronger—mood they have sometimes been so quick to fear Communism in movements of reform that their influence can seem reactionary. However unfair, the image of America as that of the Marines, highly armed with shocking weapons, supporting corrupt, authoritarian régimes and trampling upon independent soil to do so, is deadly to their reputation. The real danger today is that American influence, with its great potential for good, will be rejected out of hand by new nations in search of a personality of their own.

Against this, the Chinese Communists and the Russians claim to be fellow Asians; to understand and start from Asian peasant life; to provide a philosophy which is modern enough to accept technology yet adapted not to the capitalist institutions and social structure of the West but to the very problems of illiteracy and village economy of the East. It is a powerful claim, less feared for its denial of individual freedom by societies which have known it only as the freedom of subsistence agriculture in the grip of uncontrolled natural hazards.

The European powers (Britain, France, and Holland) are all handicapped in various degrees by their colonial past. Britain suffers from her close association with America in the eyes of Cambodia and Burma, and from her sponsorship of Malaysia in the Indonesian and Communist camp. Yet a good deal of unassertive aid, particularly in skilled men, comes from Britain, and her prominent part in the Colombo Plan is valued. Although Britain has long recognized Peking, she remains committed to the democratic world and has not followed the initiative of France in attempting to avoid the odium of American action in Viet-Nam.

When it becomes possible without betraying allies and commitments, an end to direct intervention by non-Asian powers in the whole area would be desirable. For there is not only a sense of nationality in each country to be affronted but a growing sense of an Asian half-world which would prefer to settle its own affairs. President Sukarno dreamed of uniting the Malay world in a single confederation of 150 million people stretching from the Philippines to the northern boundary of Malaya, a block big enough to stand without outside aid. Even if this dream has not finally failed, the individual countries of South-East Asia will need friends in the Eastern world if they wish to counter-balance the thrust of Communism from Peking. India, China, Japan, Australia, and New Zealand can be felt as part of this Asian complex. Britain has a link through the Commonwealth, and it is as a Commonwealth member (not as a world power) that her influence and aid can be most valued. Indeed, both Australia and New Zealand have been building increasing goodwill in South-East Asia; their universities accept a large and growing number of Asian students, and their experts have been responsible for many excellent projects in the area. Japan, too, is capable of influence and aid. Her economic miracle is admired and her technical help and investment are growing fast. There are still suspicions and resentments from the evil memories of Japanese occupation in the War; but they will pass with the generation which suffered it, and the reparations paid have helped to heal the wounds.

Little has been said of the Indian subcontinent, from which so much of South-East Asian civilization was founded. At present influence from either Pakistan or India is at its lowest ebb, not only because of their bitter quarrel but because Pakistan particularly is involved in Russian-Chinese rivalry and the East-West Cold War. These are complications which are unwelcome to those countries of South-East Asia which would like to maintain a neutralist, independent position. But it is worth looking a little farther ahead.

Indian influence has to be assessed at two levels. The Indian immigrants in South-East Asia have mainly occupied either a humble status as labourers or commercial positions in which they often attracted racial jealousy. In consequence they do not give any prestige to the image of India in the countries where they settled. But there is another India—a country of 450 millions, the bearer of an ancient and rich culture, which is striving, not without success, to maintain a fully democratic system; engaged in an immense development effort, including major industrialization; neutralist, and capable of providing neutralist Asian leadership. Indian universities accept many students from South-East Asia, and Indian experts play a considerable part in programmes of technical assistance. Moreover, India has had to face so many of the problems which beset South-East Asia—a population explosion, a vast educational expansion, a language problem, bitter communal divisions, and the immense challenge of peasant agriculture. Indian experience of tackling these tasks as an independent nation is longer and more varied than that of South-East Asia, and the planning and administrative system based on New Delhi is one of the most experienced and sophisticated in the world.

Obviously India underestimated the difficulties of maintaining a neutral, pacifist position in the jungle of modern international politics and in the pride of her own nationalism; threats to her own interests have produced a very un-pacifist response. She has fallen from the position of idealist leadership which Nehru once held. But after the painful reappraisal which must now be going on, she may well emerge with increasing stature and be able to contribute far more to the countries of South-East Asia. If she can achieve economic success as a free political system and as an Asian peasant society, India would surely be the most attractive counter-model to the Communism of China as a source of experience in handling common problems. She might find it easier to associate with South-East Asian countries than would Japan, or Australia-New Zealand, or Europe or America, because of the capitalist, or ex-imperialist, or racial associations which still surround them.

Diversity and Unity

To bewail or to applaud the end of the colonial system is beside the point. It is enough to note that in its days of strength it provided a framework of political power within which economic energy and the first benefits of science could grow. Because external domination is in some degree self-interested, this growth was bound to be distorted. But, more importantly, because it excludes politics, it postponed the real growth of responsibility. Thus, after its departure, it may seem for many years that the gains of science and economics are being squandered in a riot of power politics, racial persecution or national belligerency. The well-ordered estates are neglected or parcelled out to tenants who cannot use them well; the rich grow richer and the poor are not fed; the delicate balances of international trade are shattered; the devotion of administrators is disheartened or corrupted by new temptations or new masters. Worst of all, acute dangers of warfare between the nationalist succession states begin to arise. These are the penalties of postponing political experience.

The period of troubles will not be shortened by outside interference, though it can be eased by outside aid. But when, in time, a more mature nationhood begins to emerge in South-East Asia, at least in those countries which can avoid absorption in the Chinese empire, there should emerge civilizations much richer in culture than those of Africa because they will be fed by the springs of history, art, philosophy, and religion which are their own. Within such nations there should be room, not only for the Chinese colonies of Nanyang, but for a better integration of the hill-tribes and the sea-going peoples, within a culture less abruptly forced into a Western pattern. The spadework of economic and technical aid must come mainly from the developed countries; but in culture and institutional forms something less alien, more Asian, is needed.

The task of combining modernity with tradition makes immense demands on tolerance and humanity, virtues which are scarce in the present world. If there is indeed to be such a thing as South-East Asian culture, or any regional culture (and this is an ideal which both Asians and Africans pursue), it cannot be found in uniformity. It must be a tapestry of great variety of racial and ethnic and cultural colours, yet still in a pattern recognizably different from that of other regions. It can only come into being by acceptance of this diversity—Thais and Malays, Muslims and Buddhists, Chinese and Hindus, cultures from the mountains and from the rice plains and from the sea coasts and islands. Some of the threads within it will be repeated in every region in the world—the linking threads of science and of economic relations which make 'one world'.

The same need for tolerance applies to Europe and America, both in internal relations and in contact with the outer world. Asians, Africans, West Indians flow increasingly to the developed countries to share in the common elements of world culture, and often to contribute skills and services to meet our needs: we, too, have underestimated the tolerance and humanity which is needed to welcome them. Westerners in turn are working in every developing country, and learning both the needs and the virtues of their pattern of life. To put too high a strain on tolerance and humanity, which grow slowly whether in Birmingham or in Burma, may be unwise. But to deny either variety or interdependence—still worse, to make a virtue of racial or nationalist exclusiveness—is to delay the growth both of nationhood and of cultural personality upon which the developing countries have set their hopes.

INDEX OF AUTHORS QUOTED

Publications to which reference is made in the text include:

APPLETON, Sheldon, 'Overseas Chinese and Economic Nationalization in the Philippines', *Journal of Asian Studies*, Vol. XIX, No. 2, Feb. 1959.

COUGHLIN, R. J., *Double Identity: The Chinese in Modern Thailand*, Hong Kong, Hong Kong University Press (distributed by Oxford University Press), 1960.

DOBBY, E. H. G., *South-East Asia*, London, University of London Press, 1st ed., 1950; 5th ed., 1956.

ELIOT, T. S., *Notes towards a Definition of Culture*, London, Faber and Faber, 1947.

FIRTH, Raymond, 'The Peasantry of South-East Asia', *International Affairs*, Vol. 26, No. 4, Oct. 1950.

FRANKEL, S. H., *The Economic Impact on Underdeveloped Societies*, Oxford, Blackwell, 1952.

FREEDMAN, Maurice, 'The Handling of Money: A Note on the Background to the Economic Sophistication of the Overseas Chinese', *Man*, Vol. LIX, Apr. 1959.

FURNIVALL, J. S., *Progress and Welfare in South-East Asia*, New York, Institute of Pacific Relations Research Series, 1941.

GRIFFITHS, V. L., 'The Contribution of General Education to Agricultural Development, primarily in Africa', paper prepared for the Agricultural Development Council, Inc. (unpublished), 1965.

HARVEY, G. E., *British Rule in Burma*, 1824–1941, London, Faber and Faber, 1946.

HUNTER, Guy (ed.), *Industrialisation and Race Relations: A Symposium*, London, Oxford University Press for Institute of Race Relations and U.N.E.S.C.O., 1965.

Institute of Traditional Cultures, for U.N.E.S.C.O., *Traditional Cultures in South-East Asia*, Madras, Orient Longmans Private Ltd., 1958.

JENNINGS, Sir Ivor, *The Changing Quality of Political Life*, Report of the Duke of Edinburgh's Study Conference, Oxford, 1956–7.

JU-K'ANG T'IEN, *The Chinese of Sarawak*, London School of Economics Monographs on Social Anthropology, No. 12, London, Athlone Press, 1950.

LE PAGE, R. B., *The National Language Question*, London, Oxford University Press for Institute of Race Relations, 1964.

MACGOWAN, Rev. J., *Lights and Shadows of Chinese Life*, Shanghai, 1909.

MAHAJANI, Usha, *The Role of Indian Minorities in Burma and Malaya*, Vor and Co. Publishers Private Ltd., Bombay, issued under the auspices of the Institute of Pacific Relations, New York, 1960.

MANNONI, O., *Prospero and Caliban*, London, Methuen, 1956.

MANSUR, Fatma, *Process of Independence*, London, Routledge and Kegan Paul, 1962.

NEWELL, W. H., *Treacherous River*, Kuala Lumpur, University of Malaya Press, 1962.

NOSS, Richard B., 'Language Policy and Higher Education in South-East Asia', Consultant's Report, U.N.E.S.C.O.–I.A.U. Joint Research Programme in Higher Education, Kuala Lumpur, 1965.

OOI JIN-BEE, *Land, People and Economy in Malaya*, London, Longmans, 1963.

POLYANI, Karl, Arensberg, Conrad M., and Pearson, Harry W. (eds.), *Trade and Market in the Early Empires*, Glencoe, Ill., The Free Press, 1957.

Les Mekhadma, Paris, Prohusa, 1960 (trans.).

PURCELL, Victor, *The Chinese in Southeast Asia*, London, Oxford University Press, 1951; 2nd ed., 1965; *Memoirs of a Malayan Official*, London, Cassell, 1965.

ROBEQUAIN, C. (trans. E. D. Laborde), *Malaysia, Indonesia, Borneo and the Philippines*, London, Longmans, Green, 1954; 2nd ed., 1958.

SHILS, Edward, *Political Development in the New States*, The Hague, Mouton and Co., 1962.

SILCOCK, T. H., and Fisk, E. K. (eds.), *The Political Economy of Independent Malaya*, Canberra, Australian National University, 1963.

SKINNER, G. W., 'Overseas Chinese in South-East Asia', *The Annals*, Vol. 321, Jan. 1959 (American Academy of Political and Social Sciences); 'Chinese Assimilation and Thai Politics', *Journal of Asian Studies*, Vol. 16, No. 2, Feb. 1956; *Leadership and Power in the Chinese Community of Thailand*, Ithaca, N.Y., Cornell University Press, 1958.

STEINBERG, David J., *et. al.*, *Cambodia*, Human Relations Area Files, New Haven, 1956; rev. ed. by H. J. Vreeland, 1959.

SWIFT, M. G., *Malay Peasant Society in Jelebu*, London School of Economics Monographs on Social Anthropology, No. 29, London, Athlone Press, 1965.

TINKER, Hugh, *The Union of Burma*, London, Oxford University Press for the Royal Institute of International Affairs, 1957.

U.N.E.S.C.O.–I.A.U., *Higher Education and Development in South-East Asia*, Paris, 1965.

WALINSKY, Louis J., *Economic Development in Burma, 1951–1960*, New York, 20th Century Fund, 1962.

WANG GUNGWU, *A Short History of the Nanyang Chinese*, Singapore, Eastern Universities Press, 1959; (ed.) *Malaysia : A Survey*, London, Pall Mall Press, 1964.

WILLMOTT, D. E., *The Chinese of Semarang: A Changing Minority Community in Indonesia*, Ithaca, N.Y., Cornell University Press, 1960; rev. ed., 1961; *The National Status of the Chinese in Indonesia*, Ithaca, N.Y., Cornell University Modern Indonesia Project (mimeograph), 1956.

GENERAL INDEX

Abaca (hemp), cultivation of, 34, 40, 86, 87
Abdul Rahman, Tunku, 52
Addis Ababa Conference (1962), 115
Africa: 2, 6, 18, 42, 62–63, 64, 65, 71, 93, 101, 108, 142, 144, 146, 150, 159, 160, 163, 165, 172; tribalism in, 18, 62, 65; religion in, 42, 146; Indians in, 60; racial problems date from colonial period, 60; culture regarded by Europeans as too primitive to preserve, 62; animism in, 63, 150; Europeans at first treated as magicians, 63; colonial powers not concerned with nation-building, 64; ethnic problems in, 65; western law in, 68; colonial rule in, 71; law and order enforced in, 74; independence for small states in, 75; nationhood in, 76; survival of aristocracy in, 79; attractions of towns in, 92; emphasis on industry in, 93; attacks on foreigners in, 101; new ideas in, 108; education in, 115; teaching of English in, 130; training of African managers, 142; education and tradition in, 144–7; 'living in two worlds', 146; secularism in, 149; cultural tradition in, 150, 172; poor in natural resources, 159; racial jealousy in, 160; advances in, 161; chiefs' loss of influence in, 162; community development schemes in, 163; one-party system in, 165
Africa, East: Indians refuse citizenship in, 55; Asians introduced into, 60; development by Europeans pays for education in, 61; minorities in, 64, 65; prospects for school-leavers in, 99; few natural resources in, 100; education in, 110, 112; polyglot children in, 133
Africa, South: minority racial rule in, 10; Asians in, 60; industrialization and race relations in, 141–2; colour prejudice in, 143
Africa, West: Money Loan Associations in, 39; foreign minorities in, 65; Marabouts in, 85
Agricultural services, 92–93, 100
Agricultural settlement schemes in Malaya, 97–98, 153
Agriculture, employment in, 13–14, 86; in Thailand, 21, 22; in Cambodia, 24; in S. Viet-Nam, 26; in Indonesia, 29; in N. Borneo and Sarawak, 32; in Philippines, 34; in Malaya, 71, 97–98, 101, 102; in Burma, 95; local advance in, 138; modernity and, 144
Alliance Party, Malaya, 32–33, 56
Ambonese people, Indonesia, 9
American aid, 169; for S. Viet-Nam, 13, 26; for Cambodia, 23; for Indonesia, 29
Americans: as business consultants in Burma, 94; as businessmen in Singapore, 97; as advisers in Malaya, 98; their advantages in business in Philippines, 98; their attitude to 'backward' countries, 107; as professors in Indonesia, 127, 148 (*See* United States of America)
Ancestor worship, 42
Angkor Wat, Cambodia, temples at, 23, 62; captured by Thailand, 23; irrigation scheme at, 159
Animism, 5, 42, 63, 86, 146, 150
Annamites, 25, 56; empire of, 3, 25
Anti-Fascist People's League, Burma, 17
Appleton, S. (cited), 40
Arabs in Indonesia, 28
Arakan, 16, 18; Mountains, 16; district, 54
Arakanese people, Burma, 149; language, 121
Army, in Burma, 18, 95–96, 114, 150, 165; in S. Viet-Nam, 26, 125; in Indonesia, 29, 165
Ashanti Kingdom, 18, 76
A Short History of the Nanyang Chinese, 36, 60
Asians in Africa, 60, 65
Assimilation: (a) of Chinese, 37, 45–49, 50–51; in Indonesia, 38, 47–49; in Malaya, 45, 52; in Thailand, 46–47, 49, 66, 124; (b) of immigrants in rural areas, 89; (c) of Indians in Burma, 123
Australia, 2, 41, 131, 170, 171
Ayuthia, Thailand, 20

Baganda people, Uganda, 65
Bahasa Indonesia language, 120–1, 126
Bajau people, Borneo, 64
Bali, Indonesia: 15, 28; Balinese language, 126

Bandung Conference (1955), 48
Bandung Institute of Technology, 29
Bangkok (-Chonburi): 20, 76, 139; population of, 21; commerce of, 35, 47, 87, 90; Chinese in, 46, 47, 65, 89, 97; industrialization of, 47, 99; University of, 109; headquarters of U.N. Economic Commission for Asia, 124
Barotseland, 76
Batak language, Indonesia, 126
Batavia, 37, 91
Beecher Commission, East Africa, 112
Belgian Congo, 71
Bengal, East, Burmese and, 16; Bengalis in Burma, 19
Beyer, M. (cited), 34
Binh-Xuyen Sect, S. Viet-Nam, 26
Blumer, Professor Herbert (cited), 141, 142, 143
Bombay cotton industry, 142
Borneo: in 'Malay world', 2, 3, 27, 33; original inhabitants of, 4; ethnic groups in, 8
Borobodur, temples at, 62
Bose, Subhas Chandra, 54
Brahminism in Cambodia, 23
British: businessmen in Burma, 18; businessmen in Singapore, 97; advisers in Malaya, 98; colonial administrators, 105–6, 132; development experts, 147 (*See* Great Britain)
British Commonwealth, 120, 170
British Council expelled from Indonesia, 127
British Empire, merits in diversity of, 16, 64, 76
British Guiana, 79
British North Borneo; sketch of, 32; and Federation of Malaysia, 32, 81–82; Chinese in, 38, 81–82; intermarriage with Chinese in, 52; its progress due to Chinese, 61; British protect indigenous peoples from Chinese, 64, 81; reconstruction after Japanese occupation, 73; present life in, 86, 105
British North Borneo Company, 37, 61
British Rule in Burma, 1824–1942, 67
Brooke Bond Tea Company, India, 142
Brooke, Rajah, 37
Brunei: does not join Federation of Malaysia, 32, 71, 80; a Muslim sultanate under British protection, 32, 80; Chinese in, 36, 38
Buddhism: in S.E. Asia, 4–5; in Burma, 18, 19, 65, 108, 148–9, 150; in Thailand, 20, 21, 76; in Cambodia, 23; in S. Viet-Nam, 26, 65, 70, 148–9; Chinese and, 41–42; impressive temples of, 62; unifying influence of, 65; laymen as temporary monks, 84, 104; modernity and, 84, 116, 145–6; former influence of, 86; in new states, 108; science and, 148; materialism and, 150; value of, 164; future of, 164, 172
Buganda, Kingdom of, Uganda, 18
Burma: part of S.E. Asian mainland, 2; Indians in, 5, 19, 43, 53–55, 57, 60, 77, 123, 132, 140; China and, 5; Chinese in, 8–9, 19–20, 38, 50, 69, 77, 142; Education in, 13, 15, 109, 110, 111, 114, 118; population of, 14–15; economy of, 14; sketch of, 16–20; British rule in, 16, 19, 53–54, 69, 107; formerly part of Indian Empire, 16, 19, 53; minorities in, 16, 17, 18, 64, 65, 76, 77–78; Revolutionary Government of, 17–18, 95, 100, 102; agricultural policy in, 17, 100, 114; middle class in, 18, 143; and Thailand, 20; rice in, 21; contrasted with Indonesia, 29; intermarriage with immigrants in, 51, 54; attitude to foreigners in, 51; Britain encouraged immigration into, 60; western law in, 67–68; bureaucracy in, 69; end of colonial rule in, 69–70, 71, 73; civil war in, 73; nationhood in, 76–77, 82; politics still supreme in, 83; religion in, 84, 108 150; former peasant life in, 86; industrial development in, 94–96; shortage of practical engineers and agriculturists in, 113; modern education in, 116; language used in education in, 120; languages in, 121, 132; immigrants' schools in, 123; English language in, 124, 131; urbanization in, 140; religious differences in, 148–9; resources of, 159; its attitude to Britain, 170
Burmese, an ethnic group in Burma, 3, 9, 15; attitude of immigrants towards, 56
Burmese language, 120–3

Calcutta University, 123
Cambodia: part of S.E. Asian mainland, 2; indigenous people, of, 3; China and, 5; Vietnamese in, 9; wealth of, 13, 14, 159; population of, 14–15, 24; education in, 15, 109, 110, 111; lack of doctors in, 15; Thailand and, 20, 22, 23; sketch of, 22–25; and Viet-Nam, 23, 25; its attitude to U.S., 23; its attitude to Britain, 23, 170; agriculture in, 24, 100; industry in,

24; Indonesia and, 28; Chinese in, 36, 37, 38, 50, 69, 89; intermarriage with Chinese in, 51; end of colonial rule in, 71, 73; religion in, 84; 'planning' in, 96; languages in, 121, 125; English language in, 131; type of government in, 165–6
Cambodia, 24
Cambodian language, 120
Cambodians, their opinion of Filipinos, 35
Cambridge Higher School Certificate, 129, 146
Canton, 65; Cantonese, 39
Cao-Dai sect, S. Viet-Nam, 26
Capitalism, in Malaya and Thailand, 96–97, 102; in Philippines, 98–99, 102; capital investment as aid to progress, 108
Cash crops, 13–14, 152
Cash economy, 156
Cebuano language, Philippines, 126
Celebes (Sulawezi): in 'Malay world', 3; Christians in, 5; population of, 15; ethnic groups in, 27; revolt in, 29; immigrants in Sabah from, 65
Centralization under new governments, 102–3, 113–14, 138, 155, 160, 162, 163
Ceylon: Buddhism spreads from, 4; emigration to Malaya from, 31, 56; experiences violence when European control removed, 66
Champa Kingdom, Cambodia, 24, 25; Cham people, 23, 25; Cham-Malays, 15, 24
Cheng-Ho, Admiral, 36
Chen-la Kingdom, Cambodia, 23
Chettiars, in Burma, 19, 87; in Malaya, 53, 56
Chiefs: in Borneo, 105; in Muslim clans in Malaya, 151, 153; in Africa, 162; in S.E. Asia, 162
Chiengmai, Thailand, 20, 21, 91, 139; University of, 103
Chin people, Burma: 3, 15, 16, 69, 76; Chin mountains, 16; Chin Special District, 16; Chin language, 121
China: and S.E. Asia, 2, 5, 11, 169, 170; emigration from, 2, 3, 4; and Viet-Nam, 4, 25; Communist revolution in, 6; Thais came from, 20; Cambodia and, 24; and Annamites, 25; cost of Communism in, 159; achievements of, 161; Communism in, 166, 170; rivalry with Russia, 170
China Sea, 4
Chinese: immigrants a problem to S.E. Asia, 5, 10, 65; immigrants a racial minority, 8, 9, 10, 15; in Indonesia, 10, 28, 38, 50, 77, 96, 127; and Malaysia, 10, 50, 166; importance of, 12; in Singapore, 14, 31, 38, 140; in Burma, 18, 19–20, 38, 49, 50, 77, 142; in Thailand, 22, 37, 38, 39, 46–47, 49, 50, 51, 66, 69, 97, 124, 140, 142; in Cambodia, 24–25, 37, 38, 49, 50, 69; in S. Viet-Nam, 27, 38, 50, 70; in Malaya, 30–31, 37, 38, 45, 70, 79, 85, 97, 132, 140, 152–3; market-gardeners in Malaya, 31, 88; and rubber, 31, 39, 40, 98, 152; in Sabah, 32–33, 37, 38, 64–65, 70, 80–81, 129–30; in Sarawak, 32–33, 37, 38, 70, 80–81, 129–30; in Philippines, 34, 35, 38, 40, 49, 50, 99; in Java, 37; in N. Viet-Nam, 38; in Laos, 38; as businessmen, 39–40, 45, 88; religions of, 41–43, 164; religious tolerance of, 42, 149; feuds among, 44; discrimination against, 50–51, 69; attitude of other nations to, 50–53, 69; contrasted with Indians, 55–57; their immigration into S.E. Asia encouraged by Europeans, 60; jealousy felt for, 68, 89; and monopolies, 70; as middlemen, 87, 88, 90, 99; and modern education, 116; their education in Malaysia, 128–31; culture of, 132; their incomes compared with those of Malays, 143; 'live in two worlds', 146; as development experts, 147; their rivalry with Malays, 149; and the future, 172
Chinese languages: 37, 41, 119; in Thailand, 37; in Indonesia, 48, 120, in Burma, 120, 121, 123, 132; in Malaya, 120, 132–3; in Cambodia, 125; in S. Viet-Nam, 125; in Singapore, 129
Chinese schools: 44–45, 132; in Thailand, 46, 124–5; in British Borneo, 81, 130; in Burma, 120, 123; in Malaya, 120, 128; in Indonesia, 120, 127; in S. Viet-Nam, 125
Chittagonians in Burma, 19
Cholon, S. Viet-Nam, 27, 70
Christianity: in Philippines, 4–5; in Indonesia, 5, 148–9; in Burma, 19, 148; Chinese converts to, 42–43; in Africa, 62; modern education and, 145–6; in S. Viet-Nam, 148–9 (*See* Roman Catholics)
Chulalongkorn University, Thailand, 20, 113
Citizenship: of Indonesia, 48; for Chinese, 51–56; offered to Indians in Burma, 55, 123; refused by Indians in E. Africa, 55; of Thailand, 124; of S. Viet-Nam, 125; of Malaysia, 127

Civil Service, 83; of Burma, 18, 69, 94, 95, 96; of Thailand, 20, 69; of French Indo-China, 25; of British Borneo, 33, 81–82; of Malaya, 33, 52, 56, 82, 98, 127; of S. Viet-Nam, 70, 126; and nationhood, 83; colonial, 102–3
Coconuts grown in Philippines, 34, 87
Coffee grown in Philippines, 36
Cold War, 146, 168, 170; in S. Viet-Nam, 27; in Indonesia, 29
Colombo Plan, 132, 147, 170
Colonial rule: influence of rulers, 4, 5–6; special cases in, 16; effects of, 20, 60–72, 171; not concerned with nation-building, 64; and linguistic policy, 64, 119–20; rulers' social system, 65–66, 68; chaotic end of, 71–72, 73; American attitude to, 107, 169; policy about languages, 119–20; subjects' dependence on, 158, 159; criticism of, 166; problems left by, 167
Commerce, new states' hostility to, 93, 94, 95
Communal differences, 8, 11, 85, 148–9, 171; defined, 8; riots due to, 162
Communism: Chinese, 5, 50, 171; and Burma, 16–17, 18, 20, 95–96; and S.E. Asia, 20, 146, 169, 170; and Indonesia, 20, 29, 85, 96, 165; and Viet-Nam, 20, 25–26; and Malaya, 20, 82; and Philippines, 35; and Chinese abroad, 52; ideological empire of, 76; and Borneo, 81, 82; and religion, 150; chances for, 155, 162, 164, 166, 167; attractions of, 159, 160, 164, 166; achievements of, 161; U.S. and, 167, 168–9; India and, 171
Communist Manifesto (1848), 6
Communists, in Burma, 16–17, 18, 19; in China, 38; in Malaya, 73; in Indonesia, 78
Community development schemes, 163
'Confrontation' by Indonesia, 29, 33, 81, 82, 127
Confucianism, 25, 26, 42, 146, 164
Copra, 87
Cosmopolitanism, 51, 53
Cottage industries, 21, 138–9, 140, 148, 161
Cotton, 86; improvements in cultivation of, 147
Coughlin, R. J. (cited), 36, 37
Creoles in Sierra Leone, 65, 77
Cuba, 34
Culture, varied in S.E. Asia, 4; Hindu, 4, 5, 23, 62; tribal, 5, 105; defined, 7–8; Chinese, 9, 132; religion and, 11; in villages, 105; education and, 115–16, 117, 138; a slow growth, 137; vulnerable, 164
Cyprus, 66

Dalat University, S. Viet-Nam, 26, 125
d'Albuquerque, Alfonso, 30
Dar ul-Islam, Indonesia, 78
Democracy, 6, 165, 167, 169; in India, 171
Dewey, Admiral, 107
Diem, President Ngo Dinh, 26, 127
Dinka people, Sudan, 64
Discrimination against (a) Chinese, 10; in Thailand, 46, 47, 50–51, 69; in Philippines, 50–51; in Indonesia, 50–51. 69; in Burma, 50–51, 69; in Cambodia, 50–51, 69; in S. Viet-Nam, 50–51, 69; in Malaya, 50–51, (b) foreigners, in Thailand, 124–5
Djakarta, 85, 87, 91, 149; University of, 29
Dobby, E. G. H. (cited), 14
Doctors, in Cambodia, 15; in Burma, 122 (*See* Medicine)
Double Identity: the Chinese in Modern Thailand, 36, 37
Dusun people, Sabah, 51, 64
Dutch: and Tonkin, 25; in E. Indies, 27, 28–29, 73, 78, 87, 107; British and, 28, 30; their estates in E. Indies, 29; as colonial administrators, 29, 106–7; defeat Portuguese, 30; and Chinese, 37, 47; encourage Chinese immigration into Indonesia, 60; in Java, 65–66.
Dutch Borneo (Kalimantan), 29
Dutch language, 119; spoken by Chinese, 49; in Indonesia, 120, 121, 127
Dyak people, Sabah, 9, 64, 151

East India Company, and Burma, 16
Economic Development in Burma, 1951–60, 94
Education:
General: Chinese superiority in, 80–81, 129–31; effects of, 102; regarded as tool for economic purposes, 104; in villages, 104–5, 111–12; as aid to progress, 108; adoption of Western, 108, 117; industrial, not cultural, 108; fall in standards of, 109–10, 112, 113, 116; as an opening for jobs, 112, 114–15, 118, 138, 139; drawbacks of, 114; and culture, 115–16, 117, 138; suggested aims of, 118; modernity and, 144; and tradition, 145, 155–6; and religion, 145–7; inadequate to balance effect of modernity, 147
In colonial times: British, 106, 107; Dutch, 106; French, 107–8; American, 107, 108

National: statistics for, 13, 15; in Philippines, 13, 35, 126; in Malaya, 13, 98, 127–9, 131; in Burma, 13, 123; in S. Viet-Nam, 26; in Indonesia, 29, 126–7; in British Borneo, 32, 80–81, 130; in Thailand, 124; in Cambodia, 125; in Singapore, 129
Primary, 92, 108, 109, 110, 111, 112, 113–14, 115, 118; failure among pupils, 102; in Thailand, 124; in Cambodia, 125; in Philippines, 126; in Indonesia, 126; in Malaya, 128; in Singapore, 129; in British Borneo, 130
Secondary, 92, 108, 109, 110, 111, 112, 113, 115, 118, 121–2; in Malaya, 98, 127, 128–9, 131; in Thailand, 120–1; in Cambodia, 125; in Philippines, 126; in Indonesia, 127; in Singapore, 129; in Borneo, 130
Technical, 108, 113, 130
University: in Malaya, 13, 127, 130–1; in Burma, 18, 114; matriculation failures, 110; demand for graduates, 112, 113, 114; in Malaysia, 127, 130; in Borneo, 130; in Philippines, 131 (*See* Languages: Schools: Universities)
Eliot, T. S. (cited), 41, 112, 115
English language, 119, 120, 121, 131–2; in Burma, 120, 121–2, 131; in Malaya, 120, 128–9, 133; in Philippines, 120, 121, 126, 131; in Thailand, 120, 124, 131; in Indonesia, 121, 126–7; in Malaysia, 121, 131; in British Borneo, 121, 130; in S. Viet-Nam, 125, 131, 132; in Singapore, 131; in Cambodia, 131
Ethnic groups: defined, 7–11; statistics of, 13, 15; in Indonesia, 29
Ethnic minorities: 9, 12; defined, 8–10; and nationhood, 11; statistics of, 14–15; in Burma, 17–18, 77–78; not taught sense of nationhood, 62; in Africa, 64–65; in Borneo, 64; in Indonesia, 65, 76, 78; no self-determination for, 75–76
Eurasians, 12, 51, 96
Europeans: colonial rule of, 2; influence of, 5–6; encourage Chinese immigration into S.E. Asia, 60; respect for Buddhism and Islam, 63; in business, 90; and Malaysia, 166 (*See* Colonial rule)
Export: built up by Europeans, 87; emphasis on, 87, 89

Federal Land Authority, Malaya, 153
Federated Malay States, 30
Fiji, threat of violence in, 66
Filipino language, 126
Filipinos: population, 15; intermarriage with Chinese, 34, 49; Cambodians view of, 35; and Chinese, 47; in Sabah, 64
Firth, Professor Raymond (cited), 88
Foochow, 39
Foreign aid, 62, 95, 132, 147–8; from France, 23; from Britain, 170 (*See* American aid)
Foreign enterprise, 87; in Thailand, 21; Cambodia, 24; Burma, 95, 102; Singapore 97
Foreign experts, 113, 138
Foreign labour, 60–61, 87, 90
Forestry, 159
Formosa, 28, 58 (*See* Taiwan)
France: and Cambodia, 23, 24–25; favour Vietnamese, 25; and S. Viet-Nam, 25–26, 70, 149; and Cochin China, 25; protectorate in Indo-China, 25, 107–8, 166; encourage Chinese immigration into Indo-China, 60; colonial administration of, 107; and need for religion, 163; handicapped by colonial past, 169; recognizes Communist China, 170
Frankel, S. H. (cited), 138, 159
Freedman, Professor Maurice (cited), 39
French language: an international language, 119; in Indo-China, 120; in S. Viet-Nam, 121, 125, 132; in Cambodia, 121, 132
Fruit-growing: by Chinese, 40; in Jelebu, 152
Fukien Province, China, 37, 39, 40
Fulani people, Nigeria, 65
Fu-nan Kingdom, Cambodia, 23
Furnivall, J. S. (cited), 61–62

Geneva Accord (1954), 26
Ghana, 18, 71, 76, 77
Gia-long (Nguyen Anh), Emperor of Annamites, 25
Great Britain: immigrants in, 11; its rule in Burma, 16, 19, 20, 69; Cambodia and, 23, 170; seizes part of E. Indies from Dutch, 28; defeats Dutch in Malaya, 30; occupies N. Borneo and Sarawak, 32; encourages immigration into Burma, Malaya and Singapore, 60; promotes development schemes, 163; supports Malaysia, 167, 170; racialism in, 167–8, 173; handicapped by colonial past, 169–70; earns odium for support of U.S., 170; Burma and, 170; aid from, 170; recognizes Communist China, 170

Griffiths, V. L. (cited), 118
Gujeratis: in Burma, 19; in Indonesia, 28; in Malaya, 56

Hainanese people, China, 39, 40
Hanoi University, 26, 79, 109
Harrisson, Tom (cited), 81
Harvey, G. E. (cited), 67
Hausa people, Nigeria, 65, 77
Health services, 15, 92, 98, 100
Henghua clan, 50
Hiligaynon language, Philippines, 126
Hill tribes, 3, 4, 5, 6, 9, 11, 15, 172 (*See* Indigenous peoples)
Hinduism: its art spreads to Indonesia and Far East, 4; influence of, 4–5; its culture in Cambodia, 23, 62; in Indonesia, 27, 78, 149, 150; its effect on Islam, 27, 43; survives in Bali, 28; modern education and, 116, 146; in Malaya and Singapore, 149; materialism and, 150
Hindus, in Burma, 19, 54; their culture needed, 172
Hindustani language in Burma, 19, 120, 123
Hla Myint, Dr (cited), 109
Hoa Hao sect, S. Viet-Nam, 26
Hokkien people, China, 39
Hoktjia people, China, 39
Holland handicapped by colonial past, 169 (*See* Dutch)
Hong Kong, 44, 64, 89, 97; University of, 41
Hua Dong communes, China, 161
Hué University, S. Viet-Nam, 26, 125
Haukka people, China, 39
Hunter, Guy (cited), 141, 142, 143
Hutu people, Rwanda-Burundi, 66

Ibo people, Nigeria, 65
Ilocano language, Philippines, 126
Immigrants: and trade, 19, 24–25, 31, 39–40, 43, 45, 68, 87, 88, 90, 99, 160–1; hostility towards, 10–11, 22, 24, 30, 46, 47, 50–51, 68, 69, 84, 89, 99, 124–5
Immigration: of Chinese, 36–53, 70–71; of Indians, 53–57; encouraged by colonial powers, 60–61; disadvantages of, 61–62 (*See* Chinese: Indians)
Imperial Chemical Industries, 137
Import-export, 25, 87, 88, 93, 95
Indentured labour, from India, 30–31, 64, 88
India: and S.E. Asia, 2, 4; Burma formerly part of, 16, 19, 132; its influence on Cambodia, 23; and Indonesia, 27; and Philippines, 33; British administration in, 64; violence experienced when British control ceased, 66; end of colonial rule in, 73; unified under Britain, 74; and Nagas, 76; communal riots in, 85; secular, 108; industrialization and race relations in, 141, 142; development experts from, 147; important for future of S.E. Asia, 170–1
Indian Education Society, Burma, 123
Indian Empire, Burma formerly in, 16, 19, 53
Indian Independence League, 59
Indian languages, 119, 120, 121, 132
Indian National Army, 54
Indian Ocean, 4
Indians: in S.E. Asia, 5, 142, 170–1; in Burma, 5, 16, 18–19, 43, 53–55, 57, 77, 132, 140; a racial minority, 8–9, 10; in Malaya, 30–32, 43, 53, 55–56, 57, 70; in Singapore, 55–56; contrasted with Chinese, 55–57; jealousy felt for, 68, 89, 99; as lawyers, 68; and monopolies, 69–70; as middlemen, 87, 88, 90, 99; and education in Malaya, 128, 131; and religious feeling, 149
Indigenous peoples: 3, 5, 9; in Thailand, 20; in Cambodia, 24; in Malaya, 30, 32; in British Borneo, 32, 70, 80–81 (*See* Hill tribes)
Indo-China: France encourages Chinese immigration into, 60; Chinese in, 88; education in, 107–8; languages in, 120; Roosevelt criticizes France over, 166
Indonesia: in 'Malay world', 2, 5; Muslim, 4; origin of name of, 4; China and, 5; ethnic groups in, 8; Chinese in, 9, 10, 38, 77, 96; minorities in, 9, 65, 76, 78; wealth of, 13; population of, 14–15; education in, 15, 29, 109, 110, 111, 113; varied cultures in, 16; and Cambodia, 23; sketch of, 27–29; early conquest of Cambodia, 28; Viet-Nam and, 28; and Thailand, 28; and Malaya, 28; Malay Peninsula colonized from, 28, 30; politics supreme in, 29, 83; 'confrontation' with Malaya, 29, 33, 81, 82, 127; Philippines and, 35; religion in, 43, 84–85, 150; intermarriage with Chinese in, 51; and Malaysia, 52; Europeans encourage Chinese immigration into, 60; discriminates against Chinese, 69; and Borneo, 71, 81; end of colonial rule in, 71, 107; Dutch in, 73; nationhood in, 82; official language of, 120; languages in, 121, 126–7, 132;

English language in, 121, 131; middle-class in, 143; Americans in, 148; religious differences in, 148–9; custom in, 151; resources of, 159; type of government in, 165
Indonesian language, 48, 120; used by Chinese, 48; Indonesian/Malay language, 126
Indonesians, population of, 15; in Philippines, 33
Industrialization: in Thailand, 21, 47; in Cambodia, 24; in Indonesia, 29; in Philippines, 34–35; in Burma, 94–95, 102; and race relations, 141–4, 155; in India, 141, 142, 171
Industrialization and Race Relations: A Symposium, 141, 142, 143
Industrial Revolution in Europe, 136, 139
Industry: employment in, 13; in Thailand, 21; in Cambodia, 24; emphasis on, 91; preferred by new states to commerce, 93–94, 101
Institute of Traditional Cultures, Madras, 116–17
Intermarriage, 4, 16, 24; with (a) Chinese, 8, 45; in Cambodia, 25, 49, 51; in Thailand, 25, 37, 46, 49, 51; in Indonesia, 28, 47–49, 51, 127; in Philippines, 34, 49, 51; in Burma, 49, 51; in British Borneo, 51, 52; in Malaya, 52; (b) Spanish, in Philippines, 34; (c) Indians, in Malaya, 52; in Burma, 54
International aid, 113, 132, 147–8
International Court of Justice, 23
International Rice Research Institute, 34
Irrawaddy, River, 3, 16, 18; delta of, 16, 17, 18, 19, 61, 87
Islam: Hinduized, 27, 43; in Indonesia, 28; in Philippines, 33–34; Chinese and, 43, 79; in Malaya, 52; converts to, 52, 54; European respect for, 63; and politics, 84–85; in villages, 104; in new states, 108; modern education and, 116, 145–6; in Asia, 150; and nationalism, 150; custom and, 151; value of 164 (*See* Muslims)

Jakun people, Malaya, 30
Japan: 2; Philippines look to, 35; rice production in, 86; Indonesia wants firms from, 96; its businessmen in Singapore, 97; development experts in S.E. Asia, 147–8; and future of S.E. Asia, 170, 171
Japanese Occupation: of Burma, 16, 17, 19, 54; of Cambodia, 23; of Indonesia, 28, 78; its effect on European prestige, 28, 72; in British Borneo, 73, 81; hatred left by, 170
Java: in 'Malay world', 3, 27, 33; population of, 14–15; cultures in, 16; converted to Islam, 28; Dutch occupy, 28; British in, 28; Chinese in, 28, 36, 37, 38, 40, 42, 48, 65, 88; predominant in Indonesia, 29; early Chinese reconnaissance of, 36; assimilation of Chinese in, 48; Sumatra's rivalry with, 78; shortage of land in, 86; unemployment in, 92
Javanese, 9
Javanese language, 126; spoken by Chinese, 48
Jelebu district, Negri-Sembilan, 151–4
Jennings, Sir Ivor (cited), 138
Jesselton, Sabah, 90
Jobs: education and, 5, 102, 112, 114–15, 118, 138, 139; reservation of, 44–45, 69; social value of, 153–4
Jogjakarta University, 29
Johnson, President Lyndon B., 169
Johe, 151; indigenous people of, 30; Chinese in, 70
Joseph, K. T. (cited), 100
Ju-K'ang T'ien (cited), 40, 49
Jurang, Singapore, 97

Kachin people, Burma, 3, 9, 15, 16, 18; state, 16; language, 121
Kalimantan, 15, 29
Kaouchow, China, 39
Karen people, Burma, 9, 15, 16, 18, 76, 78, 149; State, 16; language, 121
Kayah (Karenni) State, 16
Kedah, 30
Kelantan, 30, 70, 127
Kennedy, President John F., 169
Kenya, 65, 71, 76, 77; Kenya Education Commission (1964), 99
Khmer people, Cambodia, 3, 15, 22–23, 24, 25, 56; in Thailand, 20; language of, 23, 125; their attitude to Chinese, 51; and urbanization, 140
Khonkaen University, Thailand, 22
Kikuyu people, Kenya, 65, 77
Kolb, M. (cited), 34
Korea, South, 167
Kra Peninsula, 2, 22, 124
Kuala Lumpur, 51, 81–82, 85, 97, 98, 111; University of, 45, 129, 130; educational research in, 111, 121
Kuching, Sarawak, 50
Kuo-Min-Tang Government of China, 38

Kwantung Province, China, 34, 37, 39, 57, 65, 88, 161

Lacquer cottage industry, 139, 148
Lampoon, Thailand, 161
Land, People and Economy in Malaya, 31, 33, 36, 38
Languages:
Colonial policy, 64, 119–20
For education: in Burma, 120, 121–3, 132; in Malaya, 120, 127; in Indonesia, 120–1, 126–7; in Indo-China, 120; in Philippines, 120, 126, 131; in Thailand, 120; in Singapore, 129; in British Borneo, 130–1; in Malaysia, 131, 132
Immigrants', 119–20; in Burma, 123
International, 109, 119, 121, 124, 131
Local, 119–20; in Indonesia, 120, 121; in Burma, 122–3; in Thailand, 124; in British Borneo, 130
National: in Burma, 120–1, 132; in Indonesia, 120–1, 126, 132; in Philippines, 120, 121, 125–6, 132–3; in Malayasia, 121, 132; in British Borneo, 121, 130; in S. Viet-Nam, 121, 132; in Cambodia, 121, 132; in Malaya, 127, 132–3; linguistic nationalism, 167
Lao people, Thailand, 15, 22, 23; language of, 23
Laos, 3; China and, 5; Thailand and, 20; and Cambodia, 24; Chinese in, 38; civil war in, 73
Latin America, Philippines compared with, 108
Laurel-Langley Agreement in Philippines, 98
Leadership and Power in the Chinese Community of Thailand, 36, 38, 46
Lebanese in W. Africa, 65
Le Page, R. B. (cited), 120, 130, 131, 133
Leprosy control, 148
Les Mekhadma, 154
Lights and Shadows of Chinese Life, 39
London School of Economics, 68
'Luksin' girls in Thailand, 46
Luo people, Kenya, 65
Luzon, 36, 147; Central, 34, 120, 126

Macassar, 78; Makassar language, 126
Macgowan, Rev. J. (cited), 39
Madinese language, Indonesia, 126
Magic, 5, 42, 145, 146, 164
Majapahit, Empire, 28, 33, 78
Malacca, 30, 37, 70
Malaku, Indonesia, 15
Malay (language): 4, 22, 30, 32, 120–1, 127–8, 131, 132; in Cambodia, 125; in British Borneo, 130
Malaya: China and, 4, 9; agriculture in, 13; tin-mining in, 13, 30, 87; Singapore Chinese and, 14; population of, 14–15; personal incomes in, 14, 33, 143; education in, 15, 109, 110, 113, 127–9; in former Indonesian Empire, 28; colonized from Indonesia, 28, 30; indigenous people of, 30; Indians in, 30–31, 43, 60; Chinese in, 37, 38, 43, 45, 61, 88, 132, 152–3; and immigration, 38, 70–71; religion in, 43, 84–85; British encourage Chinese immigration into, 60–61; British law in, 68; end of colonial rule in, 71–72; and communists, 73; rural development in, 97–98, 101, 102; languages in, 120, 127, 132–3; industrialization and race relations in, 141; custom in, 151–5
Malaya, Federation of, a possibility in 19th Century, 28; established (1948), 30; population of, 31; Chinese in, 70
'Malay' Indonesia, 27
Malaya, Indonesia, Borneo and the Philippines, 28, 34, 36, 40
Malayalis, 30–31
Malayan Chinese Association, 43
Malayan Indian Congress, 43, 56
Malayo-Polynesian languages, 126
Malay Peasant Society in Jelebu, 151–4, 155
Malay Peninsula, part of 'Malay world', 2, 3; colonization of, 3, 28, 30; original inhabitants of, 3
Malays: in Thailand, 15, 69, 76, 124; not indigenous in Malays, 30, 127; their percentage in Malaya, 32; in Philippines, 33; and Chinese, 41, 44–45, 155; in Sabah, 65, 80, 130; in Sarawak, 80, 81; and modern education, 116; and urbanization, 140; their incomes compared with those of Chinese, 143; their rivalry with Chinese, 149, 152–3; racialism among, 167; future of 170
Malaysia: A Survey, 81, 100
Malaysia, Eastern, 130
Malaysia, Federation of: in 'Malay world', 5; China and, 5; emphasis on, 12; wealth of, 13; population of, 14–15, 32; education in, 15, 111; dangers to, 20; Indonesian confrontation of, 29, 33, 81, 82, 127; sketch of, 30–33; a plural society, 30; British Borneo and, 32, 79–80, 81–82; politics in, 32–33; incomes in, 33; Singapore leaves, 33, 53; Chinese needed

in, 41; racial compromise in, 51–53; and Singapore Chinese, 52; Indonesia and, 52, 71; Indians in, 55–56; minorities in, 64; Chinese in, 65; nationhood in, 77, 79, 80; professional men prominent in, 83; industrial development in, 96–98; effect of British administration in, 107; languages in, 121, 129, 132; Chinese education in, 131; type of government in, 165–6; Britain supports, 167, 170
Malay Sultans: 150, 151; in Malay Peninsula, 4; in Malacca, 30; in Brunei, 32, 71, 80; cultural separation checked by, 130; representative of their peoples' culture, 161
'Malay world', 2–4, 32, 33, 35, 56, 130
Managerial skills, 95, 96, 97, 137, 140; shortage of, 94, 148; and cottage industries, 139
Managers: Malays trained as, 97; Africans trained as, 142
Manchu Emperors of China, 36, 37, 50
Mandalay, 3, 16, 17, 148
Mandarin language, 39, 44, 49, 133; Mandarin system of administration, 25, 26
Manila (-Quezon), 33, 34, 63, 65, 87, 91, 98, 99, 107; University of, 109
Mannoni, O. (cited), 157
Mansur, Dr. Fatma (cited), 150
'Maphilindo', 35
Marabouts in W. Africa, 85
Marakayars in Malays, 56
Masai people, Kenya, 64, 65
Mason, Philip (cited), 66
Massacres: of Indians in Burma, 19, 54; of Chinese in Philippines, 36; of Chinese in Indonesia, 37, 65, 77; of aliens, 89
Materialism: in new states, 6, 108, 116, 117; of Chinese, 41–42, 57, 164
Matrilinear system, 151–2, 154
Medical College, Singapore, 129
Medicine, 15, 128; modernity and, 144
Mekong, River, 3, 22, 23, 25, 159
Memoirs of a Malayan Official, 68
Middle class, 5, 7, 101, 146–7, 148; in Burma, 18, 143; in Thailand, 22; its birth in England, 138; created by industrialization, 143–4; in Sahara, 154
Middlemen, 87, 88, 90, 99
Minangkabau, Sumatra, 151; language, 126
Mindanao, 33, 34
Ming dynasty, 36; rituals of, 49
Mining of precious metals, 87 (*See* Tin)
Minorities, 7, 11–12; in Indonesia, 9; in Burma, 16, 17–18, 64, 65, 76, 77–78, 123; in Thailand, 22, 124; in Cambodia, 24; languages of, 125
Minorities Commission, Nigeria, 71
Missionaries, 42, 62, 63; mission schools, 109, 122
Modernity in S.E. Asia: 2, 53, 136–48; and religion, 6, 148–51; aim of new leaders, 6–7; its effect on peasant economy, 91–93, 102; and culture, 116–17, 148, 150–1; failures of, 147; discontent caused by, 147, 155; dangers of, 158–65
Moluccas, 5, 28, 29, 84
Money Loan Associations, 39
Monopolies, 68–70
Mon people, Burma, 16, 121; their language, 23; Mon-wa people, Burma, 15; Mon-Khmer languages, 121, 125
Morris, Professor David, 142
Muria, Sultan of Demak, 42
Muslims: in Malaya, 4, 5, 30, 33, 52; in Philippines, 4, 5, 15, 33–34; in Burma, 16, 18–19, 54, 123, 148; in Thailand, 22, 124; in Cambodia, 24; in Indonesia, 27, 28, 148–9, 150, 165; in Brunei, 32, 80; in Nigeria, 63, 65; future of, 172 (*See* Islam)

Naga people, 76; Naga Mountains, 16
Nanyang (i.e. overseas China), 36–41, 172; Nanyang University, Singapore, 110, 129
Nanyang Chinese, able, 41, 45; materialistic, 41–42, 57, 164; and Communism, 50; contrasted with Indians, 57 (*See* Chinese)
Napoleonic wars, Indonesia during, 28, 30
Narla Venkatesvara Rao (cited), 117, 164
National income, 14; in Burma, 17; in Thailand, 21; in Cambodia, 24; in Malaya 33, 143; in Philippines, 34
Nationalism, 92, 101, 136, 167, 171–2; and creation of a nation, 6–7, 10–11, 74–76, 85; in Burma, 17, 19, 96, 122; in Philippines, 98; politics of, 108; aims of, 117; and religion, 146, 150–1
Nationalization, in Burma, 17, 19, 95; in Indonesia, 96
Nation-building, 2, 6, 11, 16–17, 64, 72, 73–85
Negri Sembilan, 30, 70, 151–4
Negritos, in Malaya, 30; in Philippines, 33
Nehru, Pandit Jawahar Lal, 108, 171
New Delhi, 171
Newell, W. H. (cited), 39, 152
New Guinea, 3, 27, 28 (*See* West Irian)
Ne Win, General, 17

New Zealand, 41, 113, 131, 147–8, 170, 171
Nguyen Anh, Annamite Emperor, 25
Nguyen people, S. Viet-Nam, 25
Nigeria, 63, 65, 71, 79
Norodom, King of Cambodia, 23, 73
Noss, R. B. (cited), 121, 126
Notes towards a Definition of Culture, 41, 112, 115
Nuer people, Sudan, 64
Nusa Trengganu, Indonesia, 15

Occupations of Chinese clans, 39–40; of races in Malaya, 71
Oil refining in Philippines, 34; oil-blending in Singapore, 97
Ooi Jin-Bee (cited), 31, 33, 36, 38
Oriyas in Burma, 19

Pacific Ocean, races in, 3–4
Pacifism in India, 171
Pahang, 30
Pakistan, 85, 170
Pakistanis: in Britain, 11; in Burma, 19; in Malaya, 31, 32, 128
Pangan people, Kelantan, 30
Pan-Malayan Independence Party (P.M.I.P.), 33
Pan-Malayanism, 35
Papuans, 27, 76; in Philippines, 33
Pathet Lao, Thailand and, 22
Peasantry, gap widens between townsmen and, 102–3, 113–14, 138, 154, 155, 162; desire modern products, 154
Peking Government: Burma and, 19; France recognizes, 23, 170; richer Chinese abroad dislike, 38, 52, 82; overseas supporters of, 44, 57; Sukarno and, 77; Britain recognizes, 170
Penang, 30, 31, 65, 70, 87, 90
People's Action Party, Singapore, 79
Pepper, 40
Perak, 30, 31, 70
'Peranakans', Indonesia, 48–49
Perlis, 30
Petaling Jaya, Kuala Lumpur, 97
Petits blancs, 90
Phibun, Prime Minister of Thailand, 46
Philippines: in 'Malay world', 2, 3, 5; Muslims in, 4, 5, 15, 33–34; Christian, 4–5; Chinese in, 5, 36, 38, 40, 88, 91; wealth of, 13; population of, 14–15, 34, 91; education in, 15, 35, 109, 111, 113; sketch of, 33–35; intermarriage with Chinese and Spanish in, 34; personal incomes in, 34; agriculture in, 34, 138; plantations in, 34, 87, 91; and Indonesians, 35, 170; and immigration, 38; culture in, 62–63, 107, 108; end of colonial rule in, 71–72; immigrants in Sabah from, 80; politicians no longer supreme in, 83; its rural life unaffected by commerce, 91; unemployment in, 92; industrial development in, 98–99; agricultural development in, 100; scheme to popularize villages in, 114; languages in, 120–1, 125–6, 130, 132; English language in, 131; anti-Spanish revolt in, 150; resources of, 159; community development schemes in, 163; type of government in, 165–6
Phnom-Penh, Cambodia, 23, 24, 25, 91, 100
'Planning', 103, 137, 155, 160; of manpower, 94, 114; by foreign experts, 113
Plantations: 90; in Cambodia, 24, 25; in Indonesia, 29, 91; in Philippines, 34, 87, 91; in Borneo, 81; started by Europeans, 86
Plural Society: common in S.E. Asia, 2, 11, 133; in Malaya, 30, 32; drawbacks of, 61–62; European rulers outside, 66; nationalism in, 75–76; sophistication needed in, 145; middle class in, 147
Political Development in the New States, 91, 150
Polonaruya dam, Ceylon, 159
Polyani, K., Arensberg, C. M. and Pearson, H. W. (cited), 153
Population: statistics, 13–14; growth in, 14, 91; in Thailand, 21; in Cambodia, 24; in Malayan Federation, 31; in Singapore, 32, 97; in Malaysia, 32; in British Borneo, 32, 80
Portuguese, 25, 30
Prek Viharn Temple, suit over, 23
Private enterprise, 20, 95, 97, 99, 160–1
Process of Independence, 150
Progress and Welfare in South-East Asia, 62
Prohusa, M. (cited), 154
Prospero and Caliban, 157
Protestants, Chinese converted by, 42
Proto-Malay people in Philippines, 33
Province Wellesley, Straits Settlements, 30, 37, 39, 152
Punjab, 160; British law in, 67
Punjabis in Malaya, 31
Purcell, Victor (cited), 36, 61, 68

Race Relations, defined, 7–11; industrialization and, 141–4, 155; policy on, 167

Racialism, 7, 8, 11, 160, 162, 173; and national unity, 10–12
Raffles, Sir Thomas Stanford, 28
Raffles College, Singapore, 129
Rangoon, 16, 69, 148; nationalization in, 17, 19, 95; threatened by insurgents, 17; Indians in, 19, 53, 55; Hindustani once main language of, 19, 120; commerce of Burma centred in, 87; University of, 109, 112
Religion: animist, 5, 42, 63, 86, 146, 150; secularism and, 6, 148–51, 156; a cause of tension, 8, 10; Indians and, 10, 149; Chinese and, 10, 41–43; and culture, 11; African and Asian compared, 62–63; in S.E. Asia, 84–85; in villages, 104; in Schools, 108; modernity and, 144–5, 150–1, 158–9; education and, 145–7; science and, 156; need for, 163–5 (*See* Buddhism; Christianity; Islam)
Rhodesia, Southern, 10, 143, 167
Rice cultivation, in Cambodia, 3, 24, 159; in Burma, 18, 21, 86, 95; in Thailand, 20, 21, 34, 86; in Philippines, 34; Chinese and, 40; in Japan, in Taiwan, 86; double-cropping, 147; governed by custom in Malaya, 151–2
Rizal (Filipino hero), 126; Province, Luzon, 34
Robequain, C. (cited), 28, 34, 36, 40
Roman Catholics: in S. Viet-Nam, 26, 70, 149; in Philippines, 35, 62–63, 107, 150, 166; Chinese converts of, 40
Roman Empire, compared with modern states, 74, 76, 78
Roosevelt, President Franklin D., 166
Rubber production: in Thailand, 21; in Cambodia, 24, 25; in Malaya, 30, 31, 45, 61; Indians and, 31, 56, 157; Chinese and, 31, 39, 40, 98, 152; introduced by Europeans, 86; world demand for, 87; enriches Malaya, 90; basis of development schemes in Malaya, 98, 100; land for, 152
Rural life: changes in, 91–93, 102; gap between towns and, 99, 102–3, 113–14, 138, 154, 155, 162; need to improve, 116, 118, 161–3; importance of, 160 (*See* Village life)
Russia: Sukarno and, 77; Burmese universities employ physicists from, 122; development experts from, 147; cost of Communism in, 159, 166; and S.E. Asia, 169; China's rivalry with, 170
Rwanda-Burundi, 66
Sabah: population of, 14–15, 80; education in, 15, 80–81; and Malaysia, 32, 79–80, 81–82; progress in, 32; politics in, 33; Chinese in, 38, 51, 65, 70; intermarriage in, 51, 52; ethnic groups in, 64–65; timber in, 90: language of, 121; languages in schools of, 129–31; English language in, 130–1; resources of, 159 (*See* British North Borneo)
Sahara, 154
Saigon, 70, 87, 91, 163; University of, 26, 110, 125
St. Thomas University, Manila, 63, 109
Salween, River, 3, 16
Sancrum, Cambodia, 166
Sarawak: Chinese in, 10, 38, 49, 61, 65, 70, 81–82; population of, 14–15, 80; peoples in, 15, 32; education in, 15, 80–81; sketch of, 32; and Malaysia, 32, 79–80, 81–82; politics in, 33; intermarriage with Chinese in, 52; peasant life in, 86, 105; languages in, 121; languages in education in, 129–31; English language in, 130–1
Sarit Thanarat, Manhal, 22
Schools:
Chinese, 44–45, 132; in Thailand, 46, 124–5; in British Borneo, 120, 123; in Malaya, 120, 128; in Indonesia, 120, 127; in S. Viet-Nam, 125
Indian, 44; in Burma, 120, 123
Pagoda, 86, 92, 104, 112, 123, 125
Koranic, 86, 92, 104, 112
in villages, 104–5
mission, 109, 122
Science, 5, 6, 53; education and, 108; English used in Burma in teaching of, 122; English used in S. Viet-Nam in teaching of, 125; Chinese students and, 128; and progress, 136; and tradition, 144–7, 156; and religion, 145–6, 156, 164; useful in such experiments, 147–8, 156
Secularism, 6, 150; in Malaysia, 53; in India, 108; and religion, 148–51, 156, 164–5
Selangor, 31, 70
Semang people, in Kedah and Perak, 30
Semarang (Java), 38, 40, 42, 48, 65–66
Senegal, 90, 163
Senoi people, Malaya, 30
Shan people, Burma, 15, 16, 78; Hills, 3, 16; State, 16, 18; language, 12
Shell International, 137
Shils, E. (cited), 91, 150
Siam, 88 (*See* Thailand)
Sierra Leone, 65

Sihanouk, Prince, 23, 150, 165–6
Sihanoukville, 100
Sikhs, in Burma, 19; in Malaya, 31, 56
Silcock, T. H. and Fisk, E. K. (cited), 143
Singapore in, 3; 'Malay world', 2, 5; Chinese in, 5, 14, 31, 38, 65, 70, 79, 89, 90; China and, 5; population of, 14–15, 32, 91; personal incomes in, 14, 143; education in, 15; sketch of, 30–33; British occupy, 30; politics in, 33, 44; breaks with Malaysia, 33, 53, 168; Philippines and, 35; British in, 37; University of, 41, 109, 129, 130; Chinese education in, 44; newspapers published in, 50; and Malaysia, 52; Indians in, 55–56; Britain encourages Chinese immigration into, 60; industry in, 97, 99; two universities in, 97; Nanyang University in, 110, 129; languages in, 129; Malay and English languages in, 131; Chinese influence in, 132; its wealth due to Chinese, 140
Skinner, G. W. (cited), 36, 37, 38, 46, 48
Socialism, 160; in Burma, 17, 18, 96, 102; immigrants under, 99; in Indonesia, 102; education and, 108; and middle class, 138; its centralized planning, 155
Soil survey, 138
Somalis in Kenya, 76
Sousi-Spanish language in Philippines, 120
South America, Philippines compared with, 108; industrialization and race relations in, 141; colour bar in, 143
South-East Asia: compared with Africa, 2, 18, 42, 62–63, 64, 65, 71, 92, 93, 101, 108, 142, 144, 146, 150, 163, 165, 172; regarded as a single region, 2; immigration into, 2, 36–57; plural societies in, 2, 11; nation-building in, 2, 6, 11, 16–17, 64, 72, 73–85; sub-divisions of, 2–4, 6; foreign policy for, 11; education in, 15, 104–33; dangers facing, 20; unemployment in, 92, 99, 114; urbanization in, 102–3, 113–14, 115, 140; modernity and, 136–65; attempt to westernize too quickly in, 137; secularism and religion in, 148–50, 163–5; rich resources of, 159; foreign intervention and, 170
South-East Asia, 14
Spanish: and Philippines, 34, 35, 62–63, 98, 107; revolt in Philippines against, 150; language, 119, 126
Spices, 40, 86, 87
Sri Vijaya Empire, 23, 28, 33, 78
Steinberg, D. J. (cited), 24
Straits of Malacca, 30
Straits Settlements, 30, 31, 37, 61
Sudan, 64
Sugar, 34, 35, 86, 87
Sukarno, President Ahmed: breaks with Dutch, 28; his influence in Indonesia, 29; and Malaysia, 35, 81; future of Indonesia when his domination ends, 52; and Chinese, 77; transforms nationalist idea, 78–79, 150; and Borneo, 82; and private enterprise, 96; and United Malaysia, 170
Sukhotai, Thailand, 20
Sulawezi (Celebes), 27
Sultans, 150; in Malay Peninsula, 4; of Malacca, 30; of Brunei, 32, 71, 80; cultural separatism checked by, 130; administration of, 151; representative of their peoples' cultures, 161
Sulu Sea, 65
Sumatra: in 'Malay world', 3; population of, 15; Sri Vijaya Empire in, 23, 28; converted to Islam, 28; Dutch in, 28; revolts in, 29; rival of Java, 29, 78; Chinese in, 36; immigration into Borneo from, 80; settlers in Malaya from, 151
Sunda Islands, Indonesia, 78; Sundanese language, 126
Sung dynasty, China, 36
Sun Yat Sen rebellion (1911), 37, 46
Swahili language, 133
Swatow, China, 39
Swedish experts in S.E. Asia, 148
Swift, Dr M. G. (cited), 151–4, 155
Syrians in W. Africa, 65

Tagalog people, Philippines: women marry Chinese, 34; language, 120–1, 126, 132–3
T'ai-p'ing-T'ien-Kuo Rebellion, S. China (1850–64), 37
Taiwan, Government of, 19, 38, 44, 57; Hindu kingdoms of Indonesia reach, 28; University of, 41; rice production in, 86
Taksin, King of Thailand, 37
Tamil immigrants, in Burma, 19; in Malaya, 30-31, 88, 90; Tamil language, 120, 123
Tan An, S. Viet-Nam, 163
Tanganyika, 71
Tang Lha Range, Tibet, 3
Taoism, 42, 163
Tata Steel Company, Jamshedpur, 142
Teacher-training colleges, 163
Tea-cultivation, 86, 87
Teak, production of, 87
Technology, modern, 6–7, 94, 113; a slow growth in the West, 137

Telegu: immigrants, in Burma, 19; in Malaya, 30–31; language, 120, 123
Tenasserim, Burma, 16
Teochiu people, China, 37, 39, 40
Textile manufacture in Philippines, 34
Thailand: part of S.E. Asian mainland, 2, 3; early Malay invasion, of, 3; China and, 5, 124; land at present sufficient in, 14, 21; wealth of, 14, 21; population of, 14–15, 21, 91; education in, 15, 109, 110, 111, 113; and Burma, 16; sketch of, 20–22; rice in, 20, 21, 34, 86; religion in, 20, 21, 84, 150; agriculture in, 21, 96–97; industry in, 21, 96–97, 143; Malays in, 22, 69, 76, 124; Chinese in, 22, 36, 37–38, 39, 45, 46–47, 49, 50, 51, 65, 69, 140; discrimination against Chinese in, 22, 46, 50, 69; and Cambodia, 23; intermarriage with Chinese in, 25, 37, 46, 49, 51; once a vassal of Indonesia, 28; control of immigration into, 38, 46; never colonized, 66, 69, 105, 124; professional classes prominent in, 83; former peasant life in, 86; unemployment in, 92, 99; British influence in, 107; University in, 109; shortage of qualified engineers and agriculturists in, 113; languages in, 120, 124; English language in, 124, 131; middle class in, 143; cotton improved in, 147; type of government in, 165
Thai language, 21, 23, 120–1, 124; spoken by Chinese, 47
Thais: empire of, 3; population of, 15; origins of, 20; their attitude to Chinese, 51, 142; India and China greater than, 56; and modern education, 116; and urbanization, 140; future of, 172
Thammasart University, Thailand, 109
The Changing Quality of Political Life, 138
The Chinese in Southeast Asia, 36, 61
The Chinese of Sarawak, 40, 49
The Chinese of Semarang, 24, 36, 38, 40, 42, 48, 65
The Economic Impact on Underdeveloped Countries, 138, 159
The National Language Question, 120, 130, 131, 133
The National Status of the Chinese in Indonesia, 48
The Political Economy of Independent Malaya, 143
Theravada Buddhism, 4, 20, 23, 26, 42
The Role of Indian Minorities in Burma and Malaya, 19, 43, 53, 54
The Union of Burma, 17, 107
Thibaw, King of Burma, 16
Thorburn, S. S. (cited), 67
'Three Religions Society', 42
Tibet, 3, 25
Tin: in Malaya, 13, 30, 44, 45, 64, 87; Chinese and, 31, 44, 45, 64; enriches Malaya, 90
Tinker, Dr Hugh (cited), 17, 107
Tobacco-growing in Philippines, 34
Tonkin, 25
Totoks in Indonesia, 48–49
Towns, drift to the, 92–93, 162 (*See* Urbanization)
Trade and Market in the Early Empires, 153
Trade Unions, 57, 91, 137
Traditional culture, 4–5, 6, 91–92, 104–5, 138; colonial rulers and, 105–8; modern education and, 108, 116–17, 144–47; modernity and, 148–65; in China and Burma, disruption of, 161
Traditional Cultures in South-East Asia, 116–17, 164
Treacher, W. H. (cited), 61
Treacherous River, 39, 152
Trengganu, 30, 70
Trinh people, Tonkin, 25
Tutsi people, Rwanda-Burundi, 66

Uganda, 18, 65, 71
Unemployment in S.E. Asia, 92, 99, 114
U.N.E.S.C.O., 92, 108, 115, 116, 148, 163; reports by, 14, 15, 110, 111, 121, 128
Unfederated Malay States, 30
United Nations: unsatisfactory size of some states in, 77; English a principal language of, 132; aid from, 148
United Nations Economic Commission for Asia and the Far East (E.C.A.F.E.), 124
United States of America: gives aid to S. Viet-Nam, 13; Cambodia and, 23; and S. Viet-Nam, 26–27, 70, 125, 167, 170; and Philippines, 34, 35, 63, 72, 108; equality of citizens in, 51; Sukarno and, 77; racialism in, 143, 167–8; and nationhood, 145; and S.E. Asia, 167, 168–9, 171; and Communism, 168, 169 (*See* Americans)
Universities:
General: modern leaders from, 5; in Burma, 18, 95, 114; Chinese go abroad to, 41; and government jobs, 102; education at, 108, 109–10, 112; in Thailand, 109; languages used in, 121–3, 126; Thais' attitude to those of Britain and U.S., 124; in Malaya, 128; and progress,

136; Asian students at those of Australia and New Zealand, 170; Indian, 171 (*See* Education)
National: of Malaya, 13, 41, 110, 113, 128; Chulalongkorn (Thailand), 20, 113; Khonkaen (Thailand), 22; Saigon, 26, 110, 125; Hanoi, 26, 79, 109; Dalat, 26, 125; Hué, 26, 125; Djakarta, 29; Bandung, 29; Jogjakarta, 29; Singapore, 41, 109, 110, 113, 129, 130; Taiwan, 41; Hong Kong, 41; Kuala Lumpur, 45, 129, 130–1; St. Thomas, Manila, 63, 109; Chiengmai (Thailand), 103; Rangoon, 109; Bangkok, 109; Thammasart (Thailand), 109; Nanyang (Singapore), 110, 129; Calcutta, 123
U Nu, 17, 84, 94, 95, 108, 150
Urbanization in S.E. Asia, 4, 13, 99, 102–3, 113–14, 115, 140
Usha Mahajani (cited), 19, 43, 53, 54

Vedda people, Philippines, 33
Vegetable-growing, Chinese and, 31, 40, 88
Viet-Cong, 26, 79, 163
Vietminh Communism, 25
Viet-Nam, partition of, 26 (*See* Indo-China)
Viet-Nam, North, 25, 26, 38, 79
Viet-Nam, South: part of S.E. Asian mainland, 2, 3; early Malay invasion of, 3; China and, 5; wealth of, 13, 14; population of, 14–15; education in, 15, 109, 111, 113; dangers to, 20; and Cambodia, 23, 24, 25; sketch of, 25–27; U.S. and, 26–27, 70, 125, 167, 170; civil war in, 26, 73; Indonesia and, 28; early Chinese trade with, 36; Chinese in, 38, 50; discrimination against Chinese in, 69; French culture in, 70; end of colonial rule in, 71; and nationhood, 79, 82; and Communism, 79; politicians still supreme in, 83; religion in, 84; languages in, 121, 125; English spoken in, 131; middle class in, 143; religious differences in, 148–9; type of government in, 165
Vietnamese, in Cambodia, 9, 15, 24; and Chinese, 41
Vietnamese language, 23, 26, 120, 125, 132; in Cambodia, 125
Village life, 4, 5, 102, 104–5; improvements in, 118, 140, 148 (*See* Rural Life)
Visaya Islands, Philippines, 33

Wa language, 121
Wachirawut, King of Thailand, 46
Walinsky, L. J. (cited), 94
Wang Gungwu (cited), 36, 60, 81, 100
Welahan, Java, 42
Westernization in S.E. Asia, 136, 162 (*See* Modernity)
Western law, bad effects of, 67–68
West Indians abroad, 11, 172
West Indies, colour prejudice in, 143
West Irian, 15, 27, 76 (*See* New Guinea)
Willmott, D. E. (cited), 24, 36, 38, 40, 42, 48, 65
World Bank, 116
World Health Organization, 128

Yangtze Kiang, River, 3
Yeats, W. B. (cited), 157
Yoruba people, Nigeria, 65
Youth Movements in S.E. Asia, 84, 162
Yunnan Province, China, 20

Zambia, 61, 76
'Zerbadis' in Burma, 54